Cable Television

CABLE
TELEVISION

A REFERENCE
GUIDE TO INFORMATION

Ronald Garay

GREENWOOD PRESS

NEW YORK • WESTPORT, CONNECTICUT • LONDON

Library of Congress Cataloging-in-Publication Data

Garay, Ronald.
    Cable television : a reference guide to information / Ronald
Garay.

    p. cm.
    Includes index.
    ISBN 0-313-24751-X (lib. bdg. : alk. paper)
    1. Cable television—United States—Bibliography.   2. Cable
television—United States—Law and legislation—Bibliography.
I. Title.
Z7711.G37 1988
[HE8700.72.U6]
016.384.55'47'09–dc19   87-24955

British Library Cataloguing in Publication Data is available.

Library of Congress Catalog Card Number: 87-24955
ISBN: 0-313-24751-X

First published in 1988

Greenwood Press, Inc.
88 Post Road West, Westport, Connecticut 06881

Printed in the United States of America

The paper used in this book complies with the
Permanent Paper Standard issued by the National
Information Standards Organization (Z39.48-1984).

10   9   8   7   6   5   4   3   2   1

CONTENTS

INTRODUCTION

This work is a bibliographical reference guide to information about cable television in the United States. Included here are titles and brief commentary on books, government documents, and periodical articles that cover an extensive array of subjects related to cable television. Most of the items noted in the reference guide have publication dates that run roughly from 1980 through 1987, a period of explosive growth in the cable industry and an equally explosive growth in publications about the industry.

This guide aims to provide a useful information source for persons interested in learning about cable television or for those seeking additional information about cable in America. The guide is not exhaustive in the information it contains, nor was it meant to be. The information flood that is inundating society with enormous amounts of data on practically every subject has also affected cable. There is an immense amount of information available on every facet of the industry. Included in this guide are more than 400 book, government document, periodical, and periodical article titles that the author has concluded would be of most help in either providing primary information on a cable-related topic or leading the user to a helpful secondary source.

The selection process for choosing the publications included here has taken into account several factors. The first has been the item's substance— the depth to which the author treated its subject. A second selection factor has been the extent to which the item has application to current and future needs of those persons researching cable television. Other selection factors considered were content utility, timeliness, and lasting value. A final factor has been accessibility. Items included in this reference guide, for the most part, should be available to most researchers through other than extraor-dinary means.

Newspaper articles have been excluded from this reference guide. While some newspaper articles on cable television certainly could be considered substantive, most contain short accounts of events that usually are treated at much greater length elsewhere. Also, since some concession had to be made to the practical limits placed by the author on what could be included here, it seemed that newspaper articles should be one likely candidate for exclusion. For the same reason, items from such newspaper format peri-odicals as *Variety*, *Multichannel News*, *Advertising Age*, and *Electronic Media* also have been excluded, although special supplements from these publi-cations having to do with cable television are noted under the appropriate headings.

Periodical articles included in this guide are highly selective and generally have been drawn from journal sources. Much the same rationale as that applied to exclusion of newspaper articles has been applied to limitations on periodical articles. Periodical titles that do appear here have been chosen because they address key issues that are spread among the several major cable-related subject areas.

This guide is divided into five chapters: general sources, cable business and economics, cable programming, cable law and regulations, and video-tex. The latter four chapters are similar in structure, with each having an established pattern of headings and subheadings.

Chapter 1 includes publications that provide general overview informa-tion about all areas of cable television. The chapter's first part examines both books and periodical articles containing content of this sort. The second part examines types of publications and other information sources that should aid researchers in finding cable television information.

The last four chapters are structured as follows: The first part of each chapter provides an issue overview essay that introduces the subject of that chapter. The issue overview is followed by a series of bibliographical essays that examine, in this specific sequence, (1) books, (2) government docu-ments, and (3) periodical articles whose major content is reflective of the general subject heading of the chapter in which the publications appear. The final portion of each chapter consists of bibliographical listings for all the publication titles noted in the chapter's bibliographical essays. Categories and subcategories of the bibliographical listings are keyed to match those of the bibliographical essays.

Cable Television

Chapter One

GENERAL SOURCES

The first chapter of this reference guide is divided into three major groupings. The first grouping contains books and periodical articles that provide the researcher with general information about cable television. With a few exceptions, most of these publications cover cable in a bare-bones fashion, describing most of the facets of the cable television industry (system operation, programming, economics, regulation, and so on) without providing any great detail on any one of them. Their purpose is to present an introductory overview of cable, and many of these publications serve that function very well.

The second grouping provides titles of periodicals that contain cable television–related information. The titles are arranged under the headings of popular readership periodicals (those commonly available on newsstands), trade and professional periodicals (those publications whose readers are usually either cable television or academic professionals), legal periodicals (law journals and reviews whose readers are usually attorneys specializing in media law), and government documents.

The third grouping provides titles of special cable information sources such as reference books, directories, indexes, dictionaries, and newsletters.

CABLE OVERVIEW PUBLICATIONS

Books and Book Chapters

Thomas F. Baldwin and D. Stevens McVoy's *Cable Communication* is the premiere textbook devoted exclusively to cable television. The book's comprehensive scope and the authors' efforts at providing readers with what is most significant about cable are *Cable Communication*'s greatest assets. The book is divided into five sections—technology, services, public policy, organization and operations, and the future—and contains excellent supplementary information in several appendices.

James W. Roman speaks of *Cablemania: The Cable Television Sourcebook* as a reference tool, but it could easily pass for a textbook as well. The book's various chapters cover the cable terrain in comprehensive fashion. Included are chapters on cable television's history, regulatory and judicial decisions affecting cable, cable technology, programming types and services available to cable, major corporations involved in cable, broadcast/publisher diversification and entry into the competing cable businesses, franchising procedures, foreign cable development, the minority-group role in cable, a public access production primer, employment opportunities in the cable industry, and cable television's future.

The Cable/Broadband Communications Book, edited by Mary Louise Hollowell, appears in three successive volumes: 1977–1978, 1980–1981, and 1982–1983. Hollowell describes her books in the introduction to volume 2 as "attempts to provide comprehensive, authoritative coverage of developments in the field" (p. ix). Drawing from the contributions of several noted authorities, Hollowell has constructed each of her *Cable/Broadband Communications Book* volumes around major issues affecting cable television during a given period of time.

One final book of a textbook nature and devoted exclusively to cable television is William Grant's *Cable Television*. Grant's book is primarily a technical overview of cable operation, although some chapters provide brief descriptions of cable television development, regulation, and related technologies.

A book chapter that is noteworthy for the concise overview of cable television in the United States is Vernone Sparkes's "Cable Television in the United States: A Story of Continuing Growth and Change," in *Cable Television and the Future of Broadcasting*, edited by Ralph M. Negrine. Sparkes's chapter includes looks at cable history, regulatory policy, programming and economic matters, and cable's role in the electronic media marketplace.

A number of books, primarily textbooks, take a more broadly based approach to examining cable television by placing cable within the context of other new or emerging electronic media. Heading this list is a massive loose-leaf volume prepared by William L. McGee, Joseph H. Caton, and Lucy E. Garrick entitled *Changes, Challenges, and Opportunities in the New Electronic Media*. The size of this book is both a help and a hindrance. Plenty of information is here, to be sure, but the researcher trying to focus on cable television might have trouble sorting out cable from the other technologies. Nonetheless, McGee, Caton, and Garrick do supply a substantive overview of the subject with helpful accompanying industry profiles and illustrations.

Lynne Schafer Gross has designed *The New Television Technologies* to provide basic information about the new technologies, chiefly to show their interrelationship with one another. The book serves as a good foundational approach to the subject. While several chapters make reference to some aspect of cable or videotex, one takes an extended look at cable, and another takes an extended look at videotex.

George E. Whitehouse devotes chapters in his short book *Understanding the New Technologies of the Mass Media* to basic principles of electronic media, the radio and television broadcast media, the microwave (terrestrial) media, and finally the cable media. Whitehouse uses his cable chapter to describe master antenna television (MATV), satellite master antenna television (SMATV), community antenna, interactive, and pay cable. A chapter is also reserved for the electronic publishing media of teletext and videotex. The Whitehouse book, with an economy of words and space, carries substantial information about the operation of the new or emerging media and supplements that information with numerous well-designed diagrams and illustrations.

Telecommunications in the Information Age is meant by its author, Loy A. Singleton, "to describe in plain language the basic features of the most asked-about new telecommunication technologies. . . . The contents of each chapter are organized under four headings: Background (how was it developed and when?); How It Works (a non-technical description of its function in everyday language); Applications (real-life examples of its use); and Forecast (upcoming developments, including legal and social issues)" (p. 2).

The Video Age: Television Technology and Applications in the 1980s is a good general overview of the emerging media marketplace, with specific chapters devoted to cable and videotex. The book opens with a chapter entitled "The Home Video Industry" in which considerable space is devoted to defining cable television's economic and programming structure. The most significant chapter in *The Video Age* regarding cable is written by Lawrence Strauss and is entitled "The Emergence of Cable TV as a Viable Medium."

Frederick Williams includes observational commentary on cable television in *The Communications Revolution*. His comments appear within the context of where the communications revolution is today and where it may be heading tomorrow. Williams talks about cable growth and cable services, particularly interactive cable, and discusses what the services are doing in comparison with what they were supposed to do. He also comments on the competition between the cable industry and the telephone industry in supplying similar services. Final cable comments in *The Communications Revolution* are reserved for cable television programs and program producers as well as future trends and possibilities for the cable industry.

Wired Cities: Shaping the Future of Communications, edited by William H. Dutton, Jay G. Blumler, and Kenneth L. Kraemer, contains several chapters that explore the concept of the wired city. Dutton, Blumler, and Kraemer define the concept and comment on the underlying assumptions of wired-city advocates. While several of the book's chapters focus on wired-city projects in other countries, at least two chapters concentrate on cable policy development in the United States. Kenneth C. Laudon's "Promise versus Performance of Cable" argues that cable television failed to provide the program diversity its promoters had promised and became successful only after adapting to a broadcast television model. Robert Pepper suggests in "Competitive Realities in the Telecommunications Web" that the role cable plays in this country's communications system is more by design than by accident and is "consistent with the basic philosophy underlying communications policy in the U.S." (p. 59).

Cable television and videotex are viewed within the context of how new technologies impact upon the broadcast media in the National Association of Broadcasters' *New Technologies Affecting Radio and Television Broadcasting*. The book's short section on cable looks at the cost and benefits to consumers of cable television and then examines the effects of cable system location on broadcast licensees. The same categories of inquiry are also applied to pay cable.

A chapter by Henry Breitrose, "The New Communication Technologies and the New Distribution of Roles," in *The Media Revolution in America and in Western Europe*, edited by Everett M. Rogers and Francis Balle, examines cable television in the nexus of other new and emerging electronic delivery systems. Breitrose separates cable from the others due to cable's interactive capabilities. The author also examines privacy issues and how such matters will impact upon the consumer. Though the Breitrose chapter is short, it does provide information with a more theoretical slant and within the context of media developments internationally.

Several textbooks devoted to a survey of electronic media provide information on cable television. Among this lot, Sydney W. Head and Christopher H. Sterling's *Broadcasting in America* ranks at the top. Several sections of the book treat cable television both separately and within the mix of other new technologies. Cable-specific sections include information on cable industry description and development; cable regulation, franchising, and copyright issues; cable economics, programming, access channels, and advertising; interactive cable; satellites and cable networking, superstations, and cable program services; and pay cable.

John R. Bittner's *Broadcasting and Telecommunication: An Introduction* runs a close second to the Head/Sterling textbook. One chapter of the Bittner book is devoted exclusively to cable television, and another is devoted exclusively to teletext/videotex. The cable chapter is arranged to define cable in conceptual terms and then to expand on cable matters ranging from a description of cable system components to cable system ownership and management problems. A separate chapter is reserved for cable regulatory issues, with an emphasis on regulatory history, franchising standards, and cable copyright issues.

Radio, TV, and Cable: A Telecommunications Approach by Marvin Smith introduces the reader to cable within the context of other electronic media. Cable television is not treated exclusive of the other media but rather as a part of the media mix that comprises the "communications revolution." One chapter in *Radio, TV, and Cable* offers a look at cable technology, economics, and business practices, and another chapter provides information on cable programming. There is very little on cable advertising or cable regulation. While this textbook plays up cable television in its title, its attention to cable is actually a bit perfunctory.

A very solid discussion of cable television development in the United States is found in Eugene S. Foster's *Understanding Broadcasting*. Foster devotes most of his attention to cable's regulatory history but does manage to cover enough territory to make *Understanding Broadcasting* worthwhile reading for the general-information seeker.

Telecommunications: An Introduction to Radio, Television, and Other Electronic Media by Lynne Schafer Gross includes a description of cable television history, system structure, regulatory matters pertaining to cable, cable programming and franchising matters, and matters pertaining to basic cable, interactive cable, and cable deregulation. All of this is contained in a single chapter of the textbook.

Several textbooks that serve as a more generalized introduction to mass communication give some attention to the electronic media but usually very little to cable television. Leading the pack in terms of space devoted to cable is Jay Black and Frederick C. Whitney's *Introduction to Mass Communication*. Chapter 8 of this textbook contains an overview of cable television functions, cable program services, pay cable, interactive cable, the role of satellites in cable television, teletext and videotex, and a brief commentary on the social impact of cable television.

A number of books project into the future to see what is in store for media and their place in society. Stuart M. DeLuca does this in *Television's Transformation: The Next 25 Years*. Chapter 7 of the DeLuca book is entitled "Cable: The Dream and the Nightmare" and begins with a description of a basic cable system design, moves to a discussion of cable's threat to broadcasting, and then talks about cable television programming development. All of this is phrased in language that is more philosophical than clinical or technical, but the chapter still only amounts to an overview of what cable is all about now and what cable will be about tomorrow.

Marvin Cetron and Thomas O'Toole, in *Encounters with the Future: A Forecast of Life into the 21st Century*, provide a very brief glimpse of the supposed growth, status, and impact of cable in years to come with respect to the family, work, education, privacy, the elderly, and competing elec-

tronic media. Even briefer than the above is Raymond Williams' account
of cable's future in *The Year 2000*. The portion of this book that deals with
cable television places the technology's future into a greater sociological
context, choosing to look at how cable will impact upon how we will live
and exchange ideas and information.

A more significant projection, and one that confines its forecasting entirely to the electronic media, is Joseph P. Martino's "Telecommunications
in the Year 2000," in *Communications Tomorrow*, edited by Edward Cornish.
Martino contends that conflicts will eventually arise between consumers in
what they demand of their cable television services and regulators and
industry leaders in what services they are willing to provide.

Periodical Articles

A number of periodical articles approach cable and related subjects in
what might be considered an overview fashion. "Overview" in this instance
should be stretched somewhat to include content with bits of critical commentary on cable television's present and future condition. Regardless of
the sprinkling of critical commentary, most of the articles noted here explore
general points of cable programming, economics, and regulation.

Heading the list are two articles that describe cable within the context of
other related technologies. Early D. Monroe's "Understanding Telecommunications Systems" aims to show how the newer telecommunication
technologies are "expanding, extending, and replacing older technologies
to create the electronic global village of the future, and in the process creating
new business opportunities for those prepared to access them" (p. 95).
Watson S. James takes an approach similar to Monroe's in "The New
Electronic Media: An Overview."

An introduction to cable television with specific attention to employment
opportunities in the cable industry is the focus of Michael Stanton's "From
Franchise to Programming: Jobs in Cable Television." The history of the
cable television industry is literally "celebrated" in a series of articles that
appear in *Cable Television Business* under the general title "20 Years of Cable
Television."

Articles whose contents bespeak a point of view on a wide range of cable-
related topics must all fall in line behind Thomas Whiteside's three-part
article that appears in the *New Yorker* under the unlikely collective title,
"Onward and Upward with the Arts." The article, in three successive *New
Yorker* installments, is really a minibook whose theme seems to be that in
a frenzy to create all the intricately interlaced components of cable television
there somehow was lost the notion of what it was that cable was supposed
to accomplish. Whiteside clearly shows the symbiotic relationships that have
evolved among cable television and other entertainment/communication
entities. He describes the history of cable in general and then briefly describes

the development of HBO, CNN, C-SPAN, MTV, and CBS Cable. Attention is also paid to the impact upon one another of cable, the movie industry, and the telephone industry. Finally, Whiteside examines cable franchising and government policy toward cable and other electronic media.

Articles are sometimes constructed to explore broad cable issues in a symposium or roundtable panel format where cable authorities in programming, economics, regulation, and so on are gathered to air their views. As an example, "Cable in Perspective" is described in the *CableVision* magazine in which the article appears as a "collection of wildly individual opinions" ranging from the optimistic to the skeptical regarding cable television. The opinions of five "prominent thinkers on the telecommunications scene," ranging from academicians to cable system executives, are included here. Describing the task set before these panelists, a preface to their comments notes, "Judging the state of the [cable] industry is like making a portrait of a 2-year-old child. It won't stay still long enough to capture" (p. 87).

"The Implications of Cable," appearing in *Technology Review*, is a lengthy article comprised of a compendium of cable topics, all of which are related to one another but are nonetheless treated as discrete units. The units in this case include Robert D. Kahn's "More Messages from the Medium"; Martin L. Ernst's "Cable's Economic Impacts"; Nicholas Johnson's "The Myth of the Marketplace"; Pamela Varley's "Cities as Operators"; and Steven L. Solnick's "The Wiring of Britain."

PERIODICAL TITLES

Popular Readership

This heading is somewhat deceptive in that some of the titles included below are really meant for special-interest readers. Nonetheless, most of the periodicals in this category are easily available to anyone in reach of a well-stocked newsstand.

The most common popular readership periodicals such as *Time*, *Newsweek*, *Business Week*, *Forbes*, and *Fortune* all carry an occasional article—most often a brief news item—about some aspect of the cable business. The latter three publications are especially important for information they contribute to cable economic matters. These publications carry articles that range from the financial status of the cable industry as a whole to the financial status of certain parts of the industry. Many of the major cable companies, whether system operators, program producers, or hardware manufacturers, are profiled in these business publications, which also carry commentary on financial trends and forecasts for the cable industry.

Panorama, *Channels* (full title: *Channels, The Business of Communications*), and *Film Comment* are special cases. While seeming to fit into the category of popular readership, none of these would have the mass readership of a

Time or *Business Week*. *Panorama* no longer exists, having ceased publication several years ago. However, before it became defunct *Panorama* was an excellent source of cable articles whose content was meant for a general readership. *Channels* carries on that tradition to some extent, though the subjects of its articles are sometimes a bit esoteric. *Film Comment* is included here because of the reviews of cable programming it contains.

Trade and Professional Readership

Three publications are specifically devoted to cable television: *Cable-Vision*, *Cable Television Business*, and *Cable Marketing*. While all three share some similarities in style and content, there are some basic differences. *CableVision* is the most general of the group, covering territory that includes practically all facets of cable television. It is the news magazine of the business. *CableVision* contains news briefs, features, and analyses under feature headings for programming, business and finance, cable personnel, and products. One important and unique feature of the magazine is the "Cable Stats" section that provides biweekly statistical updates on system performance, franchising, cable penetration, and program service subscribership.

Cable Television Business (formerly *TVC*) carries articles of varying lengths on the business aspects of cable television. Its articles usually concentrate on system and personnel management and methods to improve business and finances. *Cable Television Business* departments carry news items about developments at cable systems and among personnel, new cable hardware, cable literature either available or planned, and financial news with an emphasis on cable system sales and acquisitions and profit/loss performance of cable program services and related businesses.

The news format of *Cable Marketing* does not vary significantly from those of the other two publications. It too carries feature articles of different lengths and several sections devoted to various kinds of cable news. *Cable Marketing*, however, concentrates on matters of marketing and management. Its feature articles cover emerging cable industry trends and developments, provide company profiles and interviews with cable business leaders, report on marketing strategies, and analyze selected cable marketing case histories.

CableAge was a separate publication until January 1985 when its content was merged with its parent publication, *Television/Radio Age*. Prior to the merger, *CableAge*, in a format similar to *Television/Radio Age*, contained special articles and sections covering such topics as cable programming, advertising, marketing, and technology. *CableAge* content was never as comprehensive as that available in competing cable magazines, but the publication's articles were thorough and an important addition to the cable literature. *Television/Radio Age* now carries one or two articles on cable television in practically every issue, but they are integrated among the magazine's other articles. It also provides a regular "Cable Report" department with brief news items about the cable industry, usually of a business or financial nature.

Community Antenna Television Journal (CATJ), a publication of the Community Antenna Television Association, might prove of some value to researchers. But while there are exceptions, most of the articles appearing in this publication slant toward the technology side of cable television.

Multichannel News is best described as the newspaper of the new or emerging electronic media industry. While news items related to other media such as SMATV and MMDS (multichannel multipoint distribution service) indeed may be found here, *Multichannel News* devotes most of its space to cable television. With a comprehensiveness similar to that of *CableVision*, the style of coverage in this tabloid-size weekly comes close to that found in a typical newspaper.

Apart from periodicals devoted entirely or almost entirely to cable television, there are some whose focus is on electronic media in general but with specific space set aside for cable. Chief among these is *Broadcasting* magazine. *Broadcasting* from time to time carries articles primarily about cable alongside those about over-the-air broadcasting. But the publication also includes a regular "Cablecastings" section with brief cable news items.

Electronic Media, *Advertising Age*, and *Marketing and Media Decisions* are other publications that frequently include articles about some aspect of cable television, as does the entertainment industry newspaper, *Variety*. Some of the above also occasionally carry special sections or entire supplements with a cable television theme.

Other trade and professional magazines that carry a fair amount of cable television articles are *Editor and Publisher* and *EMMY Magazine*. One publication that has carried a number of cable/videotex articles, at least in its earlier format, is *Optical Information Systems*. Though the periodical has assumed a more technical orientation of late, its content was more general when published under the title *Videodisc and Optical Disk*, and before that, *Videodisc/Videotex Magazine*.

Scholarly journals contain an assortment of articles that either report on research into some matter related to cable television or that comprise intellectual commentary or analyses of a cable-related subject. The three journals in which most of the articles of this kind may be found are *Journal of Broadcasting and Electronic Media* (formerly just *Journal of Broadcasting*), *Journalism Quarterly*, and *Journal of Communication*.

Legal and Government Readership

Publications under this heading fall into four categories: law journals, judicial reporters and documents, regulatory reporters and documents, and congressional documents. There are few law journals in which cable-related articles have not appeared. Article size ranges from the lengthy analysis and commentary usually on some regulatory practice to the brief note reviewing the substantive issues of a court decision. While many journals carry such articles, five should be considered the most prominent simply because of their emphasis on media matters. The five are the *Federal Communications Law Journal*; *COMM/ENT Law Journal* (*Hastings Journal of Communications and Entertainment Law*); *Communications and the Law*; *Cardozo Arts and Entertainment Law Journal*; and *Publishing, Entertainment, Advertising, and Allied Fields Law Quarterly*.

Cable television has been and likely will continue to be involved in legal disputes that must be resolved in court. *Media Law Reporter* summarizes not only the most important of these cases argued in courts of both state and federal jurisdiction, but also decisions of administrative agencies. All cable cases argued in the federal district courts are reported in the *Federal Supplement*. All those that are argued before the U.S. courts of appeals are reported in the *Federal Reporter*, and all cases that are argued before the U.S. Supreme Court are reported either in *United States Reports* or *Supreme Court Reporter*. The latter is cross-indexed to the former for ease in dual citation.

Many of the decisions in adjudicatory matters related to cable that come before the Federal Communications Commission are reported in *Federal Communications Commission Reports* and *Federal Communications Commission Record*. The *FCC Record* replaced *FCC Reports* as of October 1986. Almost all of the commission's rules and special reports have been published in *FCC Reports* and henceforth will appear, along with key policy statements, in *FCC Record*. Many of the FCC's decisions, rules, and reports—oftentimes those not appearing in *FCC Reports* or *FCC Record*—appear in *Pike and Fischer Radio Regulation*. *Pike and Fischer* is cross-indexed to *FCC Reports* and *FCC Record* for ease in dual citations. *Pike and Fischer* also provides verbatim transcripts of important court decisions involving the electronic media. Many of the notices required of the FCC by law appear in the *Federal Register*. Of particular importance are the notices of proposed rules and the actual rules and arguments supporting or opposing the rules promulgated by the FCC that are published in the *Federal Register*. A codification of all FCC rules affecting cable television is contained in the appropriate volume of the multivolume *Code of Federal Regulations*.

Practically all congressional activity having anything to do with cable eventually finds its way into some published form. Bills containing proposed legislation are the starting point. Copies of bills and resolutions are compiled and maintained by some libraries either in their original form or in microform. Many libraries, however, dispose of them.

Whenever bills are considered by a committee, a hearing may be called to allow testimony on the substance of proposed legislation. Hearing transcripts are usually published (often long after the date or dates of the hearing), and it is here that a wide assortment of information awaits the enterprising researcher. Not only do the transcripts contain views and comments of leading authorities on particular subjects, but supplementary reports and documents pertinent to the matter under discussion also are included. Several cable-related hearings have been conducted through the years by both congressional houses. Those hearings are examined in later sections of this reference guide.

Congressional committees often release information that comes to their attention as Senate or House prints and documents. These publications are sometimes used as vehicles for studies on legislative matters conducted by the Congressional Research Service (CRS). The CRS is an arm of the Library of Congress that conducts research for members of the U.S. House and Senate. CRS studies are available directly from the Library of Congress or from the congressional committee or committee members for whom the CRS studies were undertaken.

Committee reports contain pertinent data about legislation that is being reported by a committee to the floor of the House or Senate. Reports summarize the major components of a bill or resolution and provide arguments supporting and/or opposing the measure.

The *Congressional Record* provides a record of floor debate and commentary on legislative matters. Detailed arguments from supporters and opponents of pending legislation are published in the *Record*, though not necessarily in verbatim form. Members of Congress reserve the right to revise their remarks prior to publication of permanent volumes of the *Congressional Record*. For those researchers seeking verbatim copies of House or Senate floor debates, video and audio recordings of the debates are available from each house. There is a fee charged for the recordings, and video recordings generally are retained for only a short time beyond each day's proceedings.

Laws of the United States and legislative histories of laws are available in *United States Statutes at Large*, *United States Code*, and *United States Code Service, Lawyers Edition*. *U.S. Statutes at Large* provides the full text of all laws passed during each session of Congress. The *U.S. Code* consolidates and codifies all U.S. laws currently in force. The *U.S. Code Service, Lawyers Edition* combines the *U.S. Code* with helpful annotations and historical notes regarding the active laws.

SPECIAL INFORMATION SOURCES

Reference Works, Directories, and Guides

Three major reference works provide an abundance of information about the cable television industry. Much of what each contains is duplicative, but there are enough features unique to each to make all three valuable research tools.

CableFile (the full title includes the year of its issue, for example, *CableFile/ 86*) is a two-volume reference set, with the first volume containing the following sections: (1) Cable Television Associations (a listing of all North American cable and SMATV association names and addresses); (2) Programming Services (data on the basic, pay, audio, regional, and nonsatellite-fed cable programming services); (3) Financial Data (a list of cable attorneys, lenders, brokers, analysts, and consultants); (4) Suppliers and Services (a list of names, addresses, phone numbers and product or service descriptions of cable and SMATV companies serving North America); (5) Index of Equipment and Services (a list of cable and SMATV products or services and the companies that manufacture or distribute them); and (6) Callbook (a telephone directory of cable and SMATV industry personnel located in North America).

The second volume of *CableFile* should be of more value to researchers since it contains a good collection of cable statistics and individual cable system data. Section 1 of this volume provides the statistics, while section 2 provides the cable system profiles. System profiles are arranged by state and provide system name and address, personnel names, and an assortment of programming and operations data. Section 3 provides similar profiles for SMATV systems. The last two sections of *CableFile*, volume 2, provide directories of names, addresses, and phone numbers for key personnel of cable and SMATV multiple-system operators (MSOs).

Television and Cable Factbook is another important reference work. It too is a two-volume set, with volume 1 devoted to television-station data and volume 2 devoted to cable and cable services. The cable volume of the *Factbook* carries a system profile feature organized by state, with pertinent data somewhat similar to that provided in *CableFile*. Similar directories also appear in the *Factbook*, but are better organized than in *CableFile*.

Broadcasting/Cablecasting Yearbook (whose full title, as in the case of *CableFile*, also includes the year of its issue, for example, *Broadcasting/Cablecasting Yearbook 1987*) also has as its major component a cable system profile section arranged by state and providing system data similar to that provided in *CableFile* and the *Factbook*. A section listing MSOs and pertinent MSO data is also provided. The *Yearbook* follows these two sections with two unique sections: the first lists U.S. broadcasters or broadcast groups who own cable systems; the second lists U.S. newspapers that program cable channels. The *Yearbook* concludes its coverage of cable with several statistical tables on cable penetration.

Paul Kagan Associates Inc., publisher of an extensive array of cable newsletters, also publishes two important cable reference works. *The Kagan Census of Cable and Pay TV* provides statistical data on basic and pay cable subscribership grouped by cable system per state, group owner, and so on.

Penetration data are also provided. *The Cable TV Financial Databook* is a source of key cable financial data. It contains analyses of the economic complexion of cable system operation, economic projections for cable's future, and a directory of capital sources for cable development.

Cable Contacts Yearbook contains information especially for public relations specialists. The *Yearbook* gives such individual cable system data as location, personnel, program service description, a listing of access channel and local origination programming, and information about contacting program producers.

The *1985 Videotex-Teleservices Directory* carries information about videotex, teletext, electronic publishing, and other electronic transactional services. Listings for videotex systems, system personnel, and hardware and software manufacturers are also included along with information about projects planned for videotex.

Four reference works of a special nature are Christopher H. Sterling's *Electronic Media: A Guide to Trends in Broadcasting and Newer Technologies, 1920–1983*; *Who's Who in Television and Cable*, edited by Steven Scheuer; *Les Brown's Encyclopedia of Television*; and *Standard and Poor's Industry Surveys*. Sterling's *Electronic Media* contains an abundance of statistical information with an accompanying text to explain the significance of the data. The following categories of measurements over various spans of years are included: growth and size of cable television systems and subscriber base, system ownership trends, cable finances, employment trends in cable, cable program sources and distribution services, and state regulation of cable.

Both Scheuer's *Who's Who* and Les Brown's *Encyclopedia* are oriented toward entertainment personalities. This is not the case, however, for the *Standard and Poor's Industry Surveys*. This publication provides a quarterly economic profile of all media components. Statistical data on media performance are available here. *Industry Surveys* describes cable's operation and the issues affecting cable television performance and then examines future business trends for the industry.

Dictionaries and Glossaries

Several dictionaries and glossaries define the terms associated with cable television. Some of the terms are standard and easily recognizable, but many are unique and have only recently become a part of the cable industry's evolving lexicon. All of the publications mentioned below follow a typical dictionary format. The terms defined in each range from nontechnical to technical to a mixture of the two.

The Random House Dictionary of New Information Technology, edited by A. J. Meadows, M. Gordon, and A. Singleton, defines both technical and nontechnical terms and is illustrated. Tracy David Connors' *Longman Dictionary of Mass Media and Communication* provides very brief definitions of generally nontechnical terms. *A Dictionary of Media Terms* by Edmund Penney has a distinct production orientation. Martin H. Weik's *Communications Standard Dictionary* carries definitions for technical terms. This dictionary would be of use to researchers interested primarily in the technology of cable television.

One of the best and most complete glossaries is the *Glossary of Cable and TV Terms* published by A. C. Nielsen. Shorter glossaries are available in special sections of *CableFile* and *Television and Cable Factbook*. Many cable television textbooks also have short glossaries. *Channels* magazine includes a useful glossary in its annual "Field Guide" issue, and *Variety* occasionally publishes a glossary of media terms.

Career Guides

For persons interested in job opportunities available in cable television, several books provide details on what to do, where to go, and what to expect. Maxine K. Reed and Robert M. Reed's *Career Opportunities in Television, Cable, and Video* heads the list with a comprehensive and well-organized text. The authors describe in detail the several occupations most common to the cable television business alone and those "crossover" occupations common to all electronic media. *Career Opportunities* consists of two parts, with television broadcasting occupations described in part 1 and cable occupations described in part 2. Each part begins with general comments on the business and production status of each medium. The key components of *Career Opportunities* are the job descriptions. Here, in very precise terms, is information that describes the various positions and duties of cable system employees, the typical salaries for these positions, employment prospects for the positions, advancement prospects for persons occupying the positions and what career ladder these persons might expect to climb, requisite education and skills necessary for the positions, opportunities for minorities and women in various cable system positions, and the union requirements associated with these positions. The Reeds conclude their career guide with three appendices containing lists of colleges, scholarships, and workshops related to training for electronic media occupations; lists of unions and associations related to the various occupations; and a bibliography.

Jon S. Denny's *Careers in Cable TV* describes the numerous jobs, positions, and career opportunities in cable and related media businesses. Denny also includes interviews with cable television professionals who tell what they do and how they came to occupy their present positions. *Careers in Cable TV* generally provides a thorough overview of the entire cable business from management to talent to technician.

Jan Bone's *Opportunities in Cable Television* describes how the cable business functions and what career areas exist in cable, offers tips on job hunting and on personal qualities that cable job seekers should have, and provides information on existing training programs. Joshua Sapan's *Making It in Cable TV: Career Opportunities in Today's Fastest Growing Media Industry* and David W. Berlyn's *Exploring Careers in Cable/TV* follow a structure similar to Bone's but concentrate more on explaining the cable television industry and what makes cable tick.

Book Lists, Bibliographies, and Indexes

What is the most obvious source of information for cable television books? There is an inclination to point to the library card catalog or equivalent online data bases. For college libraries, these sources generally yield titles in numbers that are usually dependent upon the presence of a communications department on campus and a major emphasis placed by that department on cable television. Cable television holdings in some libraries are substantive, whereas holdings in others are meager.

Besides library catalogs, there are a number of book-title sources that will supply plenty of titles but hardly a complete listing of cable television books. Some of the book lists are easy to locate, while some effort must be expended to locate the others. A good cable bibliography published on a regular basis is *Communication Booknotes* (formerly *Mass Media Booknotes*). *Communication Booknotes* ranges far afield to cover many aspects of communication but does manage to remain fairly up-to-date with its annotated cable-related book lists.

A bibliography that researchers might find useful for the listings that cover cable television topics from the industry's birth through the mid–1970s is Felix Chin's *Cable Television: A Comprehensive Bibliography*. Another bibliography of a much more general nature but that does provide some cable listings is Benjamin F. Shearer and Marilyn Huxford's *Communications and Society: A Bibliography on Communications Technologies and Their Social Impact*.

One bibliography that may be difficult to locate is "The NAB Library and Information Center Book Exhibit." This bibliography is prepared by the National Association of Broadcasters Library staff to accompany its book display at the annual NAB convention. It provides an excellent source of current book titles and is updated fairly often. The NAB also publishes *Broadcasting Bibliography: A Guide to the Literature of Radio and Television*. The cable-related listings in this paperback publication are limited, and its infrequent appearance (last edition, 1984) makes the bibliography useful only if nothing better happens to be available.

Similar to the NAB's bibliographic contribution is that of the American Newspaper Publishers Association's "Cable TV Resource Guide," published in 1984. Although brief, the bibliographic portion of this guide covers the necessary territory with its title listings.

Special cable television bibliographies appear in a variety of publications. For example, the Congressional Research Service (CRS) of the Library of Congress has prepared several cable bibliographies over the years, generally as accompaniments to CRS reports on legislative efforts leading to passage of the 1984 Cable Act.

Broadcasting/Cablecasting Yearbook contains a brief bibliography, and due to the annual appearance of the *Yearbook* the bibliographical listings are current. The drawback here is the concentration on broadcasting instead of cable books.

Special cable bibliographies may also appear among articles in academic and legal journals. An example is Frank G. Houdek's "Nonbroadcast Video—Programming and Distribution: A Comprehensive Bibliography of Law-Related Periodical Articles" in *COMM/ENT Law Journal*.

Books on cable and textbooks also provide some of the best bibliographies. Many of the books mentioned throughout this reference guide contain excellent bibliographies that may lead the researcher to an extensive array of literature focusing on the specific subject area of the book in which the bibliography appears. Media textbooks are an especially good bet to have general bibliographies that cover a wide range of topics. As an example, Sydney W. Head and Christopher H. Sterling's *Broadcasting in America* carries an eighteen-page bibliography, and many of the bibliographical listings are cable-related. The problem with bibliographies that appear in books is datedness. In the case of the Head/Sterling text, as good as the bibliography is, it leaves a gap between the time when the listings were compiled and the present.

The remedy to the dated bibliographies problem is a periodical that appears frequently and contains a good reporting system for newly published literature. *Journalism Quarterly* (*JQ*) provides not only an annotated bibliography to recent periodical articles, but also a thorough book review section. Though not a bibliography in the rigid sense, the *JQ* book reviews serve the bibliographical purpose just as well. Not to be overlooked are book review sections in other journals. The *Journal of Broadcasting and Electronic Media* has its own extensive review section, as does the *Journal of Communication*. Book reviews also appear on an infrequent schedule in such publications as *Broadcasting* and *Multichannel News*.

Somewhat distant from typical bibliographical sources are the bibliographies that appear in master's theses and doctoral dissertations. These may be the most thorough bibliographies available on the specific thesis or dissertation topic. Scholarly papers prepared for convention delivery also fall into this category in that their bibliographies can be extensive and certainly current. Footnote or endnote citations in these papers as well as citations in published journal articles are also the source of some good, solid bibliographic information. This is especially true of articles appearing in law journals and law reviews. Footnote citations for these articles are so voluminous that they sometimes occupy more space than that of an article's text. Researchers should not overlook the storehouse of reference material located here. An added benefit to those engaged in legal research is the abundance of case citations contained in law or regulatory article footnotes.

One of the best ways of staying abreast of cable television books that are either new on the market or planned for future publication is from publishers' mailings. Major publishers of communication books often prepare elaborate brochures to announce new books. These brochures sometimes contain lists of other books available from the publisher. A communication-specific list of publishers is included in "The NAB Library and Information Center Book Exhibit" and the NAB's *Broadcasting Bibliography: A Guide to the Literature of Radio and Television*, both mentioned previously. Publisher names may also be drawn from bibliographies in cable books and textbooks as well as from the books mentioned throughout this reference guide.

The extensive array of articles on cable television that have been written in the past few years are found in a wide assortment of publications. Most of these have been indexed somewhere. Researchers should be acquainted, of course, with the more familiar indexes such as *Readers' Guide to Periodical Literature*, *Social Sciences Index*, or *Business Periodicals Index*. Less familiar, though, might be important indexes such as the *Public Affairs Information Service (PAIS) Bulletin* that indexes articles, reports, hearings, and so on from general readership periodicals as well as government documents, or the *Index to Current Urban Documents* that provides detailed descriptions of major government documents issued by the largest U.S. municipalities and counties. A good reference librarian, especially one who has at least a general familiarity with the electronic media, is most important for a cable television researcher seeking guidance to proper indexes and online data bases.

One index to articles appearing only in electronic communication periodicals is *Topicator*. Though *Topicator* may sometimes be inaccurate with location information, it nonetheless remains current and provides listings and cross-listings under specific subject areas. The periodicals indexed in *Topicator* are the ones that contain most of the articles dealing with practically every facet of cable television. Among those included are *Advertising Age*, *Broadcasting*, *Channels*, *Editor and Publisher*, *Journal of Broadcasting and Electronic Media*, *Journal of Communication*, *Media and Marketing Decisions*, *Television/Radio Age*, *TV Guide*, and *Variety*.

Complementing *Topicator* is *Communication Abstracts*. This index contains annotated references to cable television books and book chapters as well as cable-related articles appearing in scholarly or academic journals and law journals.

Many academic and professional journals also have their own cumulative indexes. The journals may be indexed annually by volume or by the irregular publication of indexes to several volumes that may stretch to a decade or more.

One note about using indexes: Do not give up the search if there are no listings under "cable television." Look for listings that may appear under other keywords. The keyword "cable television" has been used widely for only a few years. Many indexes of the 1970s and early 1980s list cable television articles under either "CATV" or "community antenna television." If none of the cable keywords are used, check the following keywords for whatever information they may yield: "broadcasting," "communication," "mass communication," "mass media," "media," "telecommunication," "television," and "video." For videotex listings, if nothing is found under the keyword "videotex" or "videotext," check "teletext" or any of the other keywords listed above.

Newsletters and Bulletins

Newsletters and bulletins generally are not as readily available to researchers as are other kinds of publications. The major reason for their scarcity is cost. An annual subscription fee that could run to $500 or more for weekly issues of a newsletter that sometimes consists of only a few pages is beyond what most libraries reasonably can afford. Since the information contained in newsletters and bulletins is usually the most current and in many cases the best available on a given subject, the researcher would be advised either to seek access to the publications from cable professionals or communication attorneys who might subscribe to them or to contact the publications' publishers for single issues of a needed newsletter or bulletin. Names and addresses for newsletters not included here may be found in directories and reference works mentioned earlier in this chapter. A particularly good source of titles is *Television and Cable Factbook*.

The number of cable-related newsletters is extensive, so extensive in fact that only those considered by the author as most notable will be described below. The best way to begin is by listing all the newsletters published by Paul Kagan Associates Inc. Information contained in this family of newsletters covers practically every facet of cable television. A brief content description will accompany each of the following titles: *Cable TV Investor* (private and public cable investments and stock values); *The Pay TV Newsletter* (subscriber, revenue, and profit analysis); *Cable TV Investor Charts* (public cable company stock price trends); *Cable TV Programming* (economics of basic and pay cable programming); *Cable TV Advertising* (commercial time sales analysis for basic and pay cable); *Cable TV Franchising* (franchise awards, renewals, and related legal matters); *Cable TV Technology* (technical information and system construction and rebuild updates); *Media Sports Business* (sports media rights and media competition for sports programming); *Marketing New Media* (sales, promotion, and marketing trends among cable and other emerging electronic media); *Electronic Publisher* (videotex and newspaper/cable developments); *SMATV News* (economic, technical, legal, and marketing matters related to SMATV); *Multicast* (matters related to multipoint distribution service); *Cable TV Finance* (investment and other financial matters affecting cable); *Cable TV Tax Letter* (cable tax shelters and limited partnership developments); *Cable TV Law Reporter* (developments in legal matters affecting cable); and *Theft-of-Service Newsletter* (methods to combat cable piracy and legal developments on the problem).

Television Digest Inc. publishes five newsletters that should be of interest to researchers. *Television Digest* carries news of a varied nature about electronic media generally with cable included. *Communications Daily* does much the same but on a daily basis. *Cable Action Update* carries news of franchising and cable system sales. *Video Week* provides information on video programming sales and finances, and *Satellite Week* carries news of the communication–satellite industry that relates to cable television.

QV Publishing Inc. publishes *Cablesports*, which reports on trends and developments in cable and pay cable sports program distribution. QV also publishes *Pay-Per-View Update*, which provides information on pay–per–view programming and distribution developments, and *Cable/Consumer Electronics*, which analyzes the place of cable system operators in the electronic marketplace of videocassette recorders (VCRs), television receive only dishes (TVROs), and other distribution technologies.

The title denotes the content of *The Lewis Letter on Cable Marketing*, published by Lewis Associates Inc. The same is true for *Worldwide Videotex Update*, whose publisher's name is the same as the newsletter's title. Another newsletter that deals with videotex is *International Videotex Teletext News*, published by Arlen Communications Inc. Arlen also publishes *Teleservices Report* and its supplement, *Teleselling Report*. These two newsletters carry information on electronic shopping, banking, and other interactive services available via cable and videotex. Television/Radio Age publishes *Connections*, which focuses on international electronic communications but occasionally contains items on U.S. cable and videotex.

The following four newsletters have a decidedly nonbusiness slant, three of them focusing more on providing information for the cable employee and consumer. *Women in Cable Newsletter*, published by Women in Cable Inc., carries news items and cable employment information of particular interest to women. The Foundation for Community Service Cable Television publishes *Cable Scan*, which examines ways for members of the public and local government to use community service cable access channels. *C-SPAN Update*, published by the Cable Satellite Public Affairs Network, carries news and information about C-SPAN programming, program topics, guests, and future schedules. Finally, there is *CTIC CableReports*, published by the Cable Television Information Center with the stated goal of providing information so that local municipal officials might make better decisions on telecommunication policies.

There are several helpful newsletters available on various aspects of legal and regulatory matters related to cable television. Kagan's *Cable TV Franchising* and *Cable TV Law Reporter* have already been mentioned. In addition to these there are the *National Association of Regulatory Utility Commissioners Bulletin, Nation's Cities Weekly, NATOA News,* and *Cable TV and New Media.* The *NATOA News* contains items for and about the National Association of Telecommunications Officers and Advisors and is published along with *Nation's Cities Weekly* by the National League of Cities. *FCC Week* contains news about FCC (Federal Communications Commission) actions affecting the telephone industry primarily but does give some attention to cable. This weekly news service, published by a commercial concern not associated with the FCC itself, also provides a service for subscribers needing to obtain FCC documents.

Reports

Reports of various kinds are good sources of cable information but unfortunately are not always easy to locate. Although some reports may be published, most are not, and while some companies such as Paul Kagan Associates Inc. prepare reports for general acquisition, most are prepared by consultants to fulfill specific requests. A consultant's report may be meant for a particular client but still may be available to others who wish to purchase it, or the report may be proprietary in nature and meant for use only by the person or company requesting it. Even when researchers find that reports may be purchased, they may not be able to afford the price. Consultants' reports may be just as expensive as the newsletters mentioned previously. However, enterprising researchers may be able to make a good-enough case for their project needs to persuade a consultant company to provide reports free of charge. Names of management, financial, program, and engineering consultants may be found in directories and reference books listed elsewhere. *Television and Cable Factbook* is an especially good source for such listings.

A few reports are published, although in somewhat crude forms at times. The Rand Corporation has sponsored publication of a bevy of reports on cable television, such as Stanley M. Besen and Leland L. Johnson's *An Economic Analysis of Mandatory Leased Channel Access for Cable Television.* A compilation of papers may also sometimes appear in report form, as in the case of excerpts presented at Columbia University's symposium on "Rivalry among Video Transmission Media: Assessment and Implications" that comprise *The Economics of Cable Television (CATV): An Anthology,* edited by Mark Nadel and Eli Noam. This anthology may only loosely be called a published volume, since it contains only working papers gathered and bound in October 1983 for use by participants at the April 1984 conference. Nevertheless, researchers may find some very useful items here.

Closely akin to the publication resulting from the Columbia University symposium are cable-related reports that are published by research centers or special programs associated with colleges and universities. An example is David N. Allen and Daniel J. Kennedy's *Municipal Regulation of Cable Television in the Commonwealth of Pennsylvania*, published by Pennsylvania State University's Institute of Public Administration. The report examines cable television regulation in Pennsylvania municipalities. A second example of the university research center report is *A Review of Telecommunications Technologies and Public Broadcasting*, prepared by John Carey and Mitchell Moss of the Interactive Telecommunications Program at New York University. The report, prepared for the Corporation for Public Broadcasting, outlines the various ways in which public broadcasters may incorporate new technologies such as cable television and videotex into their programming plans. *Issues Facing Cable Television*, published by the Center for Research on Communication Technology and Society of the University of Texas at Austin and supervised by Sharon Stover, is yet a third example of a report generated by a university research center. As its title suggests, this fifty-page report briefly reviews the status of a variety of cable television issues.

Other examples of published reports that might be of use to the researcher are Barry Orton's *Cable Television and the Cities: Local Regulation and Municipal Uses, The Process of Cable Television Franchising: A New York City Case Study*, and Benjamin M. Compaine's *Chronology of Telecommunications and Cable Television Regulation in the United States*. The first of these reports consists of the proceedings from a University of Wisconsin conference meant to enlighten municipal regulators about cable deregulation. *The Process of Cable Television Franchising* is a product of the New York Law School's Communications Media Center. It analyzes big-city cable franchising problems by using New York City cable franchising as a model. The Compaine report is a product of Harvard University's Program on Information Resources Policy. An outstanding feature of this publication is a tabular format that includes in adjacent columns arranged on a year-by-year basis from 1947 to 1983 brief notes on cable industry developments; state legislative, judicial, and regulatory developments; and federal judicial and administrative developments.

Published reports also are prepared by federal and state government agencies. An example is the FCC's *State Legislation 1982*, a state-by-state review of legislative activity affecting cable television prepared by the commission's Cable Television Bureau.

Finding out about unpublished reports is often difficult. The researcher generally must keep on his toes by observing news items that appear in the cable periodical literature about report preparation or presentation. *CableVision, Broadcasting*, and *Multichannel News* often carry news articles about reports that have been commissioned by some cable interest and brief summaries of reports that have been released to the press. Sometimes these summaries will follow presentation of reports during cable meetings or conventions. These three periodicals also list dates for upcoming cable meetings and conventions. Researchers may attend these conventions and pick up reports or information about reports in person, or they may wait for news articles to appear with information about the reports.

One excellent source of unpublished reports is government documents, particularly U.S. House and Senate committee hearing records. Witnesses appearing before committees sometimes will introduce either whole reports or excerpted portions of reports they have prepared for insertion into the hearing transcript.

A special kind of report is the annual report issued by major cable companies and MSOs to their stockholders. Histories of companies, their organization, structure, and especially their financial status are included prominently in these annual reports. Many libraries receive annual reports from major companies. If not available in a library, copies of reports may be requested from the issuing companies themselves. Most companies usually are happy to comply with such requests.

Academic Papers

Academic papers on cable matters, somewhat akin to reports, are presented at conventions, meetings, and other similar gatherings and usually are unpublished. Some of these papers eventually may appear in such publications as the *Journal of Broadcasting and Electronic Media* or *Journalism Quarterly* if they contain substantive information of value and if they pass muster before a panel of referees. Papers not published by a journal may be available in a semipublished form through the Educational Resources Information Center (ERIC). ERIC is a document networking system that makes available documents, including scholarly papers, in microform or full-size hard copy. Many libraries house their own ERIC microform collection. The collection may be accessed through the *Resources in Education* index.

A paper not available through ERIC may be obtained in person at the meeting where the paper is presented or by writing to the paper's author. The trick here, of course, is to know what meetings to attend and when and where the meetings will be held. Some of the organizations that sponsor meetings where cable-related papers are most likely to be presented include the Broadcast Education Association (BEA), Association for Education in Journalism and Mass Communication (AEJMC), International Communication Association (ICA), and the Speech Communication Association (SCA). The AEJMC also sponsors regional meetings where papers are presented. Moreover, there are four separate regional speech communication associations that also sponsor paper presentations at their own annual meetings. Meeting dates and locations for all of these organizations are published in the *Chronicle of Higher Education. Broadcasting* also publishes meeting dates and places for the BEA, which meets in conjunction with the annual convention of the National Association of Broadcasters.

Information about papers planned for presentation at meetings of these organizations is found in convention programs. These programs are available in advance of the actual meetings and usually may be obtained (sometimes at a slight cost) by requesting copies from the organizations' headquarters. Since the programs provide paper titles and author names and addresses, researchers wishing a copy of a convention paper may contact the author by phone or mail with a request for the copy. A cautionary note for persons who travel to a meeting hoping to hear or obtain a copy of a scholarly paper: Academicians are notorious for failing to appear at panel sessions, for failing to supply copies of their paper, or for having prepared only a portion (sometimes only an abstract) of the paper they have been scheduled to present. Moreover, convention paper titles can be deceptive since they may suggest that a paper's content will be far more substantive than what the text actually can manage to deliver.

Other Information Sources

There are several sources of information that do not fit neatly into other categories. For instance, cable-related organizations sometimes publish booklets containing concise but useful information about particular matters. One such booklet is the National Cable Television Association's *A Cable Primer*. The *Primer* actually is a minitextbook (fifty-four pages, including appendices) divided into five sections on cable technology, economics, franchising, programming, and federal and state cable regulation. An even shorter booklet (twenty-seven pages) is *Community Guide to Cable TV*, written by Stan Tamai for the Foundation for Community Service Cable Television. The main purpose of *Community Guide* is to introduce persons and groups to cable television's potential as a public service medium through local origination programming. Advice on producing such programming is provided alongside names and addresses of organizations that lend assistance to these endeavors.

Another publication prepared with a public interest objective is Bruce D. Jacobs, Marsha D. Krassner, and Cheryl R. Suchors' *Own Your Own Cable System*. The booklet describes the benefits of cable cooperative ownership whereby cable system subscribers also own the system. The authors suggest ways of starting and financing such a cooperative venture and provide pointers on constructing a cable franchise proposal.

Many libraries maintain files for cable-related items such as brochures, press releases, special mailings, and the like. Treasures may exist in these files, which researchers often overlook. Sources of another kind exist for researchers investigating local cable systems. These sources fall into written and unwritten categories.

In the written category are cable franchise documents and other municipal documents and records that are available and open to the public. Included here are franchise proposals, transcripts of franchise negotiations, cable consultant reports, cable performance reports, and a host of other important documents. Documents may also be available from local municipal cable oversight offices and state cable regulatory bodies. For cable systems that have been involved in litigation, court records and trial transcripts yield much information about the systems. Cable operators may also provide written information about their system, although persons engaged in a private business are less inclined to share information in the same way as public officials who may be required to do so. Local newspapers usually publish a good share of articles on local cable systems. Researchers may also count on state and city magazines to supply articles on local cable television.

For unwritten sources, researchers need look no further than the authors of all the documents and the reporters for the newspapers and magazines described above. Interviews with municipal officials, cable system personnel, cable consultants, and anyone else directly involved in the development and operation of a local cable television system should be the source of an abundance of information. Add to these the magazine writer who has spent days and weeks researching a story on cable television or the newspaper reporter whose beat or specialty may be cable matters. Certainly not to be overlooked by nonacademicians engaged in cable research are the academicians at local universities whose area of expertise may include cable television.

GENERAL SOURCES BIBLIOGRAPHY

Cable Overview Publications

Books and Book Chapters

Baldwin, Thomas F., and D. Stevens McVoy. *Cable Communication*. Englewood Cliffs, N.J.: Prentice-Hall, 1983.

Bittner, John R. *Broadcasting and Telecommunication: An Introduction*. 2d ed. Englewood Cliffs, N.J.: Prentice-Hall, 1985.

Black, Jay, and Frederick C. Whitney. *Introduction to Mass Communication*. Dubuque, Iowa: Wm. C. Brown, 1983.

Breitrose, Henry. "The New Communication Technologies and the New Distribution of Roles." In *The Media Revolution in America and in Western Europe*, edited by Everett M. Rogers and Francis Balle. Norwood, N.J.: Ablex, 1985.

Cetron, Marvin, and Thomas O'Toole. *Encounters with the Future: A Forecast of Life into the 21st Century*. New York: McGraw-Hill, 1982.

DeLuca, Stuart M. *Television's Transformation: The Next 25 Years*. New York: A. S. Barnes, 1980.

Dutton, William H., Jay G. Blumler, and Kenneth L. Kraemer, eds. *Wired Cities: Shaping the Future of Communications*. Boston, Mass.: G. K. Hall, 1987.

Foster, Eugene S. *Understanding Broadcasting*. 2d ed. Reading, Mass.: Addison-Wesley, 1982.

Grant, William. *Cable Television*. Reston, Va.: Reston Publishing, 1983.

Gross, Lynne Schafer. *The New Television Technologies*. 2d ed. Dubuque, Iowa: Wm. C. Brown, 1986.

—————. *Telecommunications: An Introduction to Radio, Television, and Other Electronic Media*. 2d ed. Dubuque, Iowa: Wm. C. Brown, 1986.

Head, Sydney W., and Christopher H. Sterling. *Broadcasting in America*. 5th ed. Boston, Mass.: Houghton Mifflin, 1987.

Hollowell, Mary Louise, ed. *The Cable/Broadband Communications Book*. Vol. 1, *1977–1978*. Washington, D.C.: Communications Press, 1977.

—————. *The Cable/Broadband Communications Book*. Vol. 2, *1980–1981*. White Plains, N.Y.: Knowledge Industry Publications, 1980.

—————. *The Cable/Broadband Communications Book*. Vol. 3, *1982–1983*. White Plains, N.Y.: Knowledge Industry Publications, 1983.

McGee, William L., Joseph H. Caton, and Lucy E. Garrick. *Changes, Challenges, and Opportunities in the New Electronic Media*. San Francisco: BMC Publications, 1983.

Martino, Joseph P. "Telecommunications in the Year 2000." In *Communications Tomorrow*, edited by Edward Cornish. Bethesda, Md.: World Future Society, 1982.

National Association of Broadcasters. *New Technologies Affecting Radio and Television Broadcasting*. Washington, D.C.: National Association of Broadcasters, 1981.

Roman, James W. *Cablemania: The Cable Television Sourcebook*. Englewood Cliffs, N.J.: Prentice-Hall, 1983.

Singleton, Loy A. *Telecommunications in the Information Age*. 2d ed. Cambridge, Mass.: Ballinger, 1986.

Smith, Marvin. *Radio, TV, and Cable: A Telecommunications Approach*. New York: Holt, Rinehart and Winston, 1985.

Sparkes, Vernone. "Cable Television in the United States: A Story of Continuing Growth and Change." In *Cable Television and the Future of Broadcasting*, edited by Ralph M. Negrine. New York: St. Martin's Press, 1985.

The Video Age: Television Technology and Applications in the 1980s. White Plains, N.Y.: Knowledge Industry Publications, 1982.

Whitehouse, George E. *Understanding the New Technologies of the Mass Media*. Englewood Cliffs, N.J.: Prentice-Hall, 1986.

Williams, Frederick. *The Communications Revolution*. Rev. ed. New York: Mentor, 1983.

Williams, Raymond. *The Year 2000*. New York: Pantheon Books, 1983.

Periodical Articles

"Cable in Perspective." *CableVision*, 10 December 1984, 87–113.

"The Implications of Cable." *Technology Review*, January 1983, 48–62.

James, Watson S. "The New Electronic Media: An Overview." *Journal of Advertising Research* 23 (August/September 1983): 33–37.

Monroe, Early D. "Understanding Telecommunications Systems." *Urban League Review* 8 (Winter 1983/1984): 95–106.

Stanton, Michael. "From Franchise to Programming: Jobs in Cable Television." *Occupational Outlook Quarterly* 29 (Summer 1985): 26–32.

"20 Years of Cable Television." *Cable Television Business*, 1 February 1984, 13–134.

Whiteside, Thomas. "Onward and Upward with the Arts." *New Yorker*, 20 May 1985, 45–87; 27 May 1985, 43–73; 3 June 1985, 82–105.

Periodical Titles

(Publication frequency is enclosed in parentheses following selected titles)

Popular Readership

Channels (eleven times annually). C. C. Publishing Inc., 19 W. 44th St., New York, N.Y. 10036.

Film Comment (bimonthly). Film Society of Lincoln Center, 140 W. 65th St., New York, N.Y. 10023.

Panorama (discontinued). Triangle Communications Inc., 850 Third Ave., New York, N.Y. 10022.

Trade and Professional Readership

Advertising Age (weekly). Crain Communications Inc., 740 Rush St., Chicago, Ill. 60611.

Broadcasting (weekly). Broadcasting Publications Inc., 1735 De Sales St., N.W., Washington, D.C. 20036.

CableAge (bimonthly until content incorporated into biweekly *Television/Radio Age*). Television/Radio Age, 1270 Avenue of the Americas, New York, N.Y. 10020.

Cable Marketing (monthly). Jobson Publishing Corp., 352 Park Ave. South, New York, N.Y. 10010.

Cable Television Business (biweekly). Cardiff Publishing Co., 6300 S. Syracuse Way, Englewood, Colo. 80111.

CableVision (biweekly). International Thomson Communications Inc., 600 Grant St., Denver, Colo. 80203.

Community Antenna Television Journal (CATJ) (monthly). Television Publications Inc., 4209 N.W. 23rd, Suite 106, Oklahoma City, Okla. 73107.

Editor and Publisher (weekly). Editor and Publisher Co., 11 W. 19th St., New York, N.Y. 10011.

Electronic Media (weekly). Crain Communications Inc., 740 Rush St., Chicago, Ill. 60611.

EMMY Magazine (bimonthly). Academy of Television Arts and Sciences, 3500 W. Olive Ave., Burbank, Calif. 91505.

Journal of Broadcasting and Electronic Media (quarterly). Broadcast Education Association, 1771 N St., N.W., Washington, D.C. 20036.

Journal of Communication (quarterly). International Communication Association, 8140 Burnet Road, P.O. Box 9589, Austin, Tex. 78766.

Journalism Quarterly (quarterly). Association for Education in Journalism and Mass Communication, University of South Carolina, Columbia, S.C. 29208.

Marketing and Media Decisions (monthly). Decisions Publications Inc., 1140 Avenue of the Americas, New York, N.Y. 10036.

Multichannel News (weekly). Fairchild Publications, 7 East 12th St., New York, N.Y. 10003.

Optical Information Systems (bimonthly). Meckler Publishing, 11 Ferry Lane West, Westport, Conn. 06880.

Variety (weekly). Variety Inc., 154 W. 46th St., New York, N.Y. 10036.

Legal and Government Readership

Cardozo Arts and Entertainment Law Journal (biannually). New York: Benjamin N. Cardozo School of Law, Yeshiva University.

Code of Federal Regulations. Washington, D.C.: U.S. Government Printing Office.

COMM/ENT Law Journal (*Hastings Journal of Communications and Entertainment Law*) (quarterly). San Francisco: Hastings College of the Law, University of California.

Communications and the Law (bimonthly). Westport, Conn.: Meckler Publishing Corp.

Congressional Record. Washington, D.C.: U.S. Government Printing Office.

Federal Communications Commission Reports, superseded by *Federal Communications Commission Record.* Washington, D.C.: U.S. Government Printing Office.

Federal Communications Law Journal (three times annually). Los Angeles: School of Law, University of California, Los Angeles.

Federal Register. Washington, D.C.: U.S. Government Printing Office.

Federal Reporter. St. Paul, Minn.: West Publishing.

Federal Supplement. St. Paul, Minn.: West Publishing.

Media Law Reporter. Washington, D.C.: Bureau of National Affairs Inc.

Pike and Fischer Radio Regulation. Bethesda, Md.: Pike and Fischer Inc.

Publishing, Entertainment, Advertising, and Allied Fields Law Quarterly (quarterly). Pittsburg, Pa.: Edward L. Graf, Jr., PEAL.

Supreme Court Reporter. St. Paul, Minn.: West Publishing.

United States Code. Washington, D.C.: U.S. Government Printing Office.

United States Code Service, Lawyers Edition. Rochester, N.Y.: The Lawyers Co-operative Publishing Co.

United States Reports. Washington, D.C.: U.S. Government Printing Office.

United States Statutes at Large. Washington, D.C.: U.S. Government Printing Office.

Special Information Sources

Reference Works, Directories, and Guides

Broadcasting/Cablecasting Yearbook (annual). Broadcasting Publications Inc., 1735 De Sales St., N.W., Washington, D.C. 20036.

Brown, Les. *Les Brown's Encyclopedia of Television.* New York: New York Zoetrope, 1982.

Cable Contacts Yearbook (annual). Larimi Communications Associated, Ltd., 246 W. 38th St., New York, N.Y. 10018.

CableFile (annual). International Thomson Communications Inc., 600 Grant St., Denver, Colo. 80203.

The Cable TV Financial Databook (annual). Paul Kagan Associates Inc., 126 Clock Tower Place, Carmel, Calif. 93923.

The Kagan Census of Cable and Pay TV (annual). Paul Kagan Associates Inc., 126 Clock Tower Place, Carmel, Calif. 93923.

Scheuer, Steven, ed. *Who's Who in Television and Cable.* New York: Facts on File Publications, 1983.

Standard and Poor's Industry Surveys (quarterly). Standard and Poor's Corp., 25 Broadway, New York, N.Y. 10004.

Sterling, Christopher H. *Electronic Media: A Guide to Trends in Broadcasting and Newer Technologies, 1920–1983.* New York: Praeger, 1984.

Television and Cable Factbook (annual). Television Digest Inc., 1836 Jefferson Place, N.W., Washington, D.C. 20036.

1985 Videotex-Teleservices Directory (future update publication indefinite). Arlen Communications Inc., 7315 Wisconsin Ave., Bethesda, Md. 20814.

Dictionaries and Glossaries

Connors, David. *Longman Dictionary of Mass Media and Communication.* New York: Longman, 1982.

Glossary of Cable and TV Terms. Northbrook, Ill.: A. C. Nielsen, 1981.

Meadows, A. J., M. Gordon, and A. Singleton. *The Random House Dictionary of New Information Technology.* New York: Vintage Books, 1983.

Penney, Edmund. *A Dictionary of Media Terms.* New York: G. P. Putnam's Sons, 1984.

Weik, Martin H. *Communications Standard Dictionary.* New York: Van Nostrand Reinhold, 1983.

Career Guides

Berlyn, David W. *Exploring Careers in Cable/TV.* New York: Rosen Publishing Group, 1985.

Bone, Jan. *Opportunities in Cable Television.* Lincolnwood, Ill.: VGM/National Textbook Co., 1984.

Denny, Jon S. *Careers in Cable TV.* New York: Barnes & Noble, 1983.

Reed, Maxine K., and Robert M. Reed. *Career Opportunities in Television, Cable, and Video.* 2d ed. New York: Facts on File Publications, 1986.

Sapan, Joshua. *Making It in Cable TV: Career Opportunities in Today's Fastest Growing Media Industry.* New York: Putnam/Perigree, 1984.

Book Lists, Bibliographies, and Indexes

Broadcasting Bibliography: A Guide to the Literature of Radio and Television. 2d ed. Washington, D.C.: National Association of Broadcasters, 1984.

Business Periodicals Index. Bronx, N.Y.: H. W. Wilson Co.

Chin, Felix. *Cable Television: A Comprehensive Bibliography.* New York: IFI/Plenum, 1978.

"Cable TV Resource Guide." Washington, D.C.: American Newspaper Publishers Association, 1984.

Communication Abstracts. Newbury Park, Calif.: Sage.

Newsletters and Bulletins

Cable Action Update (weekly). Television Digest Inc., 1836 Jefferson Place, N.W., Washington, D.C. 20036.

Cable/Consumer Electronics (monthly). QV Publishing Inc., 250 E. Hartsdale Ave., Hartsdale, N.Y. 10530.

Cable Scan (quarterly). Foundation for Community Service Cable Television, 5010 Geary Blvd., Suite 3, San Francisco, Calif. 94118.

Cablesports (weekly). QV Publishing Inc.

Cable TV Advertising (monthly). Paul Kagan Associates Inc., 126 Clock Tower Place, Carmel, Calif. 93923.

Cable TV Finance (monthly). Paul Kagan Associates Inc.

Cable TV Franchising (monthly). Paul Kagan Associates Inc.

Cable TV Investor (monthly). Paul Kagan Associates Inc.

Cable TV Investor Charts (monthly). Paul Kagan Associates Inc.

Cable TV Law Reporter (monthly). Paul Kagan Associates Inc.

Cable TV and New Media (monthly). Leader Publications, 111 Eighth Ave., New York, N.Y. 10011.

Cable TV Programming (monthly). Paul Kagan Associates Inc.

Cable TV Tax Letter (monthly). Paul Kagan Associates Inc.

Cable TV Technology (monthly). Paul Kagan Associates Inc.

Communications Daily (daily). Television Digest Inc.

Connections (biweekly). Television/Radio Age, 1270 Avenue of the Americas, New York, N.Y. 10020.

C-SPAN Update (weekly). Cable Satellite Public Affairs Network, 400 N. Capitol St., N.W., Washington, D.C. 20001.

CTIC CableReports (monthly). The Cable Television Information Center, 1500 North Beauregard St., Suite 205, Alexandria, Va. 22311.

Electronic Publisher (monthly). Paul Kagan Associates Inc.

FCC Week (weekly). Capitol Publications Inc., 1300 N. 17th St., Arlington, Va. 22209.

International Videotex Teletext News (monthly). Arlen Communications Inc., 7315 Wisconsin Ave., Bethesda, Md. 20814.

The Lewis Letter on Cable Marketing (monthly). Lewis Associates Inc., Housatonic, Mass. 01236.

Marketing New Media (monthly). Paul Kagan Associates Inc.

Media Sports Business (monthly). Paul Kagan Associates Inc.

Multicast (monthly). Paul Kagan Associates Inc.

National Association of Regulatory Utility Commissioners Bulletin (weekly). National Association of Regulatory Utility Commissioners, 1102 Interstate Commerce Commission Building, Washington, D.C. 20044.

Nation's Cities Weekly (weekly). National League of Cities, 1301 Pennsylvania Ave., N.W., Washington, D.C. 20004.

NATOA News (bimonthly). National League of Cities.

Pay-Per-View Update (biweekly). QV Publishing Inc.

The Pay TV Newsletter (monthly). Paul Kagan Associates Inc.

Satellite Week (weekly). Television Digest Inc.

SMATV News (monthly). Paul Kagan Associates Inc.

Teleservices Report (monthly). Arlen Communications Inc., 7315 Wisconsin Ave., Bethesda, Md. 20814.

Television Digest (weekly). Television Digest Inc.

Theft-of-Service Newsletter (monthly). Paul Kagan Associates Inc.

Video Week (weekly). Television Digest Inc.

Women in Cable Newsletter (monthly). Women in Cable Inc., 2033 M St., N.W., Washington, D.C. 20036.

Worldwide Videotex Update (monthly). Worldwide Videotex Update, Babson Park Branch, Boston, Mass. 02157.

Reports

Allen, David N., and Daniel J. Kennedy. *Municipal Regulation of Cable Television in the Commonwealth of Pennsylvania*. University Park, Pa.: Pennsylvania State University Institute of Public Administration, 1982.

Besen, Stanley M., and Leland L. Johnson. *An Economic Analysis of Mandatory Leased Channel Access for Cable Television*. R–2989-MF. Santa Monica, Calif.: Rand Corp., 1982.

Carey, John, and Mitchell Moss. *A Review of Telecommunications Technologies and Public Broadcasting*. New York: New York University Interactive Telecommunications Program, 1984.

Compaine, Benjamin M. *Chronology of Telecommunications and Cable Television Regulation in the United States*. Cambridge, Mass.: Program on Information Resources Policy, Harvard University, 1984.

Federal Communications Commission. *State Legislation 1982*. Washington, D.C.: FCC Cable Television Bureau, 1982.

Nadel, Mark, and Eli Noam, eds. *The Economics of Cable Television (CATV): An Anthology*. New York: Columbia University, 1983.

Orton, Barry. *Cable Television and the Cities: Local Regulation and Municipal Uses*. Madison, Wis.: University of Wisconsin—Extension, 1980.

The Process of Cable Television Franchising: A New York City Case Study. New York: Communications Media Center, New York Law School, 1980.

Stover, Sharon. *Issues Facing Cable Television*. Austin, Tex.: Center for Research on Communication Technology and Society of the University of Texas at Austin, 1986.

Academic Papers

Academic organization addresses:

Association for Education in Journalism and Mass Communication, University of South Carolina, Columbia, S.C. 29208.

Broadcast Education Association, 1771 N St., N.W., Washington, D.C. 20036.

International Communication Association, 8140 Burnet Road, P.O. Box 9589, Austin, Tex. 78766.

Speech Communication Association, 5105 Backlick Rd , Suite E, Annandale, Va. 22003.

Chronicle of Higher Education (weekly). The Chronicle of Higher Education Inc., 1255 Twenty-Third St., N.W., Washington, D.C. 20037.

Resources in Education. Washington, D.C.: U.S. Government Printing Office.

Other Information Sources

A Cable Primer. Washington, D.C.: National Cable Television Association, 1981.

Jacobs, Bruce D., Marsha D. Krassner, and Cheryl R. Suchors. *Own Your Own Cable System.* Washington, D.C.: National Consumer Cooperative Bank, 1983.

Tamai, Stan. *Community Guide to Cable TV.* San Francisco: Foundation for Community Service Cable Television, 1984.

Chapter Two

BUSINESS AND INDUSTRY/SYSTEM ECONOMICS

ISSUE OVERVIEW

The business and economic landscape of cable television in the 1980s represents an incredible topography, pockmarked by years of ups and downs and starts and stops. Wherever the financial paths have led and whatever the obstacles that have impeded economic progress, venturesome cable entrepreneurs have plunged ahead. Success stories and failure stories galore abound in the cable television business. For those in the industry who have struggled for financial stability, though, the effort finally may be paying off.

System Financial Structure

To set the proper stage for what is to follow, here is a brief explanation of the financial structure of the cable business. Initially, a substantial expenditure must be made in order to construct the cable system. The debt that must be incurred at this point requires that lenders and investors be capable of sustaining monetary losses that may be heavy until the completed cable system can begin generating revenue.

Several important factors affect the amount of revenue that a cable system is likely to generate. One of these is density, or the number of households per cable mile. The more households there are per mile, the greater the chance for maximum subscribership at a minimum cost. Another factor that works in tandem with density is penetration. Penetration is determined by the number of homes that subscribe to cable as against the number of homes passed by cable. Revenue itself comes in the form of subscription fees for the basic cable program service and pay cable services (called "added-on" services). Some revenue is generated by special cable services such as home security, information services, and data transfer services.

Operating expenses for cable systems include franchise fees paid to the municipal franchising authority, copyright fees for distant signal importation, utility pole attachment fees, distant signal transmission costs, and expenses associated with local origination and access facilities.[1] Cable operators must also pay a fee to many of the originating sources that provide programming. Although several of the basic network services support themselves through advertising and provide their programming free, others charge local cable systems anywhere from three cents to twenty-two cents per system subscriber. The standard payment to a superstation is about ten cents per subscriber.[2]

Capital costs for a cable television system include expenses associated with headend equipment (everything necessary to receive and process a signal), distribution plant (the equipment, including the cable itself, and the facilities, which might be underground or overhead, that are necessary to relay a signal from the headend to the subscriber), subscriber equipment (installation and converter), labor, and maintenance.[3]

Cable Industry Economic Vista

"If you went by the ratings of the cable networks, you'd have to say that cable hasn't amounted to very much thus far in the 1980s," declared one commentator, who continued, "But if you looked at the advertising revenues, you'd be surprised at how far it's come. And if you looked at the balance sheets of cable owners, or at the prices paid per subscriber to acquire existing systems, . . . or at the heavy action in buying and selling systems, you'd be mighty impressed."[4] Regarding the purchase of a cable system, the purchase price formula now includes a figure of $1,500 per subscribing household. That compares with the average of approximately $300 per subscriber in the mid–1970s.[5]

This assessment fairly well underscores the optimistic image of the cable industry today, but at the same time it calls attention to a checkered past. Just how checkered is best described through year-by-year accounts as seen through the eyes of persons well versed on the subject. As an example, cable television in 1980, with a 24 percent penetration of television households,[6] was seen as expanding rapidly into the major markets. A *Business Week* report assessed the situation as "the race to plug in." "Bidding for cable-TV franchises is at a fever pitch as companies put up millions to get a foothold in the industry," the magazine's report read. But it cautioned that "cable may well prove to be its own worst enemy. Because of the high cost of wiring each home, the cable industry will need huge amounts of capital. Many of the companies that are gambling millions on the industry's future may not be around to collect on their bets."[7]

The rosy economic picture for cable in 1980 continued into the next year as advertisers discovered the medium. A *Dun's Review* article stated that "cable TV is well on the way to developing the infrastructure it needs to become a major advertising vehicle. More than two dozen national cable networks have already sprung up to create programming and sell commercials and others are emerging almost monthly." Cable television's advertising revenue for 1981 was expected to double 1980's $50 million, which itself had jumped from a 1978 total of $5 million.[8] One of the reasons cited for the increased interest in cable advertising was the medium's expected climb to nearly 30 percent penetration by the end of 1981. The 30 percent mark had long been regarded by the advertising industry as the watershed point at which cable would become a serious advertising medium.[9]

Cable television's economic status during 1982 and 1983 was characterized in somewhat bleak terms. "Is Cable Television Losing Its Luster?" asked James Mann in a 1982 issue of *U.S. News and World Report*.[10] A 1983 article in *Business Week* was headlined "The Rush into Cable TV Is Now Turning into a Retreat."[11] Cited as some of the reasons for economic problems facing cable were fierce competition among cable companies "for recession-squeezed advertising dollars" and "troublesome conflicts with communities negotiating over awards of cable franchises."[12] An industry that had expanded too fast too soon, forcing numerous mergers, was also seen as the root of cable's economic ills. Money that was being so readily dumped into creating programming was not being returned. CBS Inc., for instance, lost $50 million on a cultural program service for cable before the service was dissolved.[13] A 1984 survey showed that of the sixteen program services then in operation, only HBO, Cinemax, Showtime, and The Movie Channel showed solid profitability.[14]

Not all news was bad during 1984. "The cable business is a lot healthier than most headlines indicate," said one industry analyst. Another said that cable, in order to be attractive to potential subscribers, had to be of the "plain vanilla" variety; that is, the system had to offer a good basic programming package with no more than about fifty channels. Some of the major cable MSOs were faring quite well. Tele-Communications Inc. (TCI), the nation's largest MSO, doubled its 1983 earnings in 1984. The second-largest company, American Television and Communications Corporation (ATC), upped its operating profits from 1983 by an estimated 25 percent. Cash flow, a barometer of a cable company's financial strength, was also at a very healthy level industrywide.[15]

All of the positive economic indicators led *Business Week* to headline a 1985 assessment of the industry "Cable TV, Older and Wiser, Looks like a Good Bet Again." Deregulation of the industry and completion of much of the costly system construction in major markets were improving cable's economic picture. In fact, construction costs that had peaked at $1.4 billion in 1982 were seen declining to about $160 million by the end of the 1980s.[16] A survey of cable's status in the top fifty television markets showed that by the end of 1985 only one market, Cleveland, had yet to award a cable franchise, and all but four of the remaining forty-nine markets had operational cable systems.[17]

Cable's penetration rate in 1985 stood at about 44.6 percent of TV households. Cable subscribers were paying approximately $8.92 per month for basic programming service and an additional $10.25 for pay or premium services. What is most important to note about the subscriber pool, according to Cable Advertising Bureau president Bob Alter, is the quality of the subscriber. Such quality creates the kind of demographics that appeal to advertisers.[18]

The positive economic signs in the cable industry that have resulted from declining costs, increased profits, and greater cash flow have turned cable companies into "net cash generators rather than net cash users," said industry analyst Paul Kagan. The increased market value of a cable system combined with a decline in interest rates also led to a flurry of cable property selling and buying in 1985.[19] Cable was being ballyhooed not just as a good buy for investors,[20] but as an industry whose "ability to raise capital both for mergers and acquisitions and for ongoing projects has never been stronger."[21]

The increased stock market value of cable stocks also reflected the strength of the cable business. What happened here, according to analyst Paul Kagan, was that cable system operators had entered a new phase. "Cable systems," said Kagan, "are typically lucrative in the franchising stage, ailing in the construction phase and fat cats when they mature." Kagan suggested that many of the nation's cable systems "are now reaching the fat cat stage." Adding to this fat cat phase was the windfall associated with the Cable Policy Act's deregulation of basic cable service rates. The law allowed a 5 percent rate increase in 1985, another 5 percent increase in 1986, and increases after that based on whatever the market would bear. Such allowances automatically increased the value of individual cable systems by $100 to $150 per subscriber.[22]

Noting the economic status of the cable industry in 1986, industry observer Cecilia Capuzzi remarked, "Cable's heyday finally has arrived, albeit not in the shape that most expected." To that assessment Colony Communications president Charles Townsend added, "The sex appeal is gone . . . and now we're down to business."[23] Some 700,000 miles of cable carried program services to nearly 47.8 percent of all U.S. television households in 1986. Total 1986 cable industry revenue, most of which was due to consumer subscription payment for basic cable services, amounted to approximately $10.5 billion.[24]

Subscriber rate deregulation that became effective in January 1987 fashioned much of the financial thinking and planning among cable system operators in 1986. "Preparing to hike basic rates come January, for instance, many cable systems began to add new services in late autumn [1986], hoping customers would, by the time rates were actually raised, recognize the added value delivered."[25] One survey of some 300 cable system operators found that an average basic rate increase of 18.5 percent (about $1.86 per month) was in the offing and that a number of strategies were planned to implement the increase.[26] One strategy, described as "tier meltdown," would have system operators who offered several basic service packages or tiers, all at different rates, collapsing these into a more "consumer-friendly" single package at one cost.[27]

Rate increases are viewed by media investors as a positive step toward building cash flow. However, ATC chairman Trygve Myhren has suggested that cable system operators whose sights are set on cash flow matters could raise rates to such an extent as not only to lose customers, but also to invite a reimposition of government rate regulation.[28] What cable system operators have been warned to bear in mind is the "price/value relationship" or the amount a cable subscriber is willing to pay before deciding that the product he receives is not worth its cost.[29]

Where is the cable television industry headed from here? Three predictions made by leading cable analysts in late 1984 and mid–1985 look to cable's economic position in 1990. Paul Kagan predicted total cable revenues of $19.2 billion, A. D. Little predicted total revenues of $16.5 billion, and T. A. Associates predicted total revenues of $20.2 billion. All saw advertising as providing the lion's share of revenues, with pay services and pay-per-view services combining to nearly equal the amount of revenue that the basic cable service will provide. Kagan saw a total subscriber count of nearly 56 million. T. A. Associates predicted about the same, and A. D. Little predicted slightly fewer, 48 million. Both Kagan and T. A. Associates predicted that 58 percent of all television households will be cable television subscribers, whereas A. D. Little predicted the penetration to reach only 51 percent. Finally, while Kagan and T. A. Associates predicted an average monthly basic cable subscription rate of about $12 and an average monthly pay cable rate of nearly the same amount, A. D. Little predicted rates of nearly $14 and $9.50 respectively.[30]

Cable System Ownership Patterns

One additional prediction for 1990 is that virtually every major population center in the United States will be wired for cable television.[31] While cable system construction continues in the yet-to-be-wired markets, many cable operators in 1985 were turning their attention not to new construction but rather to extending their service to suburban growth areas and to replacing aging system components.[32] A kind of reconstruction also occurred in the mid–1980s—but only on paper. Many cable system operators in the halcyon days of franchising too often had made blue-sky promises about services and 100-plus–channel systems that were unrealistic. As a result, these same operators found themselves later returning to the franchising authority seeking relief from their earlier promises. As city councils across America reluctantly agreed to these requests, the cable operators could proceed unhindered to build more economically rational cable television systems. Systems of between 30 and 55 channels appear to be the most feasible to operate. Many older cable systems spent the mid–1980s either upgrading or planning to upgrade their typical 12-channel service to the 30-channel minimum.[33]

Cable industry construction slumped in 1986 to its worst year since 1979. Less than $1 billion was spent on construction-related activity, and for the first time newbuild construction mileage was outpaced by system rebuild and upgrade construction. A turnaround was seen for 1987, where a 45 percent increase over 1986 spending was predicted for newbuilds, rebuilds, and upgrades. Much of the system construction that ordinarily would have occurred in 1986 was deferred for one year due to an unusual flurry of cable system buying and selling during the year.[34] System acquisition has resulted in many cases in upgrading system channel capacity in order to increase cash flow. Replacement of aging systems and franchise requirements for state-of-the-art technology have spurred rebuild activity. There also has been growing interest of late in existing cable systems that will extend into areas beyond the "40 home-per-mile density circle" of the specific franchise territory.[35]

Cable system acquisition went on a rampage in 1986. According to one account, "The potential for higher subscriber fees and cash flow, coupled with the lowest interest rates in nine years and investors' rush to beat 1987's new tax laws, made cable systems among the hottest media properties in 1986." Cable property sales of between five and six billion dollars were transacted.[36] The tax law incentive that played such a key role in 1986 cable system transfers placed both a higher capital gains tax and a higher tax on corporate asset liquidations on the sale of a cable system after 1 January 1987.[37]

Ownership in the cable television industry has evolved from a small town "Mom and Pop"–owned and operated cable system to a multiple system–owned and operated corporate enterprise. The evolution should have been no surprise, said industry observer Chuck Moozakis. "The inexorable demand for new capital needed to fuel cable's growth required no less." Moozakis continued,

It was also no surprise that in many cases the new owners of the cable industry were ones which had made their marks in affiliated fields—fields which included commercial broadcasting and/or magazine and newspaper publishing. . . . Whether fueled by the potential of new revenue sources created by cable investments—or, in some cases the fear of competition *from* cable—these companies were attracted to the industry.[38]

The major media owners who are also the major cable television system owners are surprisingly few in number. The top ten MSOs, however, collectively service 42 percent of the approximately 39.5 million basic cable subscribers—a number that likely will increase in years to come as small and medium-sized MSOs continue to be purchased by the major MSOs. The top ten MSOs and their total number of subscribers in rounded figures as of winter 1986–87 included TCI (3.9 million), ATC (3.2 million), Storer Cable Communications (1.5 million), Cox Cable Communications (1.4 million), Continental Cablevision (1.3 million), Warner Cable (1.3 million), Comcast (1.1 million), United Cable (1 million), Newhouse Broadcasting (1 million), and Heritage Communications Inc. (1 million).[39]

The size and influence of MSOs came under scrutiny in 1986 when the FCC considered rules that not only would limit future MSO cable system acquisitions, but also might require divestiture by MSOs of some cable systems already owned. Specific rule provisions called for a prohibition on ownership of systems serving more than 50 percent of cable subscribers in one state or 25 percent nationwide.[40] Action on this matter was pending as this reference guide went to press.

Cable Management

The cable system manager of today is the link between cable subscribers and what is often an MSO absentee owner. Not so long ago the manager usually owned his system, having built it from scratch. His skills usually were confined to electronics and not to the intricacies of overseeing personnel, marketing his product, and finessing the franchise authority. Things have changed in the industry. Now the cable system manager must be capable of doing all the above if his system is to succeed.

In terms of who the typical cable manager is, a 1986 survey found that he (78 percent of all managers are male) is thirty-eight years old, has had a little less than seven years of cable management experience but has worked in the cable business for ten years, has a salary of $37,000, and manages thirty-four employees. About 80 percent of the managers attended some college, with about three-quarters of them receiving degrees ranging from associate to postgraduate. Most degrees held by cable managers are in either business management (34 percent) or electronics/engineering (23 percent). As for the typical system that he manages, it is most likely to be among the 92 percent of all cable systems affiliated with an MSO, it is in a market of 29,100 households, it serves 16,200 subscribers, and it has a channel

capacity of thirty-seven channels with four of the channels reserved for pay
services. The typical cable system in 1986 was about fifteen years old.[41]

When quizzed about problems they had to deal with, most cable managers
rated finding qualified personnel as the most pressing, followed by churn,
customer/community relations, and controlling expenses and making a
profit.[42] Finding and retaining personnel is, of course, troublesome in most
businesses. In fact, all the above problems with the exception of churn are
not necessarily uncommon to other businesses. But so problematical is
churn that it was cited in another survey as cable management's number
one problem.[43]

What is churn? More specifically, what is pay churn? Churn is the cable
industry term for the voluntary cancellation or disconnection of cable service
by a subscriber. Pay churn is the voluntary disconnection of a pay cable
service or services. Industry observers say that subscribers to pay cable
services are disconnecting because of incessant program (usually movie)
repetition and because there is little difference between one pay service and
another.[44] As for churn in general, the quality of pay cable seems but one
of a number of reasons for disconnections. Others include customer service
dissatisfaction, subscriber rate increases, frequent system outages, and
moves from the service area. In order to minimize churn, one industry
leader has suggested that cable system operators pay particular attention to
satisfying any and all of their customers' service needs.[45]

Service is the key to keeping the cable subscriber satisfied. Some companies work hard at creating an efficient and effective service routine,[46]
while others place service in a secondary position. One cable researcher
suggests that cable companies could improve customer satisfaction "by
adding more phone lines so subscribers could reach the company, by pushing basic over pay services, and by having salespeople make regular follow-
up calls to subscribers."[47]

Keeping customers happy is one matter, but finding new customers is
another. The rate of growth for basic cable subscribers slowed considerably
by 1985.[48] This trend is bothersome to the cable industry, since finding new
customers really is the only way to compensate for those lost through
disconnection. Moreover, new customer subscription fees are also necessary
for cable companies to increase their profits. Additional income was at one
time anticipated from basic cable service subscribers who decided to up
their subscription fee by "adding on" one or more pay services. But as
income per household leveled off in the mid–1980s, so did the attraction of
pay cable. The subscriber fee as a base of financial support assumes even
greater significance when one considers the reluctance of advertisers to fully
commit to buying time on cable (a matter more fully explored later) and
the growing competition that other technologies, particularly videocassette
recorders (VCRs), bring to the cable marketplace.[49]

Cable Advertising and Marketing

Cable television as an advertising medium has had its image problems. But cable began to emerge in 1985 as at least a respectable member of the Madison Avenue fraternity. According to a representative of one of the biggest advertising agencies, BBDO, "Cable is more and more being thought of as mainstream." It is being placed in the same advertising mix plans as the more traditional media, and once clients use the medium they continue to budget money for it.[50]

In purely monetary figures, total cable television advertising revenues for 1987 were estimated as exceeding $1 billion. Nearly $900 million of that sum was projected to be heading toward the national cable networks, and about $250 million was projected for local cable systems. Revenue totals for cable advertising in 1990 have been estimated as nearing $2 billion; for 1995 the total will double the 1990 mark. Factors cited in the upward trend for advertising revenue are cable's efforts at continually improving program offerings and a more cost-effective buy for advertisers as measured by the cost-per-thousand (CPM) formula. This formula, an advertising industry yardstick to determine the cost per medium to an advertiser of reaching a thousand viewers, when applied to the value of cable television advertising has shown the cable CPM to be from 50 to 70 percent of that for broadcast network television.[51]

A. C. Nielsen statistics support the cable industry's pronouncement of improved viewing figures. Viewing measurements recorded for the October through January 1986–87 television program season showed that the share of audience for advertising-supported basic cable networks increased while the share for broadcast networks as well as for pay cable services declined.[52]

Regardless of the optimistic status of cable advertising and the rosy forecasts for a bright future, matters could be better. Advertising agencies "still view cable as a second-class buy," and "generally spend no more than 5 percent of their media budgets on cable buys and frequently less," according to a J. Walter Thompson advertising executive.[53] Advertising industry leaders insist that cable television must generate at least a 20 percent share of the television audience in order to compete on equal footing with the broadcast networks for advertising dollars.[54] Cable is steadily nearing that benchmark. The share of the total television audience viewing just cable networks stood at 10 percent in early 1987. Viewing figures for cable subscriber households alone gave cable networks an 18 percent share of the audience. Figures in both viewing categories were significantly higher than those for the previous year.[55] While there is no doubt that advertiser spending for cable is also growing, the problem is that the rate of that growth is disproportionate to the growth of cable's share of the television audience. Reasons for the stunted growth are numerous. Most important, perhaps, is the disruption cable has caused in what had become a routine system of media buying when there were only broadcast television network outlets on which to place commercials.[56]

What will improve cable's advertising image and make it a bona fide member of the Madison Avenue fraternity mentioned earlier? Education of advertising executives certainly is one condition of improvement. Other conditions are intrinsic to the cable industry itself. Consolidation of local cable systems into regional markets and development of cable research statistics are necessary,[57] as is an effort by the local cable operator to improve sales and promotion.

Taking these conditions one by one, here is what the cable industry is doing to prove its worthiness to advertisers. First, education. The formation in 1981 of the Cabletelevision Advertising Bureau (CAB), a trade organization whose members include local cable operators, MSO representatives, and advertising-supported cable network representatives, has done much to carry cable's story to advertisers and agencies. The CAB president described the organization's efforts and its successes in these terms:

The agencies have a bias toward broadcast television for some reason. . . . We're changing the rules. There's a network TV–agency establishment, and some of them wish we'd just go away. Anytime you try to change the existing order of things you're going to be met with resistance. People basically don't like change. We're intruding on a lot of comfort zones.[58]

The advantages that cable television advertising offers the client are numerous. "Cable, of course, is television and has all of the persuasive, intrusive, memorable, credible, and production qualities of television. Cable, however, is more *selective* than over-the-air television. Advertisers can buy spots in programs appealing to more narrowly defined market segments, which is often referred to as *narrowcasting*."[59] Cable's ability to narrowcast has been more figuratively termed the medium's "boutique factor."[60] Besides narrowcasting advantages in cable advertising, "costs are very reasonable, especially when compared with those of conventional television; there is flexibility in the length of commercials; exclusive sponsorships are available that closely tie the advertiser to the program; and cable has proved itself in very successful direct response advertising campaigns."[61]

One item not to be overlooked is the lifestyle of the cable television subscriber. As compared with the nonsubscriber household, the basic cable subscriber household is generally more affluent, has a younger head of household, and spends more leisure time viewing television. Pay cable subscribing households are even more affluent than the basic cable subscriber household, have an even younger household head and more persons in the household, and watch slightly more television. What may be more important is the pay cable subscriber's greater openness to various forms of advertising and to new products.[62]

The next measure of cable worth is in the degree by which several local cable systems may interconnect to form regional advertising media. Interconnection is especially important to regional advertisers whose product market may be too limited to require purchase of cable network time but too widespread to purchase time on local cable systems only. Local cable systems that agree to interconnect themselves so that the commercials of these regional advertisers may reach beyond the local audience are increasing in number and are attracting a growing number of advertising dollars. The technical arrangement by which cable systems interconnect should be noted. There are "hard" interconnects where participating systems are linked by microwave or wire and allow signals, and thus commercials, to be fed from one cable system to another. "Soft" interconnects have no operational links joining participating cable systems. Systems joined by soft interconnects simply agree to run their own copies of a particular commercial simultaneously.[63]

The potential for reaping tremendous financial returns as a result of interconnections is within the grasp of local cable operators. Regional sales representative firms are also in place to lend their assistance. Nonetheless, a major problem exists that is impeding implementation of interconnects: the reluctance of some cable operators to cooperate with one another. According to one source, the reluctance stems from a fear among operators in a marketplace that consolidation of efforts might result in a single system within the group emerging as the dominant one and thus the one that controls major advertising and business decisions.[64]

Another condition if cable television is to rise to a full-fledged advertising medium is accurate and acceptable subscriber viewing figures as determined by audience research. "As long as advertisers are paying the freight, it's necessary for these companies to determine how many people have access to their commercials—also known as the eyeball effect. Simply explained, the more eyeballs, the better the ratings; the better the ratings, the higher the ad rates."[65]

The rule of the land has changed, though, given the introduction of so many competing video delivery technologies into the household. This "multichannel environment" has led those in the audience-research business to fine-tune measurement techniques in order to better gauge who is watching what and for how long.

Still, for all intents and purposes, when it comes to measuring the new forms of electronic media, a reliable yardstick has all but eluded the research industry. The sheer number of viewing choices makes it difficult for traditional measuring devices—meters, diaries and telephone coincidentals—to be as reliable as they once were. This reduction in effectiveness has led ad agencies in particular to question the validity of these techniques, and redouble their search for more precise viewership information.[66]

So far, the most common audience-research method for measuring cable viewership is A. C. Nielsen's diary and supplementary metered-household sampling. The diary method, though, has not been held universally in high esteem because of its underreporting of cable viewership in television households by as much as 55 percent.[67] A research tool that shows more promise is the people meter. The people meter could provide a more precise viewing measurement because it requires that all individuals in households where the meters are placed actually indicate their viewing by pressing code numbers on a meter-attached keyboard. While the people meter may be an improvement over diaries, there are critics who contend that the scheduled fall 1987 implementation date of its use is premature, pending a more thorough study of meter results. One critic in particular cited the typical television viewer's passivity as indicating an unwillingness to push meter buttons at the proper time.[68]

The final condition that local cable system operators must meet is improvement of their audience promotion and sales efforts. A new emphasis on local advertising sales has already begun in many markets.[69] MSOs are constructing well-organized sales apparatus to assist their local cable systems,[70] and local operators are finding the value in paying top salaries to create a competent local sales team.[71] As for audience promotion, the importance of cable's entry into the "traditional battle for the eyeballs" is underscored in these terms:

The promise and problems of cable are legion, but few are as prominent as its seeming inability to successfully market itself. The industry's initial obsession with technology and immersion in city council franchise wrangles took precedence over the designing of marketing programs to lure new subscribers. That mentality has hurt.

With cable's subscriber growth slowing, the industry is facing tasks which require marketing skills rather than technical acumen to upgrade its public image and convince reluctant consumers that cable has something for everyone.[72]

Marketing campaigns thus far have been multifaceted. Direct mail, radio, and newspapers have been used to emphasize basic cable instead of pay cable, partially as a result of public disenchantment with pay cable in general. Cable operators also have been emphasizing individual program services to potential cable subscribers instead of an entire program package. Lastly, cable marketers have made efforts at creating an awareness of the way nonsubscribers perceive how they use television and the amount of time they spend with it.[73]

Competing Delivery Technologies

How consumers use television is becoming a greater economic concern to the cable industry because of the number of delivery systems (traditional as well as nontraditional media) that are competing to carry programming into the household. Referring to the phenomenon, a *Fortune* magazine article stated, "Everyone in TV is struggling to understand the changing character of the new world now taking shape, but at least one attribute is already apparent: it will be a tougher world, even for the winners."[74] The suggestion that there will be winners and losers, not merely coexistence, is most bothersome to cable's economic future. The irony is that cable television's surge during the 1980s was a major factor in pulling viewers away from over-the-air network television.[75] Now, cable is finding its own audience eroding as a result of the industry's competition.

In some cases cable television interests are joining, or at least assisting, cable competitors. Private cable systems, called satellite master antenna television (SMATV), that wire hotels, apartment complexes, and other multidwelling units have been shunned by pay cable networks for years in deference to local cable systems. HBO, realizing that it was losing nearly $100 million annually from its failure to deal with SMATV, decided in 1985 to change its policy.[76]

Another cable competitor whose success may be just around the corner is multichannel multipoint distribution service (MMDS), known more simply as "wireless cable." MMDS systems transmit over-the-air television signals much like broadcast television but in the much higher microwave frequency range. Thus MMDS subscribers must have special antennas to receive the MMDS signal, which is capable of carrying some thirty program services. Areas where MMDS is or will most likely be successful are cities where cable has been slow to enter or small towns where cable likely never will enter. As of late 1986 MMDS systems were serving an estimated 40,000 subscribers in about a dozen cities.[77]

Other cable competitors are not faring as well. The home satellite television dish, called a TVRO for "television receive only," that plucks what is often a pay cable signal out of the air for its owner's television set is the object of an intense scrambling effort by the cable industry. Cable system operators and cable network programmers oppose the idea of a cable nonsubscriber getting for free what the cable subscriber must pay for.[78] By mid–1986 there were nearly 1.6 million TVRO owners in America when the major pay cable services and some basic cable services began scrambling or "encrypting" their satellite signals. The TVRO home dish business took a nosedive, with sales plummeting from approximately 70,000 dishes in September 1985 to about 15,000 in February 1986. TVRO owners were given opportunities to receive clear signals by first purchasing a decoder for around $400 that would descramble the encrypted satellite signals and then by paying monthly or annual fees to the cable services whose programming the TVRO owners wished to receive. That fee could range from about $130 to $155 annually, a price that when added to the cost of a decoder was too much for all but about one percent of TVRO home dish owners to pay. While complaints about what TVRO advocates see as excessive program service fees are being addressed in Congress, most TVRO dish owners must remain content with receiving whatever remains of the unscrambled programming beamed from satellites.[79]

The most potent cable competitor is the home videocassette recorder (VCR). Just how the presence of a VCR affects pay cable or cable in general is still under investigation. Some feel that the VCR's "time shifting" capability will boost pay cable subscriptions since VCR owners theoretically would be able to record pay cable movies to view at a more convenient time or to retain in a movie library. Others feel differently. Since prerecorded videocassette movies are becoming increasingly available in the marketplace, pay cable network interests fear that they will have a tough time competing.[80] Those who share the first view have embarked upon a marketing strategy to convince VCR owners of VCR/cable compatibility. This strategy has been highly visible in markets where VCR penetration is especially high (50 percent or above).[81]

What pay cable is counting on most heavily to ward off any serious defection from the subscriber ranks is pay-per-view (PPV). PPV is a pay cable offshoot that allows cable subscribers to choose to view one-time-only events and to pay only for those events that are viewed. In order to activate the PPV system, the subscriber must have an addressable converter attached to his television set that allows a cable company to channel the PPV signal into the proper set at the subscriber's request. A number of PPV services are now in existence, providing such things as adult movies (Playboy Channel's "Private Ticket") and first-run movies that are available to the PPV service for airing at the same time they are released on videocassette.[82] Perhaps one of the biggest PPV attractions may be sports events. Several professional baseball and basketball teams and at least one college football team have allowed PPV cablecast of their games and have met with some success.[83]

Those directly involved in PPV—the companies providing PPV services—are banking heavily on its success, and some cable industry analysts are lending encouragement to that end.[84] Even the Hollywood film industry is pulling for PPV to succeed in view of how it might counteract the slumping receipts at the theater box office.[85] There are skeptics aplenty, however, who claim that the "impulse buy" marketing strategy for attracting PPV customers will not work. Pay cable subscribers who already pay a basic cable fee plus a pay cable fee, so say the skeptics, will be more selective about the added expense of PPV.[86]

The key to PPV's success will be the cable industry's ability to sell the service. Indeed, one cable official labeled PPV a "marketing-intensive business."[87] Selling the service may not be so easy, though, since there are complications galore that may eventually dissuade anyone from sampling

PPV or those who have sampled from doing it again. Four particular problem areas include ordering, product selection, pricing, and scheduling. Once the customer has made a decision to order a PPV program, there usually is nothing that can be done to cancel the order. In terms of available product, there still are too few special events or movie titles available to help distance PPV from videocassettes. Convenience is the only factor that really separates the two in the product selection category, and even convenience loses some ground when price is considered. Most PPV movies still cost customers more than the rental fee for a videocassette movie. The PPV fee falls between four and five dollars. Special events such as ball games and prizefights usually will cost what the market will bear. One championship prizefight has gone for as high as $30. Finally, PPV program scheduling is still too rigid, due in part to its single-channel availability. The only solution to such confinement may rest in multichannel PPV.[88]

One problem attached to PPV is far beyond cable system operator control. That is the matter of addressable converter electronics and cost. The ten companies that either were manufacturing the converters or had plans to manufacture them as of late 1986 were placing a price tag of nearly $100 on each converter. Moreover, because the converters were not always electronically compatible with VCRs, they were less than welcome in VCR households.[89] Uncertainty among cable operators about converter performance fueled a drop in purchases of the addressable hardware from 4.3 million units in 1985 to 3.7 million units in 1986. But that trend was expected to be reversed in 1987 with the advance in converter technology.[90] Moreover, a study by market researchers Frost and Sullivan Inc. predicted "explosive growth" for the addressable converter industry from 1987 to 1990 as cable system operators turn in ever greater numbers to providing PPV services for their subscribers.[91]

SOURCE OVERVIEW

Books and Book Chapters

Financial and economic matters related to cable television naturally overlap with matters of cable television law and regulations. This is particularly true regarding cable system ownership. Efforts have been made to include books and other publications in this chapter whose orientation seems heavily weighted toward business and economics but that nonetheless contain substantive comments on law and regulation as well. It is therefore recommended that readers consult categories both in this chapter and in the law and regulations chapter for the most complete references on a particular subject.

General Survey

The most thorough economic analysis of all phases of cable television is found in G. Kent Webb's *The Economics of Cable Television*. Webb defines the purpose and scope of his book in these terms:

This book identifies the market and regulatory forces that have shaped the cable-television industry. More important, it presents an investigation of the issues of price, design, and regulation. These issues are important to corporate planners who are responsible for the billions of dollars invested in cable each year, to municipal authorities who have regulatory jurisdiction over cable, and to anyone who may sometime want to use a cable system. (p. xv)

Webb bases much of his analytical commentary on the observed behavior of a computer model designed to simulate the economic conditions of an actual cable television system. He describes the results of the simulation in general terms, with specific technical details confined to appendices. *The Economics of Cable Television* is somewhat technical in places, providing the economic equations used for Webb's analyses, but there is plenty of information here for persons not as technically inclined. There are, among the book's several chapters, specific ones on overall costs of cable television (equipment costs, program costs, operating expenses, and so on), cable service pricing mechanisms, and cost-benefit analyses of cable system design, and an especially good final chapter on the economics of cable television system franchising.

Attention must once more be drawn to the textbook treatment given the cable television industry in Thomas F. Baldwin and D. Stevens McVoy's *Cable Communication*. One part of this book, "Organization and Operations," carries chapters that are noteworthy in terms of describing the economics and business concerns of a local cable television system operator. The four chapters included here are "Ownership," "Audiences and Programming," "Marketing and Advertising," and "Business Operations." The "Franchising" chapter also contains a significant amount of economic/business–related information.

At least three Practising Law Institute (PLI) books contain articles and commentary to a varying degree on cable television business and economic matters. The significance of the PLI book series is noted more extensively in the law and regulations chapter of this reference guide. A sampling of content from these books includes sections on the financial impact of cable industry developments on owning and operating a cable television system, acquisition and sale of a cable system, and labor relations.

Cable System Ownership, Operation, and Competition

The Ira C. Stein book, *Cable Television: Handbook and Forms*, the Morton I. Hamburg book, *All about Cable*, and the Daniel L. Brenner and Monroe

E. Price book, *Cable Television and Other Nonbroadcast Video: Law and Policy*, all contain ownership regulation chapters. In particular, Stein includes chapters with copious information and examples of legal documents on cable television system financing, system purchase and sale, system construction, utility pole attachments, cable system use of public easements, programming regulations, cable system subscriber relations, cable system personnel relations, cable system advertising, public access requirements, and cable system–telephone company relationships.

Hamburg's *All about Cable* does not contain as much as the Stein book, nor is the information spread about as much. However, at least one chapter of the Hamburg book is devoted entirely to cable television business matters. *All about Cable* also contains examples of a program license agreement, a network affiliation agreement, and a leased-channel agreement used by cable system operators.

Daniel L. Brenner and Monroe E. Price's *Cable Television and Other Nonbroadcast Video: Law and Policy* is organized in a style similar to the other two books. Three chapters in the Brenner/Price book that are of particular note in the context of cable television business and economics cover cable system franchising, ownership, and operations.

Two important essays appear in *Proceedings from the Tenth Annual Telecommunications Policy Research Conference*, edited by Oscar H. Gandy, Jr., Paul Espinosa, and Janusz A. Ordover. The first is Kenneth Gordon's "FCC Policies on Cable Ownership." Gordon examines the disputes surrounding cable television system ownership rules and concludes "that in the cases of broadcast-cable and network-cable crossownership the costs of uniform rules probably outweigh the benefits—principally because the benefits appear to be quite small" (p. 158). He is less certain about the telephone-cable cross-ownership rules due to antitrust complications. Gordon has divided his essay into three parts in order to discuss the rationale for cross-ownership rules, the links between economics and goals of cable television regulation, and competition in the marketplaces where cable television systems operate.

The second essay appearing in the *Proceedings* is Eli Noam's "The Political Economy of Cable Television Regulation." Noam "analyzes the consequences of monopolistic control of channel access by local cable system operators on the diversity of programming and on the free flow of information" (p. 118). He suggests that such monopoly control of local cable television systems is not conducive to either program diversity or access rights. Noam examines three methods of cable regulation—common carrier status, public ownership, and direct program regulation—to ascertain the most beneficial program control method and finds that all are wanting. He concludes that the most effective way of countering local cable monopoly is to open cable television to competition from the telephone company. Noam makes lengthier but essentially the same arguments in his "Local Distribution Monopolies in Cable Television and Telephone Service: The

Scope for Competition" essay in *Telecommunications Regulation Today and Tomorrow*, which is also edited by him.

Yet another Eli Noam essay, "Private Sector Monopolies: The Case of Cable Television Franchises," appears in *Productivity and Public Policy*, edited by Marc Holzer and Stuart S. Nagel. Noam uses in his essay a number of economically oriented statistical formulae to calculate the productivity of local cable systems as they function as monopolies. In very technical terms Noam examines policy implications and needed changes in an industry— cable television—that is comprised almost entirely of monopolies.

Three important essays that appear in *Policy Research in Telecommunications*, edited by Vincent Mosco, examine matters of cable television system ownership and concentration of media control. Eli M. Noam's "Competitive Entry into Local Cable Transmission" is an analytic piece, replete with a scattering of economic equations, that investigates "the economies of scale in cable television operations, and . . . the variation in these economies over the range of output. The results," says Noam, "are intended as an empirical contribution to the question of whether competition among rival cable television operators is likely" (p. 190).

"Market Delineation, Measurement of Concentration, and F.C.C. Ownership Rules" by Jonathan D. Levy and Florence O. Setzer derives from a report supplied to the FCC in response to the commission's request for comments on its 1982 proposal to eliminate its broadcast television network–cable television system cross-ownership prohibition. The final chapter noted here from *Policy Research in Telecommunications* is Janet Wasko's "New Methods of Analyzing Media Concentration." In view of the FCC's concern over the issue of concentration of media control in single markets and the economic dynamics that contribute to that concern, Wasko describes methods that she has developed to better analyze media concentration.

Eli M. Noam enters the picture one more time as the editor of *Video Media Competition: Regulation, Economics, and Technology*. This book contains an excellent collection of articles by noted authorities on key matters of video technology economics. Noam divides his book into three parts: empirical studies of media competition, regulatory issues in media competition, and international outlook. Although the book's content pertains to all the video technologies, there is a heavy concentration of commentary on cable television subjects. Part 1 of *Video Media Competition*, for instance, contains Jane B. Henry's "The Economics of Pay-TV Media," Jonathan D. Levy and Peter K. Pitsch's "Statistical Evidence of Substitutability among Video Delivery Systems," Eli M. Noam's "Economies of Scale in Cable Television: A Multiproduct Analysis," Kenneth Thorpe's "The Impact of Competing Technologies on Cable Television," and Walter S. Baer's "Telephone and Cable Companies: Rivals or Partners in Video Distribution." Part 2 of *Video Media Competition* contains Michael Botein's "The FCC's Regulation of the New Video Technologies: Backing and Filling on the Level Playing

Field" and Lawrence J. White's "Antitrust and Video Markets: The Mergers of Showtime and The Movie Channel as a Case Study."

Robert Pepper's "Competition in Local Distribution: The Cable Television Industry" in *Understanding New Media: Trends and Issues in Electronic Distribution of Information*, edited by Benjamin M. Compaine, is a lengthy essay that examines the implications of the cable television industry's development of "the technical ability and the incentive to utilize its rights of way to provide specific services in direct competition with regulated traditional common carriers" (p. 157). Pepper says that a "result of the trend of deregulation at the federal level converging with the development of infrastructures for potential use in local distribution is that in many cities cable has an option to become an unregulated competitor of the telephone company for private line, enhanced data, access bypass, and other specialized telecommunications services" (p. 157). He concludes, "Several technologies are emerging as potential competitors in the local distribution market, with cable television potentially the most powerful among them.... In developing its local distribution potential, cable itself will face competition from other technologies vying for part of the local distribution market" (p. 177).

Copyright

Daniel Kelley's "The Economics of Copyright Controversies in Communications" in *Policy Research in Telecommunications*, edited by Vincent Mosco, "argues that the economic and legal institutions that developed to compensate intellectual property owners before the development of television are largely, but not wholly, adequate today" (p. 220).

Cable System Management, Marketing, and Sales

Broadcast and Cable Management by Norman Marcus provides commentary on management problems shared by both the broadcast and nonbroadcast electronic media. One chapter of the book, "Cable Management: Pay Your Money, Take Your Choice," does examine the functions of the various positions within a cable television system and does provide some brief comments on cable economics, but the reader is left with having to apply general management skills mentioned in other chapters to particular cable management situations.

William E. McCavitt and Peter K. Pringle's *Electronic Media Management* carries a chapter entitled "Managing the Cable Television System" that is brief but nonetheless inclusive of major management matters affecting cable television. The chapter contains information on the following: the growth and importance of cable, cable system franchising and refranchising, cable system operation and staff responsibilities, cable system economics with methods for determining system revenue, cable regulations, factors in program selection, and local origination and public access programming.

Two excellent books give a thorough overview of cable television advertising. The first, *Cable Advertising: New Ways to New Business*, is written by Kensinger Jones, Thomas F. Baldwin, and Martin P. Block. It includes chapters on why advertisers should choose cable, how cable advertising works, exclusive cable advertising opportunities, cable program sponsorship, buying and scheduling techniques for cable, and evaluating cable advertising. *Cable Advertising* provides three appendices, one of which is a simple audience-research project. The book is well illustrated and concludes with a glossary and basic information on cable television technology.

The other excellent cable advertising book is Ronald B. Kaatz's *Cable Advertiser's Handbook*. There is a cornucopia of solid information in this book, which the author says "is targeted at everyone involved in planning, buying, selling, and developing advertising for—or just learning about—cable and other new media" (p. xvii). *Cable Advertiser's Handbook* is well illustrated and carries numerous graphs, charts, and tables that help explain and supplement the text. A chapter-by-chapter content summary includes a history of cable television that concentrates on the medium's advertising potential, a brief description of cable and other new electronic delivery systems, commentary on the number of entertainment/media viewing options for consumers, the impact of the new media (called "Videotech" by the author) on the old media, understanding cable television's potential and deficiencies as an advertising medium and planning strategies for using cable, using cable as a local and national marketing tool and targeting the cable audience, creating and producing cable advertising, local market selling ideas for cable television systems, techniques for measuring cable advertising results, and suggestions for promoting cable television.

Elizabeth J. Heighton and Don R. Cunningham's *Advertising in the Broadcast and Cable Media* is somewhat deceptively titled in that there is little direct concentration on cable advertising in the book. But the relevance of advertising techniques and methods to the electronic media in general is fairly similar across the board. In other words, what applies to broadcast television more often than not will apply to cable television as well. A reader who makes allowance for this should find the Heighton/Cunningham textbook quite useful. Structurally, the book is divided into sections on media description, procedures for constructing advertising campaigns, and advertising buying and selling techniques. Regulations affecting the advertising industry are examined, as are specific social issues affecting the advertising industry.

The basics of his subject are covered in Samuel Barr's *Advertising on Cable: A Practical Guide for Advertisers*. Barr includes chapters that explain, among other things, why cable television advertising is effective, planning strategies for cable advertising, cable advertising research, national and local cable advertising, direct-response and co-op advertising on cable television, and cable television advertising standards and practices. Barr concludes *Advertising on Cable* with appendices on how cable television works, a cable network directory, and a glossary of cable television and related advertising terms.

Charles Warner does not treat cable television as a separate category in *Broadcast and Cable Selling* but rather includes cable with other media to provide information on "up-to-date professional selling methods, plus techniques based on theoretical research in the behavioral sciences and sales performance" (p. v). The book is divided into five parts. Part 1 describes selling and marketing concepts, and part 2 covers in detail the psychological skills necessary for the salesperson to possess. The next part concentrates on particular information (such as interpretation of research data) that salespersons should possess. Parts 4 and 5 of *Broadcast and Cable Selling* describe selling opportunities in the sales profession. Warner concludes his book with useful appendices that carry examples of successful sales presentations, examples of helpful sales tools, rate structure models and sales contract content suggestions, a checklist of regulations affecting selling methods, and a glossary of electronic media sales terminology.

One chapter of David Poltrack's *Television Marketing: Network, Local, and Cable* examines cable television's past, present, and future, particularly its economic status in the media marketplace and the competition it provides for other media. Poltrack looks especially at the potential for advertiser-supported basic cable program services and includes charts for calculating the potential cable advertising revenue that such services could provide. Another chapter in *Television Marketing* looks at opportunities for the advertiser in using the diversity of cable television services to reach a viewing audience. Poltrack, at one point, gives a general assessment of cable television's marketing potential, saying that "implications of the growth of cable television for the advertiser are twofold." In the first place, "The advertiser has to consider the impact of cable television growth on the television networks and television stations, the primary sources of advertising impressions. Future television campaign planners must adjust for this new competition." Second, contends Poltrack, "The advertiser must assess the advertising opportunities provided by the new cable services. These include the national advertising availabilities offered by the advertiser-supported cable networks, the local and regional advertising opportunities offered by the local cable systems and multiple-system operators, and the as yet unavailable advertising potential represented by the pay cable services" (p. 3).

Susan Tyler Eastman and Robert A. Klein have compiled a comprehensive assortment of textbook information in their book *Strategies in Broadcast and Cable Promotion*. The book is divided into three parts covering the role of promotion, audience promotion, and sales promotion and ends with a glossary and guide to suppliers and consultants. The wide-ranging scope of *Strategies in Broadcast and Cable Promotion* includes attention to cable television most often in the context of other media. Only one of the book's chapters, Robbin Ahrold's "Pay-Television and Cable Promotion," pertains to cable television specifically.

In view of the National Retail Merchants Association's prediction that "by 1990 one-third of all merchandise sales will be non-store purchases," (p. 1) R. C. Morse and Karen L. Burns have prepared *Cable/Videotex: A Compendium for Direct Marketers* as a "guide" and "tool" to introduce direct marketers to the electronic media through which much of non-store purchasing will occur. The coeditors include nearly fifty brief essays in *Cable/Videotex* that not only describe cable television and videotex, but also provide case histories on how these media have been or might be used for marketing purposes. The book's essays are clustered into five major sections: a primer on new electronic media in general, an overview of marketing/new electronic media integration potential, views on cable-specific marketing matters, views on videotex/teletext marketing matters, and comments on future electronic media and their marketing potential. A sample of the essays in *Cable/Videotex* includes Charles Mozur's "Direct Mail and Direct Response Find New Meaning in Cable," Robert M. Jeremiah's "The Power of Direct Response with Narrowcasting," Neil Orr's "Case Histories in Local and National Direct Marketing via Cable TV," and Mark Plakias' "A Very Short Course in Interactive Transactional Technology."

Jerome D. Williams says in "Cable Television: New Electronic Media for New Nonprofit Marketing Strategies" in volume 1 of *Advances in Nonprofit Marketing*, edited by Russell W. Belk, that the availability of cable television and other new information technologies will have a significant impact on marketing the "product" of the nonprofit organization. "Because most nonprofit product offerings tend to be more in the service, idea, issue, or cause domain," comments Williams, "they are better suited to the use of information. . . . " (pp. 247–48). In this lengthy piece the author covers such territory as describing cable television marketing applications for various nonprofit groups and discussing the implications of such marketing strategies.

Hugh Malcolm Beville, Jr.'s *Audience Ratings: Radio, Television, and Cable* is a fascinating book that is possibly the only one of its kind. It is packed with information on electronic media audience measurement. Beville describes measurement methods and audience ratings uses and provides a detailed history of the companies and their products that created the ratings industry in the United States. The "Cable Ratings" chapter isolates audience measurement as it relates to cable television with content that describes cable programming and the audience measurement problems that have bothered the medium for so long. The most substantive portion of this chapter is the author's comments on the various syndicated cable audience measurement services and the several methodological studies that have been undertaken in "the quest for better diary measurement of audience to cable-originated programs" (p. 169). Beville concludes the cable chapter by discussing various qualitative measurement studies conducted to determine characteristics of cable television viewers and viewing habits.

Charles F. Keown and Leslie Freundschuh report on a research project designed to ascertain cable television viewer reaction to product commercials of special length and content format in "Alternative Advertising Formats for Cable Television" in *Current Issues and Research in Advertising 1985*, vol. 1, *Original Research and Theoretical Contributions*, edited by James H. Leigh and Claude R. Martin, Jr. Keown and Freundschuh look primarily at how different commercial formats especially designed for cable's unique characteristics might be most effective.

Competing Delivery Systems

Besides its use as a general information book on cable television, Loy A. Singleton's *Telecommunications in the Information Age*, noted in chapter 1 of this reference guide, provides a thorough examination of all the various competing and emerging electronic media. Most important is that much of the information here appears within the context of media economics.

Government Documents

Hearing transcripts from the House Subcommittee on General Oversight and Minority Enterprise of the Committee on Small Business entitled *Media Concentration (Part 2)* carry two good inserts that deal mainly with media ownership concentration in the newspaper, radio, television, and cable television industries. Both inserts are compliments of Benjamin M. Compaine. One is an assortment of information he submitted on media ownership (pp. 11–26) and the other is a chapter excerpt (pp. 100–124) from Compaine's book *Who Owns the Media? Concentration of Ownership in the Mass Communications Industry*.

The Senate Subcommittee on Communications of the Committee on Commerce, Science, and Transportation's *Rural Telecommunications* hearing transcript examines how the telecommunications industry, particularly cable television, plans to provide service to rural areas. A good discussion of the logistics and economics involved in such service is included.

The purpose of hearings conducted by the House Subcommittee on SBA and SBIC Authority, Minority Enterprise, and General Small Business Problems of the Committee on Small Business and reported in *Cable Television Industry* was to find out how small and minority businesses participate in the cable television industry and what the future holds for such participation. Inserts that appear in *Cable Television Industry* are particularly important and are noted here in the order of their appearance in the hearings transcript. Included are a copy of the "NLC Franchising Code" (pp. 8–11) reprinted from *Nation's Cities Weekly*; a National League of Cities (NLC) report, "Regulating Cable Television" (pp. 15–82); an NLC-prepared summary, "Constitutionality of Federal Law Prohibiting State or Municipal Ownership of Cable Television Systems" (pp. 83–93); a statement by Alan Pearce of Pearce Enterprises, "The Structures of the Cable TV and Program Production Industries in the United States" (pp. 97–114); "The Cox Minority Purchasing/Contracting Program" (pp. 164–70); reprints of "Cable Fever" (pp. 213–15) from *TV Guide* and "Cable TV: Electronic Redlining" (pp. 216–20) from *Black Enterprise* magazine; testimony of National Cable Television Association (NCTA) president Thomas Wheeler with attached data on black/minority ownership in cable television (pp. 227–53); and a reprint of "Cable TV and Public Power Belong Together" (pp. 285–92) from *Public Power* magazine on municipal ownership of cable television systems.

In its legislative report *Small and Minority Business Ownership in the Cable Television Industry* the U.S. House Committee on Small Business "sought to determine, in specific, those impediments faced by small and minority business in owning, constructing and servicing cable television systems and whether these small concerns are receiving access to programming, business opportunities, joint ventures, capital, and tax incentives" (p. 3).

A report by the Majority Staff of the Subcommittee on Telecommunications, Consumer Protection, and Finance of the U.S House Committee on Energy and Commerce entitled *Telecommunications in Transition: The Status of Competition in the Telecommunications Industry* contains "the first comprehensive review of competition in the telecommunications industry" (p. iii) ever undertaken by Congress or any other federal agency. It was prepared pursuant to congressional consideration of the 1934 Communications Act rewrite. The report includes much technical information on market competition within the telecommunications industry and how FCC regulations affect such competition. While focusing primarily on the telephone industry, the report does include some significant information about competition within what is termed the "information industry." Chapter 11 contains a brief regulatory history of cable television (pp. 250–54), characteristics of cable ownership and program sources (pp. 290–302), cable availability in local markets (pp. 348–54), and levels of cable competition with other media in local markets (pp. 354–77). The concluding portion of the chapter examines barriers to future market competition among all media and future trends in competition (pp. 378–90).

Periodical Articles

Various facets of cable system ownership are viewed in the following articles. Leo W. Jeffres reports on public attitudes toward a municipally owned cable system in "Public vs. Private: Attitudes toward Ownership of Cable TV Systems." The function that cable television is to perform in particular social settings as a determinant of cable system ownership and/

or control is the subject of "Social Justice and a Community Information Utility" by Clifford G. Christians and Leon Hammond. Thomas A. Hart, Jr.'s "The Evolution of Telco-constructed Broadband Services for CATV Operators" analyzes the regulatory impediments to telephone company ownership of cable systems. Minority participation in the cable industry is the subject of "Now You See It, Now You Don't: Minority Ownership in an 'Unregulated' Video Marketplace" by Allen S. Hammond IV.

Articles that lend different economic perspectives to cable system franchising, particularly with respect to market competition, include Thomas W. Hazlett's "Private Monopoly and the Public Interest: An Economic Analysis of the Cable Television Franchise" and "Competition vs. Franchise Monopoly in Cable Television," and Bruce M. Owen and Peter R. Greenhalgh's "Competitive Considerations in Cable Television Franchising."

James G. Webster examines who the cable audience is and how it reacts to the medium in "Audience Behavior in the New Media Environment." Why persons are attracted to cable is viewed by Joey Reagan, Richard V. Ducey, and James Bernstein's "Local Predictors of Basic and Pay Cable Subscribership" and by Janay Collins, Joey Reagan, and John D. Abel in "Predicting Cable Subscribership: Local Factors." James T. Rothe, Michael G. Harvey, and George C. Michael look at attitudes of cable subscribers and nonsubscribers toward one another and the effects of cable on subscriber purchasing habits in "The Impact of Cable Television on Subscriber and Nonsubscriber Behavior." Long-term subscriber attitude change toward cable television is examined by Vernone M. Sparkes and NamJun Kang in "Public Reactions to Cable Television: Time in the Diffusion Process."

Sonia Yuspeh and Garth Hallberg report on the style and effect of the cable television advertising message as being a departure from that of the broadcast television commercial in "The Radical Potential of Cable Advertising." The authors contend, as do Alan J. Bush and James H. Leigh in "Advertising in Cable versus Traditional Networks," that cable advertisers do not recognize the medium's innovative potential for delivering advertising messages.

NOTES

1. *A Cable Primer* (Washington, D.C.: National Cable Television Association, 1981), pp. 10–13.

2. "A Guide: Satellite Channels," *Channels 1986 Field Guide*, pp. 57–64.

3. *A Cable Primer*, p. 12.

4. "Who's Got the Clout and How They're Using It," *Channels*, March 1986, p. 39.

5. Cecilia Capuzzi, "Wall Street's Affair with the Wire," *Channels Field Guide '87*, p. 69.

6. "Cable Industry Growth Chart," *CableVision*, 21 July 1986, p. 78.

7. "Cable TV: The Race to Plug In," *Business Week*, 8 December 1980, p. 62.

8. Niles Howard, "Madison Ave. Tunes In to Cable Television," *Dun's Review*, May 1981, p. 60.

9. Ibid., p. 63.

10. James Mann, "Is Cable Television Losing Its Luster?" *U.S. News and World Report*, 22 November 1982, p. 71.

11. "The Rush into Cable TV Is Now Turning Into a Retreat," *Business Week*, 17 October 1983, p. 135.

12. Mann, "Is Cable Television Losing Its Luster?" p. 71.

13. "The Rush into Cable TV Is Now Turning into a Retreat," p. 135.

14. Morrie Gelman, "Cable Still Searching for Its Pot of Gold," *Electronic Media*, 28 June 1984, p. 22.

15. "The Surprising Success Stories in Cable Television," *Business Week*, 12 November 1984, p 81.

16. Mark N. Vamos, "Cable TV, Older and Wiser, Looks like a Good Bet Again," *Business Week*, 22 July 1985, pp. 126–27.

17. "Franchising in the Top 50 Markets," *CableVision*, 17 February 1986, p. 57.

18. Judith Gross, "The State of Cable: An Industry Catches Its Breath," *BM/E*, May 1985, p. 74.

19. James F. Peltz, "Market Heats Up for Cable-TV Properties," *Dallas Times Herald*, 1 September 1985, p. 11F.

20. Joel C. Millonzi, "Wall Street Still Considers Cable a Good Investment," *CableAge*, 27 May 1985, p. C–19.

21. Virginia Munger Kahn, "Fountainheads of Capital: At Peak Flow with No End in Sight," *CableVision*, 9 September 1985, p. 27.

22. Alex Ben Block, "Fat, Wired Cats," *Forbes*, 25 February 1985, pp. 84–88.

23. Capuzzi, "Wall Street's Affair with the Wire," p. 68.

24. Ibid.

25. "Rate Deregulation Sparked Moves to Adjust Cable Pricing, Marketing," *Multichannel News*, 29 December 1986, p. 3.

26. Ibid.

27. Merrill Brown, "The Business Side: Cable's Dereg Dilemma," *Channels*, January 1987, p. 22.

28. Ibid.

29. Capuzzi, "Wall Street's Affair with the Wire," p. 69.

30. Tom Kerver, "Judging the Forecasts," *Cable Television Business*, 1 July 1985, p. 28.

31. Don Veraska, "Cable Nears Reality in Big Markets," *Electronic Media*, 17 March 1986, p. C6

32. Fred Dawson and Cecilia Capuzzi, "The New Era in CATV Construction," *CableVision*, 4 March 1985, p. 32.

33. Theresa Izzillo and Jeffrey L. Wolf, "Cable: Banking on a Windfall," *Channels 1986 Field Guide*, p. 38.

34. Roger Brown, "Construction Survey Finds Market Booming," *CableVision*, 2 March 1987, p. 26.

35. Jill Marks, "Rebuild/Upgrade Trends 1987," *Cable Television Business*, 15 February 1987, p. 22.

36. Capuzzi, "Wall Street's Affair with the Wire," p. 69.

37. Stewart Schley, "Tax Reform, Eager Buyers Stir Flurry of System Sales," *Multichannel News*, 10 November 1986, p. 49.

38. Chuck Moozakis, "Cable: Who Controls the Industry?" *Cable Television Business*, 1 January 1984, p. 27.

39. "Cable Stats," *CableVision*, 5 January 1987, pp. 62–63.

40. J. L. Freeman, "MPAA Leads Charge in Urging Limits on Cable Ownership," *Multichannel News*, 28 July 1986, p. 40.

41. Chuck Moozakis, "The 1986 General Managers Survey," *Cable Television Business*, 1 November 1986, pp. 28–30.

42. Ibid., p. 40.

43. Madeline Hardart, "Churn Tops Operators' List of Woes," *Electronic Media*, 30 May 1985, p. C1.

44. Ibid.

45. Simon Applebaum, "Taking a Bite out of Churn," *CableVision Plus*, 9 July 1984, p. 10. See also William F. Stubler, Lewis F. Hanes, and Margaret Richebourg, "Measuring Customer Satisfaction," *Cable Television Business*, 1 July 1986, p. 32.

46. Julia Reed, "Cable's Service Problem," *Channels*, March 1986, pp. 50–52.

47. "Customer Service Still Key to Cable, Researcher Says," *Multichannel News*, 3 December 1984, p. 65.

48. Block, "Fat, Wired Cats," p. 88.

49. Vernone M. Sparkes, "The Half-Wired Nation: Cable Television's Fifty-five Percent Penetration Barrier" (Unpublished paper prepared for the National Association of Broadcasters, February 1985), pp. 1–2.

50. Theresa Izzillo, "Cable Advertising Makes Its Move into Mainstream on Madison Ave.," in "Spotlight on Cable TV Advertising" supplement to *Multichannel News*, 28 April 1986, p. 2.

51. "Great Oaks from Little Acorns," *Broadcasting*, 30 March 1987, pp. 155–56.

52. John Motavalli, "Basic Nets' Viewership Surges Ahead," *CableVision*, 16 March 1987, p. 26.

53. Don Veraska and Len Strazewski, "Industry Works to Improve Fuzzy Image," *Advertising Age*, 5 December 1985, p. 15.

54. Wayne Walley, "Industry Pushing Its New Image to the Public," *Advertising Age*, 30 March 1987, p. S–4.

55. "Facts and Figures," *Multichannel News*, 4 May 1987, p. 62.

56. Cecilia Capuzzi, "How Deep Is the Commitment to Cable on Madison Avenue?" *CableVision*, 25 March 1985, pp. 33, 40.

57. Theresa Izzillo, "The View from the Agencies: A Rosy Future for Cable . . . If," *Multichannel News Supplement*, 25 March 1985, p. 3.

58. Theresa Izzillo, "CAB Aims to Guide Cable Ad Sales Growth," *Multichannel News Supplement*, 25 March 1985, p. 15.

59. Charles Warner, *Broadcast and Cable Selling* (Belmont, Calif.: Wadsworth, 1986), p. 203.

60. Victor Livingston, "Words vs. Deeds: Ad Agency Attitudes Bug Cable Net Execs," *CableAge*, 11 November 1985, p. C7.

61. Elizabeth J. Heighton and Don R. Cunningham, *Advertising in the Broadcast and Cable Media*, 2d ed. (Belmont, Calif.: Wadsworth, 1984), p. 41.

62. Dean M. Krugman, "Evaluating the Audiences of the New Media," *Journal of Advertising* 14 (1985): 22–23.

63. Richard Zacks, "Cable Systems Banding Together to Boost Ad Sales," *Electronic Media*, 13 December 1984, p. 22.

64. Cecilia Capuzzi, "Ad Sales and Interconnects: Getting the Gravy Train on Track," *CableVision*, 31 December 1984, pp. 20–21.

65. Chuck Moozakis, "Audience Research: What's New," *Cable Television Business*, 1 August 1985, p. 42.

66. Ibid.

67. John Motavalli, "The People Meter Quandry," *CableVision*, 19 January 1987, p. 42.

68. Theresa Izzillo, "Cable, Broadcast Execs Voice People Meter Concerns," *Multichannel News*, 15 December 1986, pp. 1, 35.

69. Peggy Ziegler, "Cable Operators Discover the Art of Audience Promotion," *Multichannel News Supplement*, 25 March 1985, p. 7.

70. Victoria Gits, "Local Ad Sales: Enterprise in Bloom," *CableVision*, 11 November 1985, p. 36.

71. Joel C. Millonzi, "Ops Reaping Profits As They Discover Advertising Sales," *CableAge*, 5 August 1985, p. C6.

72. Judith Reitman, "Basic Cable Gets Fancy and Learns to Sell Itself," *Marketing and Media Decisions*, November 1985, p. 56.

73. Ibid., pp. 56–58.

74. Geoffrey Colvin, "The Crowded New World of TV," *Fortune*, 17 September 1984, p. 156.

75. Ibid.

76. James Traub, "If You Can't Beat 'Em...," *Channels*, May/June 1985, p. 6.

77. John Wolfe, "MMDS Coming Alive despite Barriers," *CableVision*, 15 December 1986, p. 34.

78. Jill MacNeice, "Satellite Dishes Mushroom across USA," *USA Today*, 21 August 1985, p. 5B.

79. Felix Kessler, "Will Captain Midnight Buy a Decoder?" *Fortune*, 4 August 1986, pp. 139–42.

80. Sally Russell, "Will VCRs KO Pay Cable?" *CableVision Plus*, 25 June 1984, pp. 4–10.

81. Larry Jaffee, "VCR Onslaught Forces Shifts in Cable Marketing Strategies," *Multichannel News*, 9 March 1987, p. 1

82. Peter Elsworth, "Cable Courts the Impulse Buyer," *Channels*, July/August 1985, pp. 46–47.

83. Alan Breznick, "A New Ball Game," *Electronic Media*, 17 March 1986, p. C7.

84. Brad Metz, "New Pay-Per-View: This Time, It Looks like a Real Business," *CableAge*, 9 December 1985, pp. C6–C12.

85. Kim Foltz et al., "Hollywood Tries for a New Hit," *Newsweek*, 8 April 1985, p. 56.

86. Jeffrey A. Trachtenberg, "Here We Go Again," *Forbes*, 26 August 1985, p. 108.

87. Cary Campbell, "Pay Per View: The Middleman Cometh," *Cable Television Business*, 1 January 1986, p. 34.

88. Ibid.

89. Roger Brown, "The Addressability Debate," *CableVision*, 10 November 1986, pp. 54–58.

90. Mark Frankel, "Forcing Open a New Window," *Channels Field Guide '87*, p. 82.

91. "Study Sees 'Explosive Growth' In Addressable Cable Converters," *Multichannel News*, 20 April 1987, p. 4.

BIBLIOGRAPHY

Books and Book Chapters

General Survey

Baldwin, Thomas F., and D. Stevens McVoy. *Cable Communication*. Englewood Cliffs, N.J.: Prentice-Hall, 1983.

Webb, G. Kent. *The Economics of Cable Television*. Lexington, Mass.: Lexington Books, 1983.

Cable System Ownership, Operation, and Competition

Brenner, Daniel L., and Monroe E. Price. *Cable Television and Other Nonbroadcast Video: Law and Policy*. New York: Clark Boardman Company, 1986.

Gordon, Kenneth. "FCC Policies on Cable Crossownership." In *Proceedings from the Tenth Annual Telecommunications Policy Research Conference*, edited by Oscar H. Gandy, Jr., Paul Espinosa, and Janusz A. Ordover. Norwood, N.J.: Ablex, 1983.

Hamburg, Morton I. *All about Cable*. Rev. ed. New York: Law Journal Seminars-Press, 1985.

Levy, Jonathan D., and Florence O. Setzer. "Market Delineation, Measurement of Concentration, and F.C.C. Ownership Rules." In *Policy Research in Telecommunications*, edited by Vincent Mosco. Norwood, N.J.: Ablex, 1984.

Noam, Eli M. "Competitive Entry into Local Cable Transmission." In *Policy Research in Telecommunications*, edited by Vincent Mosco. Norwood, N.J.: Ablex, 1984.

————. "Local Distribution Monopolies in Cable Television and Telephone Service: The Scope for Competition." In *Telecommunications Regulation Today and Tomorrow*, edited by Eli Noam. New York: Harcourt Brace Jovanovich, 1983.

————. "The Political Economy of Cable Television Regulation." In *Proceedings from the Tenth Annual Telecommunications Policy Research Conference*, edited by Oscar H. Gandy, Jr., Paul Espinosa, and Janusz A. Ordover. Norwood, N.J.: Ablex, 1983.

————. "Private Sector Monopolies: The Case of Cable Television Franchises." In *Productivity and Public Policy*, edited by Marc Holzer and Stuart S. Nagel. Beverly Hills, Calif.: Sage, 1984.

Noam, Eli M., ed. *Video Media Competition: Regulation, Economics, and Technology*. New York: Columbia University Press, 1985.

Pepper, Robert. "Competition in Local Distribution: The Cable Television Industry." In *Understanding New Media: Trends and Issues in Electronic Distribution of Information*, edited by Benjamin M. Compaine. Cambridge, Mass.: Ballinger, 1984.

Stein, Ira C. *Cable Television: Handbook and Forms*. Colorado Springs, Col.: Shepherd's/McGraw-Hill, 1985.

Wasko, Janet. "New Methods of Analyzing Media Concentration." In *Policy Research in Telecommunications*, edited by Vincent Mosco. Norwood, N.J.: Ablex, 1984.

Copyright

Kelley, Daniel. "The Economics of Copyright Controversies in Communications." In *Policy Research in Telecommunications*, edited by Vincent Mosco. Norwood, N.J.: Ablex, 1984.

Cable System Management, Marketing, and Sales

Barr, Samuel. *Advertising on Cable: A Practical Guide for Advertisers*. Englewood Cliffs, N.J.: Prentice-Hall, 1985.

Beville, Hugh Malcolm, Jr. *Audience Ratings: Radio, Television, and Cable*. Hillsdale, N.J.: Lawrence Erlbaum Associates, 1985.

Eastman, Susan Tyler, and Robert A. Klein. *Strategies in Broadcast and Cable Promotion*. Belmont, Calif.: Wadsworth, 1982.

Heighton, Elizabeth J., and Don R. Cunningham. *Advertising in the Broadcast and Cable Media*. 2d ed. Belmont, Calif.: Wadsworth, 1984.

Jones, Kensinger, Thomas F. Baldwin, and Martin P. Block. *Cable Advertising: New Ways to New Business*. Englewood Cliffs, N.J.: Prentice-Hall, 1986.

Kaatz, Ronald B. *Cable Advertiser's Handbook*. 2d ed. Lincolnwood, Ill.: National Textbook Company, 1985.

Keown, Charles F., and Leslie Freundschuh. "Alternative Advertising Formats for Cable Television." In *Original Research and Theoretical Contributions*, vol. 1 of *Current Issues and Research in Advertising 1985*, edited by James H. Leigh and Claude R. Martin, Jr. Ann Arbor: Division of Research, Graduate School of Business Administration, University of Michigan, 1985.

McCavitt, William E., and Peter K. Pringle. *Electronic Media Management*. Boston, Mass.: Focal Press, 1986.

Marcus, Norman. *Broadcast and Cable Management*. Englewood Cliffs, N.J.: Prentice-Hall, 1986.

Morse, R. C., and Karen L. Burns. *Cable/Videotex: A Compendium for Direct Marketers*. Monograph series, vol. 6. New York: Direct Mail/Marketing Association, 1982.

Poltrack, David. *Television Marketing: Network, Local, and Cable*. New York: McGraw-Hill, 1983.

Warner, Charles. *Broadcast and Cable Selling*. Belmont, Calif.: Wadsworth, 1986.

Williams, Jerome D. "Cable Television: New Electronic Media for New Nonprofit Marketing Strategies." In *Advances in Nonprofit Marketing*, vol. 1, edited by Russell W. Belk. Greenwich, Conn.: JAI Press, 1985.

Competing Delivery Systems

Singleton, Loy A. *Telecommunications in the Information Age*. 2d ed. Cambridge, Mass.: Ballinger, 1986.

Government Documents

U.S. House. Committee on Small Business. *Small and Minority Business Ownership in the Cable Television Industry*. 97th Cong., 2d sess., 1982. H. Rept. 97–976.

————. Subcommittee on General Oversight and Minority Enterprise of the House Committee on Small Business. *Media Concentration (Part 2)*. 96th Cong., 2d sess., 1980. Hearing.

————. Subcommittee on SBA and SBIC Authority, Minority Enterprise, and General Small Business Problems of the House Committee on Small Business. *Cable Television Industry*. 97th Cong., 1st sess., 1981. Hearing.

————. Subcommittee on Telecommunications, Consumer Protection, and Finance of the House Committee on Energy and Commerce. *Telecommunications in Transition: The Status of Competition in the Telecommunications Industry*. Report by the Majority Staff. 97th Cong., 1st sess., 1981. Committee Print.

U.S. Senate. Subcommittee on Communications of the Senate Committee on Commerce, Science, and Transportation. *Rural Telecommunications*. 97th Cong., 1st sess., 1981. Hearing.

Periodical Articles

Bush, Alan J., and James H. Leigh. "Advertising in Cable versus Traditional Networks." *Journal of Advertising Research*, 24 (April/May 1984): 33–38.

Christians, Clifford G., and Leon Hammond. "Social Justice and a Community Information Utility." *Communication* 9 (1986): 127–49.

Collins, Janay, Joey Reagan, and John D. Abel. "Predicting Cable Subscribership: Local Factors." *Journal of Broadcasting* 27 (Spring 1983): 177–83.

Hammond, Allen S., IV. "Now You See It, Now You Don't: Minority Ownership in an 'Unregulated' Video Marketplace." *Catholic University Law Review* 32 (Spring 1983): 633–63.

Hart, Thomas A., Jr. "The Evolution of Telco-constructed Broadband Services for CATV Operators." *Catholic University Law Review* 34 (Spring 1985): 697–735.

Hazlett, Thomas W. "Competition vs. Franchise Monopoly in Cable Television." *Contemporary Policy Issues* 4 (April 1986): 80–97.

————. "Private Monopoly and the Public Interest: An Economic Analysis of the Cable Television Franchise." *University of Pennsylvania Law Review* 134 (July 1986): 1335–1409.

Jeffres, Leo W. "Public vs. Private: Attitudes toward Ownership of Cable TV Systems." *Journalism Quarterly* 61 (Summer 1984): 325–31.

Owen, Bruce M., and Peter R. Greenhalgh. "Competitive Considerations in Cable Television Franchising." *Contemporary Policy Issues* 4 (April 1986): 69–79.

Reagan, Joey, Richard V. Ducey, and James Bernstein. "Local Predictors of Basic and Pay Cable Subscribership." *Journalism Quarterly* 62 (Summer 1985): 397–400.

Rothe, James T., Michael G. Harvey, and George C. Michael. "The Impact of Cable Television on Subscriber and Nonsubscriber Behavior." *Journal of Advertising Research* 24 (August/September 1983): 15–22.

Sparkes, Vernone M., and NamJun Kang. "Public Reactions to Cable Television: Time in the Diffusion Process." *Journal of Broadcasting and Electronic Media* 30 (Spring 1986): 213–29.

Webster, James G. "Audience Behavior in the New Media Environment." *Journal of Communication* 36 (Summer 1986): 77–91.

Yuspeh, Sonia, and Garth Hallberg. "The Radical Potential of Cable Advertising." *Journal of Advertising Research* 23 (August/September 1983): 51–54.

Chapter Three

PROGRAM SERVICES, PROGRAM CONTENT, USES AND EFFECTS, VIEWING HABITS, AND CRITICISM

ISSUE OVERVIEW

A cornucopia of program and service selections is available to the cable television subscriber. The subscriber has far more channels moving into his home via cable than ever came over the air. Cable systems are also capable of narrowcasting content matter into selected subscriber homes. Two-way or interactive cable services make it possible in some markets for the subscriber not only to receive cable content but to originate it as well. Perhaps the ultimate service offered by cable television is linkage of the cable transmission system with a computer-generated data system such as videotex.[1] While all these things are possible, there is still no clear vision as to which of the program channels or services is the most practical, useful, or desirable. Cable program and service content, then, is the one area of the entire cable enterprise that is least settled and most dynamic.

Program Services in General

Cable program services are grouped into three categories: basic, pay, and interactive. Basic or primary-tier cable is comprised of those program services that the subscriber pays a monthly fee to receive. Such programming may be imported from a distant origination point by satellite and is usually produced especially for cable distribution. Signals of "superstations" may also be carried on basic cable. Superstations are independent television stations generally located in major markets like New York, Chicago, and Los Angeles whose over-the-air signals are relayed by satellite to cable systems around the country. Rounding out the basic service are local origination

(LO) programs that may be cablecast projects of the cable system (for example, coverage of local sports events or a local cable newscast) or public access programs (for example, coverage of local city council meetings or programs produced by citizens independent of the cable system).

The second tier of cable programming is comprised of pay or premium services. These are services available at extra cost to basic cable subscribers who are interested in viewing movies or other special programs originated at a distant location and made available to the local cable system via a satellite relay. Most pay cable services are available to subscribers on a continuous basis and require payment of a monthly fee. However, pay-per-view (PPV) services are available on a one-time, one-payment basis. PPV programs usually consist of special movies or sports events.

Interactive cable provides the subscriber with a host of services ranging "from home banking, energy management, and security alarms to medical referrals and information-retrieval systems." The most publicized interactive cable system probably has been that of Warner Amex's QUBE. Located in several major cities, QUBE was seen as a breakthrough technology when it was introduced. QUBE subscribers were able to "talk back" to their television sets by responding to polling questions, judging beauty contests, and calling plays in football games. However, the discovery by subscribers and program producers alike that the utility of interactive programming is definitely limited has stymied interactive program system development. Added to this is a growing concern that interactive cable could be used to invade the privacy of the cable subscriber by creating a computer dossier on his viewing, opinion, and buying traits.[2]

Basic Cable

One count of available basic cable program services or networks places the number at 48 national services and 14 regional services. The cable system affiliate numbers for the national services run from a low of 5 systems carrying the International Television Network to more than 14,000 carrying ESPN.[3] Ironically, even with so many program services to choose from, many cable systems have channel space that remains unused. One study showed that an average of 6.1 channels remain open on 14- to 34-channel capacity cable systems and that 13.8 channels remained open on 35- to 53-channel capacity systems.[4]

Program content types available from basic cable services have been grouped into the following ten categories: "sports; news, information, public affairs; music; arts, culture; games, children's; full service, women's; adult; religious; foreign language, ethnic; and educational, instructional."

Basic cable networks are typically advertiser supported, and about half of them use program forms similar to those of broadcast television. The other half represent innovations in long-form content (all-weather, all-health) or adaptations from other media (games from computerized software, teletext-type news and financial information adapted from print media). Many forecasters predict that less than two dozen of these basic services will survive as national services. At present, four basic networks lead the field: ESPN in sports, CBN in religion, CNN in news and USA Network in full-service programming.[5]

According to A. C. Nielsen third-quarter 1986 audience research figures, the top basic cable program services arranged in descending order by the number of households viewing the service included WTBS, ESPN, CNN, TNN (The Nashville Network), USA Network, MTV, CBN, Lifetime, and Arts and Entertainment. The WTBS audience nearly doubled the size of its nearest competitor, ESPN. While the above list pertains to prime-time viewing (Monday to Saturday, 8 P.M. to 11 P.M., and Sunday, 7 P.M. to 11 P.M.), the ranking did not change appreciably when total day viewing was measured, with the one exception that Nickelodeon appeared in second place to WTBS.[6]

A full list of basic cable services is not provided here, but the reader is directed to at least two good sources of information on the subject. *CableVision*, in its "Cable Stats" section, frequently updates a list of basic services along with their affiliate and subscriber counts. The annual *Channels Field Guide* goes a bit further, though, by supplying the name, owner, and launch date of each basic service as well as the number of homes reached by each service, whether the service scrambles its signal, and program content characteristics of each service.

Local Origination and Access

Local origination (LO) or cablecasting refers to programming produced by a cable operator especially for his system's subscribers. LO programming was at one time viewed as an irritant by many cable operators, but it is emerging as both an important promotion tool and a viable addition to the programming mix. Some cable systems have even built special production units that produce a variety of sophisticated programs.[7] Perhaps one of the most common LO productions is the newscast that provides what one observer has described as "probably the most highly localized news coverage ever to appear on television. And, in contrast to broadcast programming, cable newscasts are produced in a world of meager resources and elusive commercial success—making them at once raw, plucky, resourceful, and, all too often, unabashedly amateur."[8]

While some LO productions may become regionalized when carried on more than one cable system, few will attain the kind of exposure that came to the Home Shopping Network (HSN). From a locally produced program available at first only in Clearwater, Florida, HSN blossomed into a national

program service. The entire service can be described as either a video merchandise catalog or a program-length commercial. Viewers may phone
designated numbers to purchase items that are displayed and described in
an originating studio and sold at a discounted price. Reflecting on the success
of his company, HSN president Lowell W. Paxon said, "We have combined
two of America's greatest loves, watching television and shopping. We
have created a romance."[9] By early 1987 some twenty-five more home
shopping cable services were either in operation or in some planning stage
for future operation.[10]

Another unique LO production that is more nearly a hybrid between
access and LO programming is "Dial-A-Teacher." This program allows
high school students to phone teachers at the local cable system studio for
help with homework. The teacher responds on camera and uses visuals if
necessary to clarify answers.[11]

Cable access channels provide a unique service to local cable subscribers.
Access programming—public, educational, and governmental—has become
institutionalized in some markets, while in others it has remained a thorn
in the side of cable operators. Access has become a controversial pawn in
some places because of cable franchise requirements that cable systems provide not only access channels, but also studio facilities and equipment with
which to produce access programming. "Providing public access can be a
budgetary problem for big systems, and a budgetary nightmare for smaller
ones, especially if operator-purchased production equipment lies unused."
As a result, "Some cable companies in larger markets are going to city
governments to request cutbacks in public access obligations or to rene-
gotiate the public access terms of their franchise agreements."[12] The irony
of this is that only 10 percent of all the cable systems in the United States
had even dedicated channels to public access, according to a 1984 study.
The record among the nation's fifty largest cable systems was little better.
About one-third of them had dedicated access channels.[13]

Opposition to access channels by some cable system operators is problematical, but so too is the content of some of the access programs. Cable
systems may charge a small fee for use of their access facilities, but they
have little control over what local self-made program producers and talent
may choose to do. Some have reached nearly the limit of propriety, as in
the case of Manhattan Cable's Ugly George, who devoted his access program to showing women on busy New York streets disrobing at his request
while he caught them in the act with his portable video camera. Others
have paid the access fee just to have a stage to display their (sometimes
limited) talent, thus making a contribution to "vanity video."

Despite all the flaws, though, cable access programming has emerged in
many markets as a vibrant adjunct to the more typical cable fare. Two
writers have even called access programming "sophisticated, original, and
fascinating" and have cited examples of access programs on a variety of

subjects produced by non-professionals that have been praised for both content and quality.[14] There is also a tremendous diversity in how communities have utilized cable access channels. A Pennsylvania school system has used cable access to carry classroom instruction to persons seeking to qualify for a general education development diploma.[15] A Michigan police department has used an access channel to instruct viewers on local law enforcement matters,[16] and the audio portion only of a cable access channel in Connecticut has been utilized to carry information to visually impaired subscribers.[17]

One of the greatest attributes of public access cable is the "blank canvas" it allows for artistic creativity.

Experimental work presented on local channels stretches the ability of the viewer to relate to television. Access channels have offered exciting and unsettling new uses of the camera in drama and dance—even for talk shows. Experimental work on local television promises to change our expectations of the medium over the next few years. . . . Television can offer us new ways of seeing, through the work being done in hundreds of local cable systems, access studios, lofts, museums, galleries, and even in the streets.[18]

Public access also assists the arts by providing a forum to bring individual artists and arts organizations into direct contact with those on whose financial support the arts often must depend.[19]

Cable access programming embodies the essence of narrowcasting, touted for so long as being one of the major advantages of cable television. Reaching and appealing to the select few instead of the mass audience gives access a unique dimension. Its participatory nature is also unique, as noted by one observer who calls public access television "community television":

Community television is a different *kind* of television, in style, content, intended audience, and equipment used. It emphasizes process rather than product, participation rather than viewing, quality information, examination of the TV environment, and critical viewing skills. In essence, it demystifies the television process and gives people skills to deal with television as a cultural phenomenon.[20]

Pay Cable

Pay cable program services provide programming that is available to systems other than cable, such as MMDS, SMATV, and direct broadcast satellite (DBS). Cable systems are nonetheless the major means of distributing these pay or premium services. There were ten national and nine regional pay services available in early 1987.[21] The general content fare of the pay services include movies (first-run, classics, children, and adult), sports, and programs especially produced for pay service distribution. The undisputed leader of the pay cable pack is HBO. HBO was the first pay cable service created (in November 1972), and its subscribership of 14.6 million is nearly three times that of its nearest competitor, Showtime.[22]

Six pay-per-view (PPV) cable services are available. Content matter of the PPV services is somewhat more specialized than the regular premium services, but not all that much. As an example, the leading PPV service, Choice Channel, launched in October 1984, provides sports and entertainment events to its nearly 4 million subscribers, for an average fee of $11 per event. The slightly newer (by one year) PPV service, Viewer's Choice, provides movies as well as sports events to its nearly 1.2 million customers. The average cost of Viewer's Choice programs ranges from a high of $20 per sports event to a low of $4 per movie.[23]

Interactive Cable

Interactive cable television is synonymous with the QUBE service initiated by Warner Amex in 1977. QUBE eventually spread to other Warner Amex cable locations and served as a model for similar interactive services at other cable systems. The basic orientation of most interactive services has focused on entertainment and merchandising. But there was hope, yet to be fully realized, that interactive cable would become an instrument of "teledemocracy," that is, a two-way system by which citizens could routinely express their voting preferences and record their opinions regarding public matters.[24]

Interactive cable may have an even greater potential for use as a marketing and product research tool. In fact, some industry observers see interactive cable as "one of the most effective and efficient data-gathering tools available for certain kinds of research." The two characteristics of an interactive service that make it so useful are its addressability—enabling commercials to be transmitted or narrowcast to a select audience—and the audience feedback that allows researchers to poll test subjects about products they have used or commercials they have just viewed.[25] Interactive cable also allows commercials to be transformed into "infomercials" whereby cable subscribers may ask questions of advertisers as well as make purchases during live, on-air product demonstrations.[26]

Audio, Text, and Data Services

Cable television systems obviously give most of their attention to video services, but some systems also carry audio or radio program services. At least nine such services are available by satellite, and one of them, Tempo Sound, is carried by 300 cable systems. Text services such as AP News Cable and Cable Sportstracker also are carried by a number of cable systems. Heading the list of eleven nationally distributed text services is UPI Data Cable, available on 450 cable systems.[27]

One particular kind of text service is videotex. So much has been written about videotex and its potential that an entire later chapter of this reference guide is devoted to the subject.

Cable Programming Costs and Sources

Basic cable television program services were to spend an estimated $500 million in 1987 for program acquisition.[28] Add to that the combined amount of expenditures by pay cable services for purchase of exclusive rights to major Hollywood film libraries (already into the billions for Showtime).[29] Such sums indicate two things about the cable industry: One is the recognition among industry leaders that programming, especially of the kind and quality that attracts viewers, is important; the other is that cable program services have the financial resources to acquire the programming. One cable executive placed both points into the following perspective:

[M]ost of the cable networks that have been in business for the last four or five years are in the black or are about to tip into the black this year [1987]. And some of them are beginning to generate some very nice profits. The economics of those networks are good, and they are on a realistic base of operation in terms of expenditures, so they're building in a very healthy way. They're not overextending themselves, and as they build more audience, as they get more advertising dollars, as they get more [subscriber] fees back from the [local cable] operators, that money is going back into the programming.[30]

The relationship between cable television and programming has evolved into something quite complex. Cable networks now provide an important market as well as program testing ground for program syndicators. Perhaps more important, though, cable networks also produce some of their own programs and thus serve as program sources as well as program buyers for syndicators.[31] The first made-for-basic-cable program was TNN's "I–40 Paradise," a situation comedy produced in 1983. Since then, not only has quality and quantity of made-for-cable programming increased, but so has the amount of money that the cable networks are willing to invest in the programming.[32] Several MSOs have even entertained the idea of forming a cooperative that would fund the acquisition and development of high-quality programming, both series and specials, that would air exclusively on cable television. The cooperative would also raise funds from its members to outbid the broadcast networks for the rights to certain sports and entertainment events.[33]

Cable Viewing Habits and Patterns

An examination of why persons subscribe to cable in the first place has been the subject of at least one study. The study showed that several lifestyle characteristics and the uses that are made of cable television distinguish the cable adopter from the nonadopter. Generally, cable subscribers "are more affluent, more likely to be married, and live in households with more children than non-subscribers." Cable television often enters the household at the request of a child and the acquiescence to that request by the child's parent. "When children leave the home, parents decline to subscribe, offering reasons which suggest that cable is a commodity which needs justification, rather than a necessity which stands alone." Cable subscribers also "read less, travel for pleasure less, and attend fewer movies than do non-subscribers." Finally, the decision both to subscribe to and to cancel cable service is usually made collectively, due in part to the lifestyle influence that accompanies cable television's arrival or departure from a home.[34]

What kind of viewing patterns are discernible for cable subscribers? According to Television Audience Assessment research firm, cable television subscribers usually watch and like television more than nonsubscribers. Cable subscribers are more satisfied with television programming in general. Television viewing averages 12.6 hours per week among noncable viewers, 13.1 hours per week among basic cable subscribers, and 14 hours per week among pay cable subscribers. Cable subscribers also watch less network programming than do cable nonsubscribers. Premium service subscribers watch even less network programming than do basic cable subscribers.[35]

Subscriber satisfaction with cable has been a major concern within the cable television industry. There is a mixed bag of attitudes on the subject. A 1984 study indicated that more than 80 percent of those surveyed were satisfied both with cable programming and service.[36] A 1986 study found that 53 percent of survey respondents said that cable programming had not changed over the past year, whereas 26 percent indicated that it had improved and 16 percent that it had deteriorated.[37] Another 1986 study of cable program network satisfaction level for regular viewers of the networks found that at least 50 percent or more were satisfied with CNN, ESPN, Financial News Network (FNN), MTV, TNN, Nickelodeon, Video Hits One (VH1) and The Weather Channel programming. The highest satisfaction level (nearly 70 percent) was accorded CNN and ESPN. At the low end of the scale were Black Entertainment Television (BET) and PTL The Inspirational Network, both of which measured only about a 30 percent satisfaction level. Among the pay cable services, Cinemax and The Disney Channel both reached a nearly 70 percent viewer satisfaction level, but HBO, The Movie Channel, and Showtime satisfied only 50 percent or less of their viewers.[38]

The low satisfaction level for the three pay services is yet another example of cable television viewers' general disaffection for pay cable—a disaffection that can be tracked over several years. A 1983 study found that the longer a cable subscriber had had cable, the more likely that basic cable was the only service he subscribed to. Of those basic service subscribers who also had subscribed to a pay service prior to the study, more than half had cancelled the pay service between 1982 and 1983. Those who dropped their pay service said that they were not getting their money's worth from the service, that movies were repeated too often, and that the quality of the movies was low.[39] A 1985 survey confirmed that subscriber cancellation of pay cable was not simply a 1983 phenomenon. Instead, it was a trend that by 1985 was described by one industry observer as "an entire rejection of the pay product on the part of many consumers."[40]

Viewer turnoff to pay cable may be measured in another more telling way. "While cable viewing is up across-the-board in pay cable households," according to 1985 figures, "pay TV viewing is flat, representing a smaller share of the total." One overriding reason for the pay cable decline is the popularity and the ubiquitous household presence of the VCR. Said one HBO official, "You don't have to be a rocket scientist to know that videocassette recorders are cannibalizing our ratings." The pay cable industry is hard-pressed to compete with such advantages of the videocassette movie as faster movie release time from theater to cassette than from theater to pay cable, single title selection, watching the videocassette movie according to the viewer's schedule, and less expense (about three times less) for a single videocassette rental than for a pay cable monthly subscription.[41]

To combat the VCR incursion, many of the pay cable services are turning to original programming.[42] Pay cable officials maintain that movies "will remain the heart and soul of the service,"[43] but they concede a need to produce programming that is new and unavailable from any other source. Ironically, original programming was used in the beginning days of pay cable primarily to fill gaps between movies. Now original programming will play the much more important roles not only of supplanting movies, but also of assisting pay cable services in differentiating themselves from one another.[44]

Basic cable program services may be holding their own in terms of audience attraction, but they too are experiencing a "fundamental shift" in program content. "The notion of many specialized channels is giving way to a system in which a few channels are aimed at mass audiences. . . . The reasons for the move toward more broadly based services are practical and economic. It seems as if many cable users never wanted the 'television of abundance' that numerous specialized channels promised."[45]

Even for those specialized channels whose programs have attracted viewers, the total number of viewers has, in some cases, not been high enough to attract sufficient advertiser support. A cable audience is normally fragmented. The more program services a cable system provides its subscribers, the more fragmented the system's viewing audience becomes. In some cases the individual audience fragments may be too small to sustain all the program services provided by the cable system.

Another factor in the cable industry's shift to program services of broader appeal is the cost of program production. Network television has conditioned viewers to expect the kind of quality programming that is usually very expensive to produce. In order to pay for such programming, viewership must be high enough to attract advertisers' dollars.[46]

An industry that is in such a state of flux must inevitably undergo a shake-out period that will determine the survival of the fittest among both pay and basic cable program services. A 1984 study to determine just what programming services would survive predicted that from ten to twelve of the national services were the likeliest candidates. Referring to content types and not to specific services, the study predicted that the survivors would include two pay cable movie services, one pay cable sports network, two news services (one feature-oriented and the other headline-oriented), a pay cable network featuring adult programming, a pay children's network, a pay music video network, a pay cultural service, and one to three basic services whose content would range from weather to general-interest programming.[47]

Cable Program Content and Viewer Effects

Regardless of cable's, especially pay cable's, ups and downs, there is no denying that the "television of abundance" made possible by cable has changed and will continue to change the cable subscriber's life. Just how significant the change will be was documented by one writer who interviewed residents living on a single street in Lanham, Maryland, shortly after their homes had been "turned on" by a new cable system.

Since their turn-on, the people of Ellerbie Street have been watching more television and staying up later to do so. They find themselves more often sitting around their TVs as a family, though with at least two televisions wired in most homes someone is usually drawn to the other set. The people of Ellerbie Street also are going to fewer movies, changing daily routines, watching more earthy films, and catching the excitement of previously unknown sports.[48]

Specific cable program content has had pronounced effects on some subscribers. Sports fanatics, for instance, need never leave their television sets to witness a never-ending parade of the traditional as well as the more exotic athletic events. What results from this? In the words of a *Sports Illustrated* writer, the product is a "channel-dazzled, game-crazed, ESPN-stoned junkie."[49] The point to note here is the amount of time and attention a cable viewer spends with his favorite programming. That point may be made even more strongly with the findings of a study conducted to ascertain MTV viewing habits. The study showed that the longer MTV is available in a household, the more attached to the cable service the viewer becomes. Younger viewers, aged twelve to seventeen, are most attracted to MTV.

This same group would also opt for MTV if faced with having to choose between it and radio.[50]

The pay cable services that bring movie buffs a steady diet of uninterrupted cinema also have caused a major viewing habit change. Gone are the commercial breaks that allowed movement, trips to the kitchen, and conversation with fellow viewers. Uninterrupted movies require undivided attention—which itself requires a discipline that is unnecessary when viewing movies aired by the commercial networks.[51]

It was noted earlier that children influence the decision to subscribe to cable television. The growing penetration of cable television into households where children are present has caused many of these youngsters to "develop a set of viewing habits and attitudes quite different from those of their unwired playmates." A Michigan State University study found that children in cable households watch more television than children in noncable households. That is not particularly unexpected; what is surprising, though, is the finding that the cable household children read more books and magazines, watch television more selectively and with greater awareness, engage in more innovative thinking, are friendlier, and are better acquainted with such technology as VCRs and computers than are their noncable counterparts. Moreover, "Parents who subscribe to cable are, according to their offspring, less likely to set rules about TV usage and more likely to let their kids watch PG- and R-rated movies and stay up late to watch TV. When they make their children study, that studying is more likely to occur in front of a TV set that is turned on."[52]

From the lower end of the age spectrum we move to the upper end, where cable television represents for the elderly not merely an entertainment medium but also an important information source and a companion. Especially valuable for those whose mobility is restricted are the special cable services that narrowcast religious, political, and health care programming. Interactive cable services now under development hold the potential for allowing shut-ins to once more become active participants in society.[53]

So far, the uses and effects of cable television have been described in ways that are intrinsic to the technology, its content, and its users' habits. Cable may also be used to affect subscribers in ways that are extrinsic to the medium's basic nature. For the unscrupulous, interactive cable television provides an excellent vehicle for invading the privacy of unsuspecting cable subscribers.[54]

Several cable services that either are available now or will be in the near future provide cable and/or service operators instantaneous access to computer data that contains information on such things as subscriber business practices, program viewing and product preferences, living habits and routines, and more. Unsecured access to and improper use of subscriber interaction with at least eight categories of cable services could lead to invasion of privacy. The eight include home banking services, shop-at-home services, information services, home and personal security services, opinion-polling services, home study services, special entertainment options or pay cable services, and religious or similar services involving organizational fund raising.[55]

Some persons envision an even greater threat to the nation's welfare as a result of cable programming coming under the control of a single entity. Citing the trend toward smaller cable television systems being purchased by large MSOs, one observer claims that eventually all wired communication systems in this country could fall into the hands of a very few or maybe only a single authority. "An agency that gained such control, if left to operate it without adequate restraints, could dictate its contents and decide its political, economic, and social applications."[56]

Cable Criticism

Much of the criticism of cable television is directed toward cable programming, and much of that criticism is embedded in the charge that cable has failed to deliver as promised. Many of the critics, as witnessed by the following comments, recount an enthusiasm followed by a disillusionment regarding the cable service they had subscribed to:

Once, cable was sold to the public as the tool to break the networks' stranglehold. It was the way to allow a thousand geniuses to blossom. Now movies are the biggest hype. Cable creativity is a Hollywood rerun and a rerun of the Hollywood rerun. . . .

The concept behind 100 or more channels was that you could have it your way. That's about as common for cable viewers today as it is for fast-food lovers. Most of the cable channels find themselves competing for popularity—the largest number of viewers. They do it, the way the networks do, by offering a low common denominator.

At the end of the cable line, we don't have choices in the real sense of that word. We just have more TV. The picture is terrific, but the purpose is way out of focus.[57]

Another critic provides an even more caustic assessment of cable television:

From the moment it began vibrating in America's collective consciousness, cable TV programming has been a mixture of unfulfilled or outright phony promises; a load of network reruns on self-declared "superstations"; repeated telecasts of movies, most of which you never would have paid to see in a theater; made-for-cable films that might just as well have been made for networks; more sports than any ordinary human could ever want, much less need; services based on the notion that more of anything, especially mediocrity, is a good thing; cultural channels that stood about as much chance of survival as ice cream in Ecuador; and, every now and then, fine programs that eventually would have made their way to public TV anyway.[58]

There are other observers who assume a decidedly different posture:

It's won us over, that fact can't be denied. Critics who attack cable for failing to meet its promise never quite get around to interpreting the medium's boffo popularity. Cable sells—now why?

Undeniably the medium's most attractive characteristic is diversity. Watch any new subscriber practicing 10-finger exercises on his channel selector, and it's apparent that quantity is king. This increased number of alternatives gives cable TV programming its unique character....

Certainly cable is America's best shot at a truly democratic mass medium, a public arena in which the tyranny of quality—as defined by an oligarchy of taste despots—has been kept in check.

Cable programming overrides parochial views of art and recognizes the true folk dimension of TV. It's reached a critical mass—not a critical mess. Viewed from this perspective, more is more.[59]

Pay cable programming, particularly the variety that has been specially produced for premium services such as HBO, has been the subject of much scrutiny. While there have been some exemplary programs to appear in the made-for-pay category, most have failed to win any notable acclaim. Why this is so has been explained by one critic:

It is depressingly familiar for anyone who has followed the history of commercial television in this country. In a nutshell: the vast majority of programming decisions take second place to business considerations. The top-executive echelons of HBO are overflowing with Harvard M.B.A.'s, lawyers and theatrical agents, who may be good people all but who lack experience in, and a commitment to, quality programming. Armed with surveys and statistics about what audiences are supposedly interested in, they devote much of their time to making constructions that should work, at least on paper.[60]

One critic has analyzed the problems that cable program services have faced with building audiences and suggests that cable does not lend itself that well to accommodating the intrinsic capriciousness of the cable viewer. Laurence Michie contends that clear winners may indeed emerge from among the numerous pay and basic cable services. But those services whose narrowcast objectives reach for too limited a target audience will likely falter. Michie views the popularity of narrowcast program services as "a short-lived fad, because program types go in and out of vogue, and the commercial television networks prosper partly because they carry all types of programming, and can shift emphasis at the drop of a share point."[61]

The positions, then, seem well established. To some critics cable television is doing well enough as is, providing the cable subscriber with a diversity of program sources and types. Others contend that more is not better—and not a great deal different than what is available from over-the-air network television. Indeed, one observer concluded, "For all of cable's revolutionary potential, as a communication institution it has been thoroughly amalgamated into the American mass media structure. Its differences with broadcasting are only those of surface and nuance, not of principle."[62]

The future for cable programming, in the view of those who share the latter of these two opinions, is that cable must "reinvent itself." "Cable has been leading from its weakness all this time. Its weakness being that it's like television," contends Les Brown. "Its strength," he says, "is that it can be different from television. That's the one thing it seems to deny." Brown sees cable's future in local public access programming and programming from independent producers whose products are placed amidst programming from a few of the major satellite-supplied cable services. This arrangement would be analogous to a shopping mall: "A shopping mall where large chains like Sears and Macy's anchor the mall. We have to do the same thing in cable and have the large chains like CNN and ESPN and HBO and the others. But in and around those chains are new things, some kind of ferment and invention going on."[63]

NOTES

1. Robert D. Kahn, "Cable Programming," *Current*, no. 251 (March/April 1983): 22–23.

2. Ibid., pp. 23–24.

3. "Cable Services Subscriber Count," *CableVision*, 19 January 1987, p. 64.

4. "Facts and Figures," *Multichannel News*, 22 September 1986, p. 45.

5. Susan Tyler Eastman, Sydney W. Head, and Lewis Klein, *Broadcast/Cable Programming*, 2d ed. (Belmont, Calif.: Wadsworth, 1985), pp. 240–41.

6. "Facts and Figures," *Multichannel News*, 10 November 1986, p. 41.

7. Simon Applebaum, "LO," *CableVision*, 25 November 1985, pp. 28–33.

8. Laurence Zuckerman, "Cable News Hits the Small Time," *Columbia Journalism Review*, September–October 1982, p. 35.

9. Paula Schnorbus, "Sold!" *Marketing and Media Decisions*, March 1987, p. 53.

10. "Home Shopping: How High Is Up?" *Broadcasting*, 9 February 1987, p. 106.

11. Barbara Zigli, "Homework Help Has Gone High-Tech," *USA Today*, 20 December 1984, p. 5D.

12. Cary Campbell, "Nine Lives of Public Access," *Cable Television Business*, 1 December 1985, p. 34.

13. Mitchell L. Moss and Robert Warren, "Public Policy and Community-Oriented Uses of Cable Television," *Urban Affairs Quarterly* 20 (December 1984): 250.

14. Jonathan Mostow and Mark Litwak, "Losing Access," *EMMY Magazine*, May/June 1984, pp. 39–41, 43.

15. Joseph H. Previty, "Cable Television: An Aid to Education," *Technological Horizons in Education Journal* 11 (January 1984): 136.

16. Donald O. Brook, "Educating Residents through Cable Television," *Police Chief*, May 1984, p. 63.

17. Bob Gottlieb, "Cable TV: Focus on the Disabled," *Journal of Rehabilitation* 50 (January/February/March 1984): 54.

18. Kirsten Beck, *Cultivating the Wasteland: Can Cable Put the Vision Back in TV?* (New York: American Council for the Arts, 1983), pp. 157–58.

19. Ibid., p. 158.

20. Jim Bell, "A Different Kind of Television," *Public Management*, June 1980, pp. 5–6.

21. "Cable Services Subscriber Count," p. 64.

22. "Pay Cable Networks," *Channels Field Guide '87*, p. 81.

23. "Pay-per-View Networks," *Channels Field Guide '87*, p. 83.

24. Ted Becker, "Teledemocracy," *Futurist*, December 1981, p. 6.

25. F. Anthony Bushman and Richard Robinson, "Two-Way Television: A Tool for New Product Research," *Business Horizons*, July/August 1981, pp. 69–75.

26. Linda Gluck, "How Cable TV Provides Instant Answers," *Stores*, July 1978, p. 44.

27. "Cable Services Subscriber Count," p. 64.

28. Cecilia Capuzzi, "Wall Street's Affair with the Wire," *Channels Field Guide '87*, p. 69.

29. John Motavalli, "In Search of a New Strategy," *Channels Field Guide '87*, p. 80.

30. "Great Oaks from Little Acorns," *Broadcasting*, 30 March 1987, p. 158.

31. John Motavalli, "Buying and Selling Programming: An Ever-Widening Two Way Street," *CableVision*, 20 January 1986, p. 26.

32. John Motavalli, "Shaking Up the Programming Market," *CableVision*, 13 October 1986, p. 26.

33. "Cable Out to Break a Leg," *Broadcasting*, 2 June 1986, p. 39.

34. John J. Bezzini and Roger Jon Desmond, "Adoption Processes of Cable Television" (unpublished manuscript, Department of Communication, University of Hartford, November 1982).

35. "Cable TV Viewers Watch, Like More," *USA Today*, 14 November 1983, p. 1A.

36. Stewart Schley, "New NCTA Study Finds Most Cable Subscribers Satisfied with Service," *Multichannel News*, 28 May 1984, p. 1.

37. John Motavalli, "Survey Shows Cable Getting Mixed Marks from Customers," *CableVision*, 15 December 1986, p. 64.

38. "Facts and Figures," *Multichannel News*, 23 June 1986, p. 54.

39. "Survey Finds Subs Unhappy with Pay TV," *Multichannel News*, 25 July 1983, p. 6.

40. Morrie Gelman, " 'Entire Rejection' Hitting Pay-TV, Study Indicates," *Electronic Media*, 12 August 1985, p. 3.

41. Victoria Gits, "The Destiny of Pay TV," *CableVision*, 3 June 1985, pp. 78–80.

42. Morrie Gelman, "Pay Cable Must Look in Its Own Back Yard," *Electronic Media*, 22 November 1984, p. 12.

43. Ibid., p. 26.

44. Ibid., p. 12.

45. Sally Bedell Smith, "Demand for Special Cable-TV Channels Doesn't Fulfill Promise," *Houston Chronicle*, 27 November 1983, sec. 3, p. 8.

46. Ibid.

47. "10–12 Nets Will Survive Shakeout, Study Predicts," *Multichannel News*, 6 February 1984, p. 33.

48. Leon Wynter, "Cable TV Changing Some U.S. Lifestyles," *Baton Rouge Sunday Advocate*, 6 November 1983, p. 7-E.

49. William Oscar Johnson, "You Ain't Seen Nothin' Yet," part 1, *Sports Illustrated*, 10 August 1981, p. 50.

50. Karen Heller, "Rock TV Channel Grabs Us over Time," *USA Today*, 30 November 1983, p. 1-D.

51. Bruce McCabe, "New Technologies Are Rechanneling Television Viewers' Ingrained Habits," *Houston Chronicle*, 28 March 1985, sec. 4, pp. 1, 4.

52. Andy Boehm, "Study Finds Cable Affects Kids' Viewing Habits, Attitudes," *Multichannel News*, 3 June 1985, pp. 68–69.

53. Richard H. Davis and Robert V. Miller, "The Acquisition of Specialized Information by Older Adults through Utilization of New Telecommunications Technology," *Educational Gerontology* 9 (March–June 1983): 225–29.

54. Deanna C. Nash and David A. Bollier, "Protecting Privacy in the Age of Hometech," *Technology Review*, August/September 1981, p. 67.

55. Alan F. Westin, "Home Information Systems: The Privacy Debate," *Datamation*, July 1982, pp. 100–103.

56. John Wicklein, *Electronic Nightmare: The New Communications and Freedom* (New York: Viking Press, 1981), p. 8.

57. Ellen Goodman, "Cable Television Put in Sharp Focus," *Baton Rouge Morning Advocate*, 12 March 1985, p. 8-B.

58. Eric Mink, "Television Viewers Could Survive Quite Well without It," *Electronic Media: Cable Special Report*, 30 May 1985, p. C8.

59. Jack Curry, "It's the Best Shot at a Truly Democratic Mass Medium," *Electronic Media: Cable Special Report*, 30 May 1985, p. C8.

60. John J. O'Connor, "Where's That Promised New World of Cable?" *New York Times*, 25 November 1984, sec. 2, p. 22.

61. Laurence Michie, "Mass and Class: The Oil and Water of Cable," *Television Quarterly* 20 (Summer 1983): 60–61.

62. Dean M. Krugman and Clifford Christians, "Cable Television: Promise versus Performance," *Gazette* 27 (1981): 204.

63. Michael Mascioni, "An Electronic Parade," *CableVision*, 10 December 1984, pp. 90–92.

SOURCE OVERVIEW

Books and Book Chapters

General Survey

The most thorough, comprehensive source of information on cable television programming is Susan Tyler Eastman, Sydney W. Head, and Lewis Klein's *Broadcast/Cable Programming*. The book incorporates cable with other media for an examination of programming strategies, audience research, and the role of ownership in program matters. Part 3 of *Broadcast/Cable*

Programming consists of five separate chapters on cable programming exclusively. Included are chapter 9, "Cable System Programming" by Eastman, which looks at components of programming selection decisions and factors affecting those decisions such as carriage requirements, cable system capacity, market needs, program scheduling practices, and so on; chapter 10, "Basic Cable Networks" by Eastman, which describes all basic cable program services, their composition, and their audience reach; chapter 11, "Premium Programming Services" by Jeffrey C. Reiss, which examines factors affecting the economics of pay cable and then describes the content and distribution features of the pay cable services; chapter 12, "Local Origination Cable Programming" by Eastman and Donald E. Agostino, which describes LO production, cable access, and such ancillary cable services as videotex; and chapter 13, "Superstation Programming" by Sidney Pike, which looks at the programming strategies of superstations for both local and national audiences.

The merits of Thomas F. Baldwin and D. Stevens McVoy's *Cable Communication* have already been mentioned, but note must be made of the cable programming portion of this comprehensive textbook. Part 2 of *Cable Communication* includes four chapters devoted to every aspect of cable television subscriber services. Chapter 6 comprises subject matter appropriate for the title "Over-the-Air, Access, Community, and Automated Channels." Chapters 7, 8, and 9 do the same under the respective titles "Satellite-Delivered Programming and Cable Radio," "Pay Television," and "Two-Way Services."

A chapter by Melinda Benedek, "Cable Television and the New Technologies: A Snapshot," appears in the *1983 Entertainment, Publishing, and the Arts Handbook*, edited by Michael Meyer and John David Viera, and is meant to provide "an overview of the trends affecting programming for cable television and the new technologies" (p. 173). The chapter is directed toward program producers who, says Benedek, are perplexed by the new technologies.

Robert Atwan, Barry Orton, and William Vesterman's *American Mass Media* contains reprints of several articles or book excerpts on cable television. Included as chapters are Ross Corson's "Cable's Missed Connection: A Revolution That Won't Be Televised," which looks at cable's lost promise in terms of program diversity; Sharon Geltner's "Matching Set: Brian Lamb and C-SPAN," which discusses the operation of the C-SPAN cable service; Tony Schwartz's "Communication in the Year 2000," which examines the future impact that cable television and videotex will have on society; and John Wicklein's "The New Communications: Promise and Threat," which looks at threats to society posed by the new electronic media and those persons who control them.

An outgrowth of the Carnegie Commission on the Future of Public Broadcasting report is Sheila Mahony, Nick DeMartino, and Robert Stengel's *Keeping PACE with the New Television: Public Television and Changing Technology*. The first section of the book recommends and states the rationale for public television's creation of a nonprofit cultural pay cable network called PACE (Performing Arts, Culture, and Entertainment). Section 2 of *Keeping PACE with the New Television* is comprised of five industry status reports on satellite communications, cable television, pay television, home video, and videotex.

Sports Junkies Rejoice! The Birth of ESPN describes the origins of the ESPN cable sports network from the perspective of its cofounder (along with his son Scott), Bill Rasmussen.

Local Origination and Access Programming

The effort of the Cable Television Information Center (CTIC) to assist city officials in formulating policy to regulate cable television and to create cable franchise provisions for local access channels has resulted in the publication of an excellent two-volume set of *CTIC Cablebooks*. Volume 2 of the set, *A Guide for Local Policy*, has a legal orientation and will be discussed in the next chapter of this reference guide. Volume 1, *The Community Medium*, edited by Nancy Jesuale with Ralph Lee Smith, contains an especially well organized selection of chapters explaining how cable television can be utilized to serve the needs of a community. Jesuale and Smith include chapters covering such topics as local government, educational and health uses of cable, cable security and fire-alarm services, interactive services, and cable system interconnection for local programming. In addition, *The Community Medium* carries four appendices with information on community television production techniques and satellite program services, a cable glossary, and a bibliography.

The publication of William Drew Shaffer and Richard Wheelwright's *Creating Original Programming for Cable TV* was sponsored by the National Federation of Local Cable Programmers. The book's purpose is to take advantage of local opportunities for diverse groups to produce cable television programs. As a way of underscoring what access channels mean to community groups, the authors say, "On the local level cities, libraries, schools, churches, hospitals, citizens, independent producers, community organizations, cable companies, businesses, and many others are beginning to communicate visually via cable. This is a new experience for most of these players; an uncharted area with precious few blueprints to follow" (p. 5). Shaffer and Wheelwright provide particular information on producing original programs for cable access channels, distributing the programs, advertising, and legal considerations pertaining to the programs.

For anyone engaged in cable access, *The Access Manager's Handbook: A Guide for Managing Community Television* by Robert S. Oringel and Sue Miller Buske is an invaluable aid. The book, a no-nonsense treatment of its subject, covers all the essentials of developing and managing a cable access center. Included are chapters on staffing the access center, creating procedural rules, equipping the center, training the production crew, assessing community cable access needs, and access program production evaluation. Oringel and Buske conclude their book with several case studies of successful cable access projects nationwide and with an appendix with resource suggestions for cable access programming.

Telecommunications and Libraries, written by a staff of writers headed by Donald W. King, concentrates on how libraries can use and are affected by new electronic media. One of the book's chapters, "Cable TV and Libraries," written by Lynne E. Bradley, mentions five levels of library involvement in relationship with cable television: basic information services about cable; video playback services in the library; the library's video production capability; use of cable access channels on shared, cooperative, or dedicated bases; and two-way or interactive cable system capabilities.

Brigitte L. Kenney, who edited *Cable for Information Delivery: A Guide for Librarians, Educators, and Cable Professionals*, remarks in the book's introductory chapter that it "is about using cable for information delivery" (p. 1) and is meant for anyone wishing to utilize cable technology to create informational programming for consumers. The primary audience of *Cable for Information Delivery*, however, is meant to be librarians. Says Kenney, "Together, video and cable constitute a powerful tool that libraries can use to reach those who might not come to the library" (p. 2). Chapters in the book describe cable television and provide information on ways for integrating cable into the information–dissemination role of the local library. A helpful appendix carries a list of sources for cable television programming available to libraries.

Cultivating the Wasteland: Can Cable Put the Vision Back in TV? by Kirsten Beck is about "community prospects for cable and the arts" (p. xv). The first part of Beck's book serves as a general introduction to the operation of a cable television system. The book turns next to an in-depth discussion of cultural programming on cable with an emphasis on the birth, struggle, and death of CBS Cable. Next comes a discussion of local cultural productions for cable that either are being done or that can be done. Beck follows this with a discussion of the cable franchising process and the role that local arts groups can play in the business of franchise agreements. The closing portion of *Cultivating the Wasteland* consists of the following three essays in a section entitled "A Guide to Understanding Television Deals": R. Bruce Rich's "Copyright Fundamentals," Richard J. Lorber's "Elements of Deal Making," and Timothy J. DeBaets' "The Concepts of Negotiation."

Fred S. Knight, Harold E. Horn, and Nancy J. Jesuale focus on the use of cable television by policymakers in their book, *Telecommunications for Local Government*. This is actually a book of readings with articles reprinted from other books and periodicals. It is intended as a resource book for city managers or municipal officials whose responsibilities pertain to telecommunications policy. *Telecommunications for Local Government* provides information about other media, but its concentration is on cable. Included in the book are articles providing an overview of cable operation, its technology, program services, access channel potential, and ways in which cities may utilize cable capabilities to provide municipal services. The concluding chapters of *Telecommunications for Local Government* deal with issues such as privacy and antitrust that might involve city officials, with special commentary on the *Boulder* decision, the major antitrust pronouncement affecting cable system enfranchisement.

Two books that focus on cable television as a medium for religious programming are John W. Bachman's *Media—Wasteland or Wonderland: Opportunities and Dangers for Christians in the Electronic Age* and Gene Jaberg and Louis G. Wargo, Jr.'s *The Video Pencil: Cable Communications for Church and Community*. Bachman criticizes the way that new media, cable in particular, are being used for evangelism and suggests alternatives in usage that would better serve the church. Jaberg and Wargo's *The Video Pencil* is a short book giving a unique perspective on integrating cable television into the life of the church. The book presents a theological justification for using this means of communication and provides advice on how to incorporate cable into the religious life of the church congregation.

One section of Stewart M. Hoover's *The Electronic Giant: A Critique of the Telecommunications Revolution from a Christian Perspective* contains two chapters primarily devoted to a discussion of cable technology and programming. An accompanying chapter examines the practitioners, leaders, and role of the electronic church in the United States. The intent of Hoover's book, although never clearly stated, appears to be a call for integration of the church with the new electronic media, particularly cable television.

Several book chapters provide information on cable access programming. Harold E. Horn's "Local Government and Cable Television" appears in *Telecommunications and Productivity*, edited by Mitchell L. Moss. Horn's chapter defines the use of access channels in terms of how and why they may be utilized but then suggests that municipal governments have made minimum effort to effectively use the channels or to see to it that others use them. Horn also examines the use of cable institutional networks that will at some point be constructed to interconnect businesses, banks, hospitals, and other institutions.

John Carey and Pat Quarles' "Interactive Television" and Martha Gever's "Meet the Press: On *Paper Tiger Television*" both appear as chapters in *Transmission*, edited by Peter D'Agostino. Carey and Quarles describe the operation of Berks Community Television (BCTV), which was begun in the mid–1970s in Reading, Pennsylvania. BCTV was created as an interactive cable television system for senior citizens and was funded by the National Science Foundation; its services were implemented by a consortium of New York University and Reading groups. BCTV was field-tested in 1975 and formally launched in 1976. Gever describes the access program *Paper Tiger Television* that appears on a Manhattan cable system. The program "attacks the ideology and economics of mass media in the context of the industry itself. 'The power of mass culture,' the *Paper Tiger* producers state, 'rests on the trust of the public. This legitimacy is a paper tiger.' Thus the series' title" (p. 217).

Interactive Cable

Maxine Holmes Jones says in the introduction to her *See, Hear, Interact: Beginning Developments in Two-Way Television* that the book seeks to examine "the potential of interactive television by providing examples of prototype systems which have already been explored" (p. ix). *See, Hear, Interact*, continues the author, "presents background information on experimental studies in several fields: education, for young people and for adults; social services; telemedicine; citizen participation; in-service information; and community services. This sampling of prototype interactive systems provides a view of everyday services which may be available in the future" (p. x). Jones concentrates on a description of some eighteen interactive television experiments conducted around the United States. Many of these have had no direct relationship to cable television but rather have been operated on a closed-circuit basis. Nonetheless, the implications for interactive cable are obvious in the potential for extending experimental interactive television systems to the level of practical public services. *See, Hear, Interact* concludes with an excellent annotated bibliography of interactive television literature.

The operation and application of more than one hundred interactive cable services in the United States are profiled in *The Interactive Cable TV Handbook*, edited by Mark R. Kimmel. The book's overview section, written by D. Stevens McVoy and Thomas F. Baldwin, introduces the technology and applications of interactive cable. The handbook then moves to its series of system-by-system interactive service profiles and follows this with listings of interactive cable hardware manufacturers and suppliers, firms offering informational and technical assistance to the interactive cable industry, state and federal cable regulatory bodies, and common carrier systems proposing to construct interactive services. Kimmel also furnishes several technical essays on interactive cable and concludes his book with a helpful glossary of interactive cable terms.

"The New Communication Technologies and the New Distribution of Roles," Henry Breitrose's short but wide-ranging chapter in *The Media Revolution in America and Western Europe*, edited by Everett M. Rogers and Francis Balle, covers several issues related to cable television but eventually concentrates on cable's interactivity. Breitrose describes interactive cable's capabilities and asserts, "Interactivity differentiates the new technology from the old. The old technology can tell, but it cannot answer" (p. 75).

Social and Institutional Implications

Although James Martin mentions cable television in a number of different contexts in *Telematic Society: A Challenge for Tomorrow*, he does devote one entire chapter of the book exclusively to cable. In the chapter he discusses the uses or applications of cable in the workplace and for recreational purposes and is perhaps one of the first to question the uses to which all of the new cable program services can be put.

Comments from several participants are included in *The Proceedings of a Conference on Cable Television and the Performing Arts*, conducted at the New York University School of the Arts. Some conferees discuss artistic productions for cable and the potential for such productions, and some, primarily theatrical producers, discuss their experiences with artistic productions for cable.

An assortment of essays on cable television as the technology applies to various social and political functions in Washington, D.C., appears in the D.C. Cable Coalition's *Cable Television: An Assessment of Critical Issues in Washington, D.C.* Grouped under the three headings of "Politics and Economics," "Quality of Life," and "Education and Culture" are such essays as Marion Hayes Hull's "Cable Issues Impacting on Local Officials," Nancy M. Caliman's "Increasing Citizen Participation in Local Government through Cable Television," Kay Pierson's "Impact of Cable on Human Lifestyles," David D. Biedler's "An Assessment of Privacy Issues Relating to Cable Television," Bette M. Rothstein's "Telecourses: Postsecondary Education and Cable TV," and Lawrence E. Molumby's "Libraries and Cable in the Information Age."

What the future holds for cable television as well as other evolving technologies entering the "automated office" and the "wired household" is the subject of Jean M. Ciano and E. Bryan Carne's chapter "Telecommunications: The Next Generation" in *Communications and the Future*, edited by Howard F. Didsbury, Jr. Ciano and Carne state:

In 1960, it would have been difficult to project the technology-rich environment of the 1980s. In the 1980s, the task of projecting technical developments in the remaining years of the twentieth century is no easier. What is certain is that the next generation of services that will be supported by these new media will be shaped by consumer demand, provider reward, the need to conserve resources, and the opportunities provided by the coming together of telephony, data processing, television, satellites, optical fibers, and integrated circuits. (p. 144)

Richard S. Hollander discusses the political role for cable television in *Video Democracy* and suggests that "communities wired for interactive cable should experiment with direct democracy" (p. 3). "What is proposed here," says Hollander, "is to merge the spirit of ancient Athens with the technologies of the twenty-first century—Pericles with digital transmission.

Direct democracy can and should have a rebirth" (p. 3). He concludes, "The time is here to make peace with the new technology. It is already in our homes. If untamed, it could devour some excellent political institutions. If domesticated, it could make the democratic experience leap from the civics text to real life" (p. 4).

Some specific ways that cable television may be integrated into the political process are described by Richard M. Neustadt in a chapter entitled "Politics and the New Media" in the already-mentioned *Communications and the Future*. Also related to cable television and politics is Joey Reagan, Thomas F. Baldwin, and John D. Abel's "The Impact of Mass Media Environments on Political Behavior" in John J. Havick's *Communications Policy and the Political Process*. Reagan, Baldwin, and Abel suggest that policymakers should examine how the availability of information via cable television might affect the citizens' political behavior.

Changing directions somewhat is John Wicklein's *Electronic Nightmare: The New Communications and Freedom*. Wicklein begins with his contention that the emergence and spread of new media technology with interactive capabilities could result in loss of individual liberties if the technology comes under the control of one all-powerful overseer. He looks at all media but concentrates in one chapter on interactive cable. Most of this chapter is devoted to the Warner Amex QUBE system and its potential for misuse. Two other lengthy chapters are devoted exclusively to videotex.

While neither Everett M. Rogers' *Communication Technology: The New Media In Society* nor Frederick Williams' *Technology and Communication Behavior* concentrate on cable television, both books incorporate cable with other new or emerging electronic media to discuss their social implications. In both cases the discussions occur within the context of communication theory. Rogers and Williams are especially interested in leading their readers to creatively investigate the research potential relative to new communication technology application. Central to both *Communication Technology* and *Technology and Communication Behavior* is not so much what cable is but rather why cable is and where society is likely to progress as a result of its interrelationship with the technology.

Cable Program Uses and Criticism

Why viewers watch cable programming is the subject of Carrie Heeter and Bradley Greenberg's chapter, "Cable and Program Choice" in *Selective Exposure to Communication*, edited by Dolf Zillman and Jennings Bryant. Heeter and Greenberg examine past research on and make assumptions about those factors that influence the process of program selection, concentrating especially on the effect that the increased number of cable channels has on choices made by cable viewers.

CNN vs. The Networks: Is More News Better News? is the Media Institute's effort to conduct a comparative study of the business and economic news

coverage by CNN and the broadcast networks according to certain eval-
uative criteria. The conclusion is that CNN indeed does outperform its
broadcast competitors.

Pat Aufderheide's "The Look of the Sound" in *Watching Television*, edited
by Todd Gitlin, explores the origins, structure, and appeal of a program
genre that has become uniquely associated with cable television: the music
video. The author concentrates her analysis of music video's popularity on
the MTV program service, whose success, she says, "has been based on
understanding that the [service] offers not videos but environment, a context
that creates mood" (p. 118). Aufderheide scrutinizes the whole arena of the
music video world—the form and substance of the art and performer, the
form and substance of the viewer, and the media chemistry that unites
them.

One book whose content does not fit neatly under any particular descriptive heading but nonetheless does have a relationship to cable television
is Christopher M. Byron's *The Fanciest Dive*. Byron tells the story of *TV-
Cable Week*, a magazine that Time Inc. "conceived of as a weekly listings
guide for cable TV viewers. Because it survived in the marketplace for less
than six months, few magazine readers knew much about *TV-Cable Week*.
But within the world of magazine publishing and the media—and most
particularly among the employees of Time Inc.—it was another story" (pp.
11–12). The purpose of relating what happened with *TV-Cable Week*, says
Byron, is "to reveal the damage that can result when corporate decision
makers become preoccupied with Wall Street to the expense of their customers; and to recreate the human drama of the magazine itself" (p. 14).

Government Documents

*Information and Telecommunications: An Overview of Issues, Technologies, and
Applications* is a report by the Science Policy Research Division of the
Congressional Research Service describing the impact of information technologies on society. The report looks at the "information age" impact in
government and society, discusses issues—national and global—of development and utilization of the technologies, and gives a description of the
technologies. One basic concentration of the report is upon the symbiotic
relationship of all the information media (mass and otherwise). The report
includes an excellent array of charts and other visuals.

The effect of cable television on the role of a particular federal service is
the focus of *Impact of New Information and Communications on Postal Service*,
a transcript of hearings conducted by the Subcommittee on Postal Personnel
and Modernization of the U.S. House Committee on Post Office and Civil
Service. One portion of this document (pp. 39–84) devotes specific attention
to the impact that cable television might have on the postal service and how
individuals might use cable to communicate in the future.

Testimony on the role of cable in conveying the proceedings of the U.S. House of Representatives and later the proceedings of the U.S. Senate is included in *To Establish Regulations to Implement Television and Radio Coverage of Proceedings of the Senate*. This hearing transcript document, a product of the U.S. Senate Committee on Rules and Administration, devotes special attention to the role of C-SPAN (pp. 53–80).

Finally, a document entitled *Minority Participation in the Media* contains testimony from a hearing conducted by the Subcommittee on Telecommunications, Consumer Protection, and Finance of the U.S. House Energy and Commerce Committee. The document examines how the telecommunications industry in general has responded and will respond in the future to minority needs in light of continued industry deregulation. There is nothing in particular about cable television here, but bits and pieces on the role of cable are spread throughout the document.

Periodical Articles

Program genres have not merited the same intense study as have other facets of cable television. But cable cultural programming (more for its failure) and cable music programming (more for its success) are program types that have been scrutinized in a number of articles. Giving attention to the first is David Waterman's "The Failure of Cultural Programming on Cable TV: An Economic Interpretation." Studies of music programming are manifested most often in the research literature by examinations of MTV. One issue of *Journal of Communication* carries several articles on the subject, among which are Barry L. Sherman and Joseph R. Dominick's "Violence and Sex in Music Videos: TV and Rock 'n' Roll," Jane D. Brown and Kenneth Campbell's "Race and Gender in Music Videos: The Same Beat But a Different Drummer," and Se-Wen Sun and James Lull's "The Adolescent Audience for Music Videos and Why They Watch."

How citizens may participate in cable television access channel utilization is examined in "Public Policy and Community-Oriented Uses of Cable Television" by Mitchell L. Moss and Robert Warren. David Katz looks at how cable may be used in the medical arena in "Cable Television and Health Promotion: A Feasibility Study with Arthritis Patients."

Choice of cable programming is seen as a routine based upon particular viewer characteristics in Carrie Heeter's "Program Selection with Abundance of Choice: A Process Model." James G. Webster's "The Impact of Cable and Pay Cable Television on Local Station Audiences" examines the impact of cable television viewing on the use of local television station programming. How viewers use cable television news services and what impact these services have on other media are the subject of Lee B. Becker, Sharon Dunwoody, and Sheizaf Rafaeli's "Cable's Impact on Use of Other

News Media" and Joey Reagan's "Effects of Cable Television on News Use."

A unique angle on the matter of viewers' changing activities as a result of cable television's presence in the household is explored in E. W. Brody's "Impact of Cable Television on Library Borrowing." Subhash Sharma, William O. Bearden, and Jesse E. Teel's "Differential Effects of In-Home Shopping Methods" concentrates on how consumer behavior and retail business are affected by cable shopping services.

The effects of interactive cable on group dynamics and sharing of ideas are examined in Eric S. Fredin's "The Context of Communication: Interactive Telecommunication, Interpersonal Communication, and Their Effect on Ideas." Mit Mitropoulos addresses some of the questions regarding interactive cable's potential impact on our lives in "Public Participation, as Access, in Cable TV in the USA."

Some observers view interactive cable's greatest potential impact to be in the way the medium could be used to invade privacy. Neil Vidmar and David H. Flaherty's "Concern for Personal Privacy in an Electronic Age" focuses on the privacy matter, as does Oscar H. Gandy, Jr., and Charles E. Simmons' "Technology, Privacy, and the Democratic Process."

BIBLIOGRAPHY

Books and Book Chapters

General Survey

Atwan, Robert, Barry Orton, and William Vesterman. *American Mass Media*. 3d ed. New York: Random House, 1986.

Baldwin, Thomas F., and D. Stevens McVoy. *Cable Communication*. Englewood Cliffs, N.J.: Prentice-Hall, 1983.

Benedek, Melinda. "Cable Television and the New Technologies: A Snapshot." In *1983 Entertainment, Publishing, and the Arts Handbook*, edited by Michael Meyer and John David Viera. New York: Clark Boardman Company, 1983.

Eastman, Susan Tyler, Sydney W. Head, and Lewis Klein. *Broadcast/Cable Programming*. 2d ed. Belmont, California: Wadsworth, 1985.

Mahony, Sheila, Nick DeMartino, and Robert Stengel. *Keeping PACE with the New Television: Public Television and Changing Technology*. New York: Carnegie Corporation, 1980.

Rasmussen, Bill. *Sports Junkies Rejoice! The Birth of ESPN*. Hartsdale, New York: QV Publishing, 1983.

Local Origination and Access Programming

Bachman, John W. *Media—Wasteland or Wonderland: Opportunities and Dangers for Christians in the Electronic Age*. Minneapolis, Minn.: Augsburg Publishing House, 1984.

Beck, Kirsten. *Cultivating the Wasteland: Can Cable Put the Vision Back in TV?* New York: American Council for the Arts, 1983.

Carey, John, and Pat Quarles. "Interactive Television." In *Transmission*, edited by Peter D'Agostino. New York: Tanam Press, 1985.

Gever, Martha. "Meet the Press: On *Paper Tiger Television*." In *Transmission*, edited by Peter D'Agostino. New York: Tanam Press, 1985.

Hoover, Stewart M. *The Electronic Giant: A Critique of the Telecommunications Revolution from a Christian Perspective.* Elgin, Ill.: Brethren Press, 1982.

Horn, Harold E. "Local Government and Cable Television." In *Telecommunications and Productivity*, edited by Mitchell L. Moss. Reading, Mass.: Addison-Wesley, 1981.

Jaberg, Gene, and Louis G. Wargo, Jr. *The Video Pencil: Cable Communications for Church and Community.* Lanham, Md.: University Press of America, 1980.

Jesuale, Nancy, Richard M. Neustadt, and Nicholas P. Miller, eds. *The Community Medium.* vol. 1 of *CTIC Cablebooks.* Arlington, Va.: Cable Television Information Center, 1982.

Kenney, Brigitte L., ed. *Cable for Information Delivery: A Guide for Librarians, Educators, and Cable Professionals.* White Plains, N.Y.: Knowledge Industry Publications, 1984.

King, Donald W., et al. *Telecommunications and Libraries.* White Plains, N.Y.: Knowledge Industry Publications, 1981.

Knight, Fred S., Harold E. Horn, and Nancy J. Jesuale. *Telecommunications for Local Government.* Washington, D.C.: International City Management Association, 1982.

Oringel, Robert S., and Sue Miller Buske. *The Access Manager's Handbook: A Guide for Managing Community Television.* Boston, Mass.: Focal Press, 1987.

Shaffer, William Drew, and Richard Wheelwright. *Creating Original Programming for Cable TV.* Washington, D.C.: Communications Press, 1983.

Interactive Cable

Breitrose, Henry. "The New Communication Technologies and the New Distribution of Roles." In *The Media Revolution in America and Western Europe*, edited by Everett M. Rogers and Francis Balle. Norwood, N.J.: Ablex, 1985.

Jones, Maxine Holmes. *See, Hear, Interact: Beginning Developments in Two-Way Television.* Metuchen, N.J.: Scarecrow Press, 1985.

Kimmel, Mark R., ed. *The Interactive Cable TV Handbook.* 4th ed. Bethesda, Md.: Phillips Publishing, 1984.

Social and Institutional Implications

Ciano, Jean M., and E. Bryan Carne. "Telecommunications: The Next Generation." In *Communications and the Future*, edited by Howard F. Didsbury, Jr. Bethesda, Md.: World Future Society, 1982.

D.C. Cable Coalition. *Cable Television: An Assessment of Critical Issues in Washington, D.C.* Washington, D.C.: D.C. Cable Coalition, 1984.

Hollander, Richard S. *Video Democracy.* Mt. Airy, Md.: Lomond Publications, 1985.

Martin, James. *Telematic Society: A Challenge for Tomorrow.* Englewood Cliffs, N.J.: Prentice-Hall, 1981.

Neustadt, Richard M. "Politics and the New Media." In *Communications and the Future*, edited by Howard F. Didsbury, Jr. Bethesda, Md.: World Future Society, 1982.

The Proceedings of a Conference on Cable Television and the Performing Arts. New York: New York University School of the Arts, 1981.

Reagan, Joey, Thomas F. Baldwin, and John D. Abel. "The Impact of Mass Media Environments on Political Behavior." In *Communications Policy and the Political Process*, edited by John J. Havick. Westport, Conn.: Greenwood Press, 1983.

Rogers, Everett M. *Communication Technology: The New Media In Society*. New York: Free Press, 1986.

Wicklein, John. *Electronic Nightmare: The New Communications and Freedom*. New York: Viking Press, 1981.

Williams, Frederick. *Technology and Communication Behavior*. Belmont, Calif.: Wadsworth, 1987.

Cable Program Uses and Criticisms

Aufderheide, Pat. "The Look of Sound." In *Watching Television*, edited by Todd Gitlin. New York: Pantheon Books, 1986.

Byron, Christopher M. *The Fanciest Dive*. New York: W. W. Norton, 1986.

Heeter, Carrie, and Bradley Greenberg. "Cable and Program Choice." In *Selective Exposure to Communication*, edited by Dolf Zillman and Jennings Bryant. Hillsdale, N.J.: Lawrence Erlbaum Associates, 1985.

Media Institute. *CNN vs. The Networks: Is More News Better News?* Washington, D.C.: Media Institute, 1983.

Government Documents

U.S. House. Subcommittee on Postal Personnel and Modernization of the Committee on Post Office and Civil Service. *Impact of New Information and Communications on Postal Service*. 98th Cong., lst sess., 1983. Hearing.

————. Subcommittee on Science, Research, and Technology of the Committee on Science and Technology. *Information and Telecommunications: An Overview of Issues, Technologies, and Applications*. Report by the Science Policy Research Division, Congressional Research Service. 97th Cong., 1st sess., 1981. Committee Print.

————. Subcommittee on Telecommunications, Consumer Protection, and Finance of the Committee on Energy and Commerce. *Minority Participation in the Media*. 98th Cong., lst sess., 1983. Hearing.

U.S. Senate. Committee on Rules and Administration. *To Establish Regulations to Implement Television and Radio Coverage of Proceedings of the Senate*. 98th Cong., 1st sess., 1983. Hearing.

Periodical Articles

Becker, Lee B., Sharon Dunwoody, and Sheizaf Rafaeli. "Cable's Impact on Use of Other News Media." *Journal of Broadcasting* 27 (Spring 1983): 127–40.

Brody, E. W. "Impact of Cable Television on Library Borrowing." *Journalism Quarterly* 61 (Autumn 1984): 686–89.

Brown, Jane D., and Kenneth Campbell. "Race and Gender in Music Videos: The Same Beat But a Different Drummer." *Journal of Communication* 36 (Winter 1986): 94–106.

Fredin, Eric S. "The Context of Communication: Interactive Telecommunication, Interpersonal Communication, and Their Effect on Ideas." *Communication Research* 10 (October 1983): 553–81.

Gandy, Oscar H., Jr., and Charles E. Simmons. "Technology, Privacy, and the Democratic Process." *Critical Studies in Mass Communication* 3 (June 1986): 155–68.

Heeter, Carrie. "Program Selection with Abundance of Choice: A Process Model." *Human Communication Research* 12 (Fall 1985): 126–52.

Katz, David. "Cable Television and Health Promotion: A Feasibility Study with Arthritis Patients." *Health Education Quarterly* 12 (Winter 1985): 379–89.

Mitropoulos, Mit. "Public Participation, as Access, in Cable TV in the USA." *Ekistics* 50 (October 1983): 385–92.

Moss, Mitchell L., and Robert Warren. "Public Policy and Community-Oriented Uses of Cable Television." *Urban Affairs Quarterly* 20 (December 1984): 233–54.

Reagan, Joey. "Effects of Cable Television on News Use." *Journalism Quarterly* 61 (Summer 1984): 317–24.

Sharma, Subhash, William O. Bearden, and Jesse E. Teel. "Differential Effects of In-Home Shopping Methods." *Journal of Retailing* 59 (Winter 1983): 29–51.

Sherman, Barry L., and Joseph R. Dominick. "Violence and Sex in Music Videos: TV and Rock 'n' Roll." *Journal of Communication* 36 (Winter 1986): 79–93.

Sun, Se-Wen, and James Lull. "The Adolescent Audience for Music Videos and Why They Watch." *Journal of Communication* 36 (Winter 1986): 115–25.

Vidmar, Neil, and David H. Flaherty. "Concern for Personal Privacy in an Electronic Age." *Journal of Communication* 35 (Spring 1985): 91–103.

Waterman, David. "The Failure of Cultural Programming on Cable TV: An Economic Interpretation." *Journal of Communication* 36 (Summer 1986): 92–107.

Webster, James G. "The Impact of Cable and Pay Cable Television on Local Station Audiences." *Journal of Broadcasting* 27 (Spring 1983): 119–26.

Chapter Four

CABLE LAW AND REGULATIONS

ISSUE OVERVIEW

The need for some degree of oversight regarding technical, economic, consumer, and program matters is the basic premise for regulating cable television. These four broad areas are all addressed originally in federal legislation but must be addressed more specifically in rules, ordinances, policies, and agreements resulting from application of federal law to specific instances. Such application falls chiefly into the provinces of the Federal Communications Commission (FCC), state legislatures, and local municipal governments, and to agencies established by the latter two.

Though by its nature regulatory responsibility for cable television is collectively shared among these federal, state, and municipal entities, each has staked a jurisdictional claim independent of the others. This multilevel regulatory scheme has resulted in numerous disputes in recent years over proper divisions as well as limits of authority. Cable operators have claimed that the hodgepodge of localized controls and requirements to which they have been subjected has too often resulted in regulatory abuse. In order to remedy the situation, Congress enacted new cable legislation in late 1984 that significantly reduces the regulatory authority of local municipalities while it increases that of the FCC.

Evolution of Cable Regulation

Joseph R. Fogarty and Marcia Spielholz have described the genesis and the evolution of cable television regulation in these terms:

The history of FCC cable regulation is a complex interweaving of FCC opinions, court decisions, and technological advances, characterized by numerous shifts in opinion concerning both the source and scope of FCC cable jurisdiction and the value of the new technology. At the heart of the development of FCC cable regulation lies the fact that until recently, the Communications Act of 1934 made no explicit provision for the regulation of cable television.[1]

The recent Communications Act provision to which Fogarty and Spielholz alluded is the Cable Communications Policy Act of 1984 (hereinafter the Cable Act) signed into law on 30 October 1984.[2] Two objectives in passing the new law were to provide some stability within the cable industry so that it might develop on a path more independent of its electronic media competitors and to establish some distance for the cable industry from the byzantine assortment of rules created by the FCC in 1972.[3] Those rules set up an intricate regulatory structure that inhibited the growth of cable television for most of the mid- to late 1970s. But a series of FCC rule repeals and judicial reversals have since aided in reducing some of the more burdensome requirements affecting the cable industry.

This period in cable regulatory history was pivotal. Prior to implementation of the 1972 rules, municipal involvement in cable television "was generally limited to authorizing use of local streets and rights of way and adopting regulations to protect the safety of life and property. The franchises which authorized [cable] operations were simple documents which reflected basic services provided by the systems."[4] But as cable expanded into more cities and became a more sophisticated signal delivery service, the municipalities responded by enacting more sophisticated franchise ordinances whose provisions covered a greater breadth of cable system operator activity.

These cable franchises dealt with matters such as service requirements and rate regulation. In addition, many franchises sought to regulate matters which were clearly of Federal rather than local concern, and this prompted specific FCC decisions to preempt such provisions. For example, the FCC held that regulation of broadcast signal carriage, certain technical standards and regulation of any aspect of pay cable service, were all matters appropriate for comprehensive and uniform Federal regulation.[5]

The package of FCC rules adopted in 1972 was supposed to have restored some balance in the cable television regulatory scheme. Included were

rules regulating television broadcast signal carriage by all cable systems; requiring the deletion of network and syndicated programming of distant television stations; and requiring cable systems located within the 100 largest television markets to have a minimum of 20 channels, two-way capacity and four dedicated access channels for public, educational, local government and leased access purposes. Systems having more than 3,500 subscribers were required to originate locally produced programming (cablecasting).[6]

One of the most important items in the 1972 rules pertained to the municipal franchising authority's jurisdiction over a cable system's rate structure. The rules required the franchisor "to specify or approve initial subscriber and installation rates; to institute a program for rate review and, if necessary, rate adjustment; and to give reasonable advance notice to the public of proposed rate changes." The FCC specified that decisions affecting cable system rates be "fair to the system and to the subscribing public."[7]

The premise behind the FCC's 1972 rules was not confined to matters of regulatory jurisdiction; there was also the matter of economic competition between cable and broadcasting. The commission "assumed cable television, through its ability to provide alternatives to local broadcast service, would divide the TV audience . . . , reduce revenues, and eventually cause harm to the ability of local broadcasters to serve the public interest."[8]

The cable television industry, never happy with the 1972 rules, almost immediately after the rules' implementation began efforts toward their dismantlement. Cable forces were successful in convincing the FCC to either extensively modify or eliminate altogether those rules governing pay cablecasting, local origination cablecasting, local franchise standards, access channels, carriage of both local and distant television broadcast signals, and protection of local broadcasters' syndicated program exclusivity.[9]

Ironically, as the FCC retreated from its somewhat heavy-handed oversight of cable television, local franchising authorities began picking up the slack. They began demanding more and more of cable system operators who were seeking a municipal franchise for their companies. Compliance with what were in many cases unrealistic demands was the price of winning the franchise, but too often cable television systems failed to achieve what was promised. "In major cities across the country, cable operators have soon after the grant of a franchise turned to the city with requests to reduce channel capacity from that bid in the franchising process, cut back on the services provided, reduce public access facilities, increase rates and slow down the timetable for construction."[10] These requests were not always honored, so cable system operators increasingly looked to the FCC for relief.

How well the Cable Act will succeed in further loosening the franchising authorities' tight reins is yet to be seen; nonetheless, the new law has settled territorial claims by creating specific boundaries that determine policy prerogatives of the FCC and those of municipal governments.

Cable Communications Policy Act of 1984

Constructing the Cable Act was no easy task. It was a struggle between two well-defined factions: the cable television industry as represented by the National Cable Television Association (NCTA) and the municipalities or franchising agencies as represented by the National League of Cities (NLC). The NLC favored a law that would ensure local cable control, a position it claimed better protected the interests of the consumer, while the NCTA favored a law that would restrict what it considered unjust local franchising authority, giving instead greater control over local cable matters to the FCC. In a letter to the chairman of the House Committee on Energy and Commerce the NLC defended its position on new cable legislation but, more importantly, found a common ground upon which both it and the NCTA could establish firm footing:

National cable policy must be forward looking and flexible, reflecting the complex relationships among communications technologies and services and the rapidly changing nature of the information industry. Access to information is now a prerequisite to full participation in the American economy and is likely to become even more important in the future. Cable systems, with their high transmission capacity and economic efficiency, are expected to become a key component of the local communications infrastructure. Consequently, Congress must establish a regulatory framework which ensures the availability of quality service to all consumers and the provision of a wide range of information services over cable systems on a competitive basis.[11]

The final draft of the measure that eventually would become the Cable Act resulted from a compromise between the NCTA and NLC. The maneuvering and debates on which the compromise was built would fit into the category of a classic. For more than two years the NCTA and NLC forces battled one another. Congress, whose role would be to shape the NCTA/NLC compromise into legislation, seemed at times little more than an arbiter between the two factions. But there were disputes to be settled among members of the House and Senate over language contained in the two slightly different versions of cable bills originating in the respective chambers. Finally, on the last day of the 98th Congress, agreement was reached and Congress passed S. 66, destined to become the Cable Act.[12] A few days prior to the bill's passage, *Broadcasting* magazine commented editorially:

Assuming all goes well in the next four days, Congress will have scrutinized, passed, conferenced, compromised and otherwise massaged into law the first-ever legislative mandate for a medium that has managed to reach almost 50% of the American TV audience following a strictly ad hoc policy pattern. As a result, cable's has been the most jerrymandered media landscape of them all, with no two jurisdictions marching to the same beat.[13]

Most major provisions of the Cable Act took effect sixty days after President Ronald Reagan's signature, but some sections of the new law allowed additional time for the FCC to devise applicable regulations. Some of the major provisions contained in the Cable Act include (1) allowing franchising authorities to require prospective cable system operators to provide public, educational, and governmental channels as a condition of enfranchisement; (2) requiring that cable system operators provide leased channel space for "non-affiliated commercial programmers"; (3) prohibiting broadcast station–cable system cross-ownership in the same market; (4) retaining municipal franchising authority but with reduced control over cable system rate regulation and program services; (5) providing greater renewal protection for cable systems whenever the system owner's franchise expires; (6) protecting privacy by requiring that cable system operators inform subscribers of any use the cable system makes of subscriber-related information; and (7) allowing for punishment of persons caught illegally intercepting cable signals.[14]

Reaction to the Cable Act was mixed. On the positive side were comments from NCTA president James P. Mooney, who said that "in essence" the new law had placed the cable industry "in a deregulated environment for the first time in its history. . . . Without rate regulation, and with their discretion sharply curtailed at renewal time, local franchising authority will have little opportunity to intrude into cable's business decisions." The NCTA president concluded that cable television "at last is ready to take its place alongside the two giants that have traditionally dominated electronic communications—broadcasting and telephony."[15] On the down side, however, came this less-than-rosy assessment from attorney Michael Botein: "The new law . . . is riddled with inconsistencies, ambiguities, and just plain glitches."[16]

The FCC on 11 December 1984 released a Notice of Proposed Rulemaking that would revise rules already in effect to bring them into conformity with the Cable Act.[17] Final rule changes were adopted unanimously by the commission on 11 April 1985.[18]

Municipal Cable Television Franchises

Local regulatory control over cable television comes in a limited degree from state agencies. But as already indicated, most local control rests in the hands of municipal governments. These governments or franchising authorities derive their regulatory powers from the traditional controls they exercise over access to city property—property that cable system operators must use in order to construct their systems.

The actual document that contains the franchise agreement reached between the municipal government and the cable system operator is enacted as a city ordinance. The ordinance is an important document, since it codifies the operational requirements of a cable television system, but it perhaps is not as important as the Request for Proposals (RFP). Prior to inviting applications for cable franchise proposals, municipal officials must first decide what it is they are seeking in a cable system in terms of its service to local citizens. Once they have made a decision, an RFP is drafted to include these specifications and when published not only serves as notification to interested cable operators that franchise proposals are being solicited, but also states what the franchising authority expects of potential applicants. Once the proposal application process is complete and the franchising authority has selected a franchisee, the two usually meet to negotiate particular items of contention found in the RFP.[19] When negotiations are complete at this stage, the resulting agreement becomes the municipal cable television ordinance.

The franchising process may give the appearance of procedural efficiency, but it has come under increasing criticism of late. One critic has described it as "a process so absurd, cynical, and self-defeating it amounts to a very nearly hilarious metaphor on the evils and folly of government intervention in the private sector."[20] Another critic has said that franchising problems most often occur initially just as cable operators are submitting franchise proposals:

After submitting proposals, the bidders battle one another through the use of such weapons as cocktail parties, media campaigns, and prominent community advocates known in the industry as 'rent-a-citizens.' The RFP process itself effectively excludes all but a few companies from offering services to potential subscribers, in that most companies do not have the financial backing to meet the city's articulated prerequisites or to engage in the political gamesmanship involved in nearly every contemporary franchise contest.[21]

One common practice among franchising authorities and the one about which cable system operators have complained the loudest has been the cable system's payment of a franchise fee. The fee is usually negotiated prior to awarding a franchise and is meant to pay the costs incurred by a municipality's cable administration activities and for the use of city property. The FCC has allowed municipalities to collect a franchise fee of up to 3 percent of the cable company's gross annual revenue, but the Cable Act now places a limit on the fee, allowing up to a 5 percent ceiling but only under certain circumstances.[22] Cable television interests continue to maintain that franchise fees are unreasonably high and that they have inhibited the growth of cable television.[23] Moreover, cable interests charge that franchise fees restrain their First Amendment rights to free speech. An Erie, Pennsylvania, court addressed that matter in April 1987, ruling that First Amendment rights of cable system operators were not violated by franchise fee requirements and that municipal authorities have a duty to impose any reasonable fee for the rental of public property.[24]

Other Cable Television Restraints

Another monetary controversy that has plagued the development of cable television has been that of pole attachment fees. Since cable systems must use utility poles to attach their cables for distribution to subscribers, it has become a convenient practice simply to lease attachment space on poles owned by local utility companies. Accusations that some utility companies were charging unnecessarily high rates eventually led to enactment of the 1978 Federal Pole Attachment Act, giving the FCC the authority to determine equitable pole attachment rates.[25] However, that authority often has been transferred to state public utility commissions whose policies, according to cable television operators, have been more in sympathy with the utility companies under their jurisdiction than with the cable systems. The result was a less-than-equitable pole attachment fee assessed many cable television system operators during the early 1980s.[26]

The whole matter seemed destined for resolution in the courts. Pushing it in that direction was a dispute that arose in Florida in 1980 over rates charged cable systems by a local utility company. The dispute, eventually calling into question the constitutionality of the Pole Attachment Act and the FCC's authority to regulate pole attachment rates, went before the U.S. Court of Appeals and was settled in favor of the utility company. That decision, however, was reversed by the U.S. Supreme Court in February 1987.[27]

Two additional controversial matters affecting cable television have been "market access" and program content regulation. "Market access" refers to the rights of a cable television system operator to locate his system in a municipality (or portion of a municipality) that either is or is not already being served by cable. A prohibition on cable system enfranchisement in a particular marketplace, assuming that the system is otherwise qualified for the franchise, conflicts directly with antitrust laws, the objective of which "is to prohibit conduct which directly or indirectly forecloses entry into and competition within any type of economic 'market'."[28] The major antitrust pronouncement affecting cable television came in the U.S. Supreme Court's *Boulder* decision. The decision resulted from the charge that the city council of Boulder, Colorado, violated the Sherman Antitrust Act when it refused permission for the local cable television system to expand its operations into other areas of the city. The Supreme Court ruled that the city of Boulder was not exempt from antitrust liability under Colorado's "home rule" authority.[29]

Cable spokespersons also maintain that antitrust laws require that cable system operators be allowed to compete head-to-head with established systems wherever they choose rather than being "assigned" an area of a city in which to locate or being preempted from the city altogether by the municipal franchising authority's enfranchisement of a competing cable system. Those who favor this kind of competition say that it would benefit consumers by forcing greater program choices at cheaper rates. A March 1985 court decision provided even greater justification for competition than just economics. In *Preferred Communications, Inc. v. City of Los Angeles*, the U.S. Court of Appeals ruled that not only were "exclusive" cable television franchises in violation of antitrust laws, but they were also in violation of the First Amendment rights of cable system operators seeking to compete in exclusive franchise markets.[30] The decision, later affirmed by the U.S. Supreme Court,[31] presents an ironic dilemma within the cable television industry. While the industry has uniformly advocated full First Amendment rights for cable television, at the same time it has informally appreciated the economic benefits that franchise exclusivity has provided many of its members. In fact, some cable television systems have gone to unscrupulous means to attain their exclusivity.[32]

There is a second ironic twist coming from the *Preferred* decision. As sometimes happens, the decision of one circuit of the U.S. Court of Appeals will conflict with a decision on a similar matter released by another circuit. Some eight months before the Ninth Circuit's ruling in the *Preferred* case, the Fifth Circuit U.S. Court of Appeals, ruling in *Affiliated Capital Corporation*, said, "Cable television, like electric utilities, is generally considered a natural monopoly. According to conventional wisdom, the extremely high fixed costs incurred in preparing a cable television company for operation prevent the survival of competition in the marketplace."[33] "What difference does it make to cable's First Amendment rights if it is a natural monopoly?" asked the author of a commentary on the *Affiliated* decision. "As a monopoly," the commentary continued, "it must be regulated to protect the public interest. And it is cable's monopoly status that seems to distinguish its legal foundation from those of the print and broadcasting media."[34] Obviously, the two conflicting points of view—the one supporting unqualified First Amendment freedom for cable television and the other supporting regulation of cable as a common carrier public utility monopoly—are far from reconciliation.

The second major matter of controversy affecting cable television is that of questionable program content. Cable television systems in many municipalities provide programs whose content is regarded as offensive by some members of the public. While those who are offended argue for restraints or censorship of such content, others insist that cable television, under the First Amendment, should be allowed to carry whatever programs a cable system operator chooses. Though some of the controversial content may deal with extreme political or religious ideologies, most of it deals with what protestors have labeled as obscene or indecent sexual themes. What some persons regard as obscene or indecent, though, is not so regarded by others, and therein lies perhaps the true nature of the controversy. The courts simply have not yet devised a definition of obscenity or indecency comprehensive enough to apply to every facet of media content, especially that of cable television.[35]

This obstacle has not stopped individuals from pressing forward with their efforts to rid cable of objectionable programming. Several states and municipalities have enacted legislation or ordinances to regulate what they regard as "cable pornography," but in most cases where cable interests have challenged the regulations' legality, courts have ruled in favor of cable— basing their decisions on First Amendment grounds.[36] One such decision, *Community Television of Utah, Inc. v. Roy City*,[37] is an especially important one. The district court ruling held that the Utah Cable Television Programming Decency Act lacked any constitutional foundation in the ban it placed on cable program content containing certain visual or verbal depictions of sexual activity. The U.S. Court of Appeals upheld the district court's decision, agreeing almost entirely with the rationale of the lower court's position.[38] The final word in the matter came in 1987 when the U.S. Supreme Court refused to review the U.S. Court of Appeals decision. Responding to the significance of the Supreme Court's action, NCTA president James Mooney said, "This case underscores the futility of legislatures trying to use so-called 'indecency' statutes to prevent people from watching in their own homes what they can see in their neighborhood movie theaters."[39]

The protest over questionable programming moved to a different venue in 1985 when several U.S. senators introduced a bill to prohibit transmitting "obscene, indecent or profane" content over cable television.[40] At the same time, a Commission on Pornography created by U.S. Attorney General Edwin Meese was busy investigating pornography in America in order to find ways to curb its growth. Cable television program content was one particular target cited by the attorney general, who remarked, "With the advent of cable TV and video recorders, pornography is available at home to anyone . . . at the mere touch of a button." A representative from the Playboy Channel cable program service responded that "the Meese concern is misplaced because cable above anything else is a medium of choice. You have to pay a premium to get it. Choice should be with the individual and not with the government."[41]

The Cable Act addresses obscene and indecent programming by allowing franchising authorities to place certain conditions on cable operators in the kind of programming they may provide subscribers. Program content determined to be obscene according to the criteria devised by the U.S. Supreme Court in *Miller v. California*[42] may either be prohibited altogether or carried at a time when children would be less likely to be viewing. The Cable Act also requires that a cable operator provide subscribers, upon request, a device referred to as a "lock box" that may be used in the home to restrict access to cable television programs at the subscriber's discretion. The "lock box" is seen as a tool that can be used selectively "without infringing the First Amendment rights of the cable operator, the cable programmer, or other cable viewers."[43]

Videotex and Interactive Cable

Cable television regulation collides with First Amendment rights in yet another way with respect to videotex. Videotex, a subject to be explored in much greater depth in the following chapter of this reference guide, is the generic term applied to services that may be supplied by cable television systems to carry information both to and from a subscriber's home. The interactive service converts a television receiver into a computer monitor and with the addition of a keyboard allows the subscriber to "access" information that will appear on the television screen. Videotex is predicted to be the key to home shopping, banking, mail delivery, and a host of other services.

One service in particular that videotex is meant to provide is that of an "electronic newspaper." Such a newspaper would provide the videotex subscriber all the news of any desired kind simply at the press of a key. In a regulatory sense, though, this electronic newspaper will differ from the traditional kind in that its content as well as its mode of delivery will be subject to FCC regulations.[44] There are obviously some very delicate problems that arise from this situation, problems that regulators must eventually resolve.

Videotex is yet another example of how technology is outpacing the ability of government to effectively deal with the technology's role in the consumer marketplace. Videotex technology, as one source put it, "gives us round pegs to fit into the square holes of old legal classifications."[45]

One other area in particular where regulation has not kept pace with technology is that of privacy. When consumers subscribe to interactive cable services such as videotex, they invite the possibility of their privacy being invaded. After all, the same wire that brings information into the household can also take information from that same household. While it may be true that telephone wires have been doing this for years, telephone wires have nowhere near the capacity of an interactive cable television wire. One commentary stated the matter in these terms:

The traditional concepts and language of individual privacy do not account for the new realities of interactive home media. For example, how are we to interpret the Fourth Amendment protections against unlawful search and seizure in the context of two-way cable, videotex, and other interactive systems that can collect countless streams of data about a person, compile that information, store it, analyze it, cross-reference it, and use it in manipulative ways without the consent of the individual or the supervision of government or the courts?[46]

Interactive cable television has not yet developed to the extent that subscriber privacy need be a major worry. However, that has not stopped
several state legislatures from enacting legislation to ensure that the privacy
of cable subscribers in their states is protected. Warner Amex Cable Communications, with cable systems located in several major cities, created its
own Code of Privacy, which carefully explains how the cable system "shall
maintain adequate safeguards to ensure the physical security and confiden-
tiality of any subscriber information."[47] The step taken by Warner Amex
is now mandated for all cable television systems by the Cable Act.

Copyright

Payment of copyright fees for programming carried on cable television
systems has been the subject of almost constant dispute since near the very
beginning of the cable industry. As cable operators began importing distant
signals for carriage on their systems, persons with copyright interests in
the programs being imported complained of copyright infringement. No
copyright fee had been paid and no permission had been granted for use of
program product, claimed the affected copyright holders. The dispute became the subject of several suits and eventually wound up in the U.S.
Supreme Court. The matter was decided in favor of cable operators who,
said the Court, did not "perform" programs they chose for their systems
but merely retransmitted them from point of origination to home viewer.

The misfortune of copyright holders derived from the fact that the applicable Copyright Act of 1909 had no provisions to support their position.
It became clear that circumstances dictated a major effort toward revision
of the outmoded 1909 law. That effort succeeded with passage of the Copyright Act of 1976. The new law extended copyright protection to any
programming carried on signals that eventually would be retransmitted by
cable systems. Cable system operators may now either purchase from copyright holders the rights to individual programs, or they may obtain a
compulsory blanket license for a statutory fee. Money from the fee payment
is then spread among all the copyright holders of programs carried on the
licensee's cable television system. The Register of Copyrights collects the
compulsory license fees, but the Copyright Royalty Tribunal (CRT) de-
termines specific fee levels. The 1976 Copyright Act granted the CRT
"explicit authority to periodically adjust the compulsory license fees to take
into account inflation (or deflation), changes in cable system subscriber rates,
and changes in FCC carriage regulations."[48]

As the FCC has loosened its heretofore tight grip on what distant signals
cable operators are allowed to choose for their cable television systems, the
CRT has exercised its mandate to increase compulsory license fees of those
operators electing to import more and more distant signals. Cable system
operators have complained that the fee adjustments are excessive and have

found a number of prominent congressional sympathizers to plead their case legislatively.[49]

Must-Carry

Cable industry critic Les Brown has characterized the FCC's "must-carry" rule as "neither complicated nor problematical. It merely requires that cable systems carry all local television stations that are 'significantly viewed' in the immediate area or that are located within 35 miles of the cable transmission center." Deletion of the rule, according to Brown, would "place the future of broadcast stations in serious question and create a media monster of cable."[50] What Brown considered his worst fears came to pass in 1985 when the U.S. Court of Appeals ruled in the *Quincy* decision that the must-carry rule violated cable system operators' First Amendment rights and thus was unenforceable.[51]

What followed from the moment the *Quincy* decision was rendered was a series of efforts to create a regulatory framework that would embody the spirit of the original must-carry rule. First came an agreement in early 1986 between representatives of the broadcast television industry (the NAB, the Television Operators Caucus, and the Association of Independent Television Stations) and representatives of the cable television industry (the NCTA and the Community Antenna Television Association) for required carriage of local broadcast television station signals by certain cable systems. Only those systems with more than twenty activated cable channels would be affected. Those systems with fewer than twenty channels would not be required to carry the broadcast television signals.[52] Within a short time following the agreement the U.S. Supreme Court upheld the *Quincy* decision by refusing to review it.[53] By August 1986 the FCC had modified the earlier broadcast/cable industry must-carry agreement, stipulating among other things that local cable systems provide subscribers with an "A/B switch" that would allow switching back and forth between cable signal and over-the-air signal.[54] All modifications were incorporated into a final must-carry rule and adopted by the FCC on 7 August 1986.[55]

On 24 December 1986, a little more than three weeks prior to the effective date for the new must-carry rule, the FCC voted to indefinitely stay the rule.[56] A redraft of the must-carry rule was adopted by the commission in March 1987 with only one substantive change from the August 1986 version. No longer would cable system operators be required to provide subscribers with "A/B switches." Instead, the operators would be required to notify subscribers of the switches' availability and to install them at subscribers' cost if requested to do so. Left intact in the FCC redraft was a controversial "sunset" provision that would delete all must-carry rule requirements within five years of the 1987 must-carry rule implementation date.[57]

Cable Signal Theft

Unauthorized interception of cable program service signals is referred to by those in the cable business as either theft of service or signal "piracy." Theft of a cable signal may take any of the following forms: "(1) Physically or electronically 'tapping' a cable running past the home; (2) Attaching to a legitimately subscribed-to cable a 'decoder,' which electronically reconstructs the 'scrambled' pay channel signals that are transmitted together with unscrambled channels over the cable; [or] (3) Installing an 'earth base' communications satellite receiver, which intercepts signals being transmitted via... communications satellites."[58] According to the NCTA's Office of Cable Signal Theft, unauthorized interception of cable service in 1986 cost cable system operators, programmers, and copyright holders an estimated $1.4 billion in lost revenue.[59]

Prosecution of persons charged with cable signal theft was pursued most often in state courts until passage of the 1984 Cable Act. But since two provisions of the act, sections 633 and 705, address the matter, it is assumed that theft of cable service cases now will be pursued more vigorously through the federal courts. Section 633 specifically sets penalties for illegally tapping or converting cable signals, while section 705 sets penalties for illegal interception of satellite signals. Persons who intercept the satellite signals on backyard TVRO dishes and use the programming for their own private viewing are exempt from section 705 enforcement,[60] thus creating what has been described as a "safe harbor" for otherwise would-be signal "pirates."[61]

Satellite Signal Scrambling

The problem of satellite signal piracy as well as that of legitimate reception of signal by TVRO dish owners has prompted a number of program suppliers to scramble or "encrypt" their satellite-distributed programs. Reception of these scrambled signals is possible only by means of a special decoder coupled with payment of a monthly or annual fee. The cost of leasing the decoder and the amount of the fee have met with opposition from the nearly 1.5 million TVRO dish owners, who claim that the two are excessive. TVRO dish owners and satellite dish dealers alike have carried their concerns to Congress, where they have found sympathetic ears. As a result, several bills have been introduced in the U.S. Senate and House seeking some form of relief for the affected parties.[62] Senator Albert Gore, Jr. (D-Tenn.), one of the leading advocates for placing greater restraints on descrambling fees, has argued,

No one can reasonably dispute the right of cable networks to be paid for their product. Controversy has risen, however, because of the timing of the net-

works' decisions and because of the amount they intend to charge for their programs. . . .

Rather than being a sincere effort by the cable industry to obtain fair compensation
for its programming, the industry's actions are actually a concerted attempt to quash
the home earth station movement in its infancy. Because of our concern over the
cable industry's effort, other members of Congress and I have taken steps to counter
its tactics and ensure that a fair marketplace for cable satellite programming is allowed
to exist.[63]

Senator Gore and his supporters have yet to muster sufficient interest among
their congressional colleagues to pass scrambling relief legislation.[64]

SOURCE OVERVIEW

Books and Book Chapters

All titles—books, government documents and periodicals—pertaining
specifically to the Cable Communications Policy Act of 1984 are included
under a special "1984 Cable Act" heading following the Source Overview.

General Survey

Most of the titles in this category are law or case study books that deal
with cable television law and regulations in an overview fashion. What is
very clear about these titles is the manner in which their authors choose to
examine cable law and regulations. Three distinct categories of investigation
emerge: (1) law, regulations, and policies affecting all new or emerging
electronic delivery systems, of which cable television is treated as only one
among several competing technologies; (2) summary of key provisions of
the FCC's 1972 cable rules (and the 1984 Cable Act for those books published
after its passage) and cases affecting or affected by FCC policy, rulemaking,
or court decisions applicable to cable television; and (3) deregulation of the
telecommunications industry.

Falling into the first category is Michael Botein and Michael B. Sprague's
"Regulation of Telecommunications in the United States" in *Telecommunications for Management*, edited by Charles T. Meadow and Albert S. Tedesco.
This essay is brief but integrates cable television with other electronic delivery systems to show how the government's regulatory scheme differs
from medium to medium.

Revolution in the Wasteland: Value and Diversity in Television is Ronald A.
Cass's examination of ways in which new regulatory theories are being
forged due to the growing diversity in the electronic media marketplace.
Old regulatory schemes will be required to adapt to the emerging electronic
media and their needs, according to Cass. *Revolution in the Wasteland* looks
at a host of new media arrivals, including cable television, and quickly

reviews cable's regulatory history and the impact that regulation has had on cable television programming capabilities.

A book whose focus is difficult to pin down is Edward V. Dolan's *TV or CATV? A Struggle for Power*. The book appears to be an overview of the struggle between regulatory policy affecting the broadcasting and cable television industries and the development of the two. *TV or CATV?* tends toward providing a historical account of both the economic and the regulatory development of cable and only slightly tilts toward the latter.

David M. Rice, Michael Botein, and Edward B. Samuels' *Development and Regulation of New Communications Technologies* is a hardback version of the *New York Law School Law Review* special edition on "Law and the Emerging Video Technologies."

At the head of the second category of titles is *National Association of Broadcasters Legal Guide to FCC Broadcast Regulations*, a publication that would seem an unlikely source on cable regulations, given the antipathy of broadcasters toward cable television. The NAB, however, has a vested interest in cable regulation, as stated in the *Legal Guide*'s preface: "Licensees of television stations should understand the impact on their operations of the FCC's cable television rules governing broadcast signal carriage, non-duplication and carriage of sports events" (p. 3). While the explanation of these rules is quite good, the reader should be cautioned that without addition of updated text inserts, rule changes, court decisions, and passage of the 1984 Cable Act will have outdistanced the usefulness of a portion of the *Legal Guide*'s chapter on cable television.

John R. Bittner includes one chapter on cable television regulation, chiefly describing the components of the cable television franchise ordinance, in *Broadcast Law and Regulation*. The author devotes some of this cable space to copyright, with information on royalty fee schedules and examples of forms used for calculation of such fees in preparation for the Copyright Office. There are some important cable-related items in *Broadcast Law and Regulation*, but Bittner covers the subject in a very routine fashion.

Marc A. Franklin's *Cases and Materials on Mass Media Law* devotes space to only two cable-related matters—copyright and restrictions on pay cable systems. More substantive are *Mass Communications Law in a Nutshell* by Harvey L. Zuckman and Martin J. Gaynes and *Mass Communication Law: Cases and Comment* by Donald M. Gillmor and Jerome A. Barron. True to their devotion to an economy of words, Zuckman and Gaynes manage in a few pages to cover extensive territory ranging from a discussion of jurisdictional divisions affecting cable television regulation to cable copyright problems and cable programming regulation. The Gillmor and Barron book covers even greater territory. This classic case study text examines the 1976 Copyright Act and the Copyright Royalty Tribunal and looks at legal problems attached thereto. The book's authors then comment on subjects that include FCC regulation of cable system franchising, mandatory carriage of local television broadcast station signals, and the significance of the *Boulder* decision for local cable regulation.

Don R. Pember squeezes quite a bit of information regarding cable television into a small space in his *Mass Media Law*. He includes here only scant mention of law and regulations pertaining to other emerging electronic media, choosing instead to look most closely at legal and regulatory matters surrounding cable. Pember's incorporation in summary fashion of information drawn from the 1984 Cable Act makes *Mass Media Law* perhaps the most useful of the numerous general media law texts available on the market.

The third category of general cable television law and regulations investigation—that of cable deregulation—begins with two books that include chapters in which the subject is examined in the broader context of general electronic media industry deregulation. Florence Heffron's "The Federal Communications Commission and Broadcast Deregulation" in *Communications Policy and the Political Process*, edited by John J. Havick, serves as an excellent "briefing" on the influences through the 1960s and early 1970s that led to the FCC's move toward deregulating the electronic media. The commission's repeal of major cable television rules is mentioned only as an example of the extent to which deregulation had progressed by the early 1980s. Covering the same territory but with the absence of Heffron's more philosophical tone is Douglas W. Webbink's straightforward "The Recent Deregulatory Movement at the FCC" in *Telecommunications in the U.S.: Trends and Policies*, edited by Leonard Lewin.

Bruce M. Owen's "The Rise and Fall of Cable Television Regulation" in *Case Studies in Regulation: Revolution and Reform*, edited by Leonard W. Weiss and Michael W. Klass, comments first on the 1972 cable rules and their impact on the cable television industry and then moves to a discussion of cable deregulation. Owen briefly speculates on the reasons for deregulation and what deregulation will mean to cable's future.

Edwin Diamond, Norman Sandler, and Milton Mueller combine an overview of regulatory policy issues with an overview of deregulatory issues affecting all electronic media in *Telecommunications in Crisis: The First Amendment, Technology, and Deregulation*. The authors comment on some of the major issues, particularly in content matters, with which regulators and Congress must grapple, but only to a limited extent do they include cable television within the context of their commentary. *Telecommunications in Crisis* makes a strong pitch for the government to retreat from any kind of editorial role relevant to the electronic media.

General Survey, Cable-Specific

Three outstanding books on cable television law and regulations are Morton I. Hamburg's *All about Cable*, Ira C. Stein's *Cable Television: Handbook and Forms*, and Daniel L. Brenner and Monroe E. Price's *Cable Television and Other Nonbroadcast Video: Law and Policy*. All three books were noted in the business and economics chapter of this reference guide, and they will be noted once more in this chapter's franchising category.

The Hamburg book is complete with up-to-date commentary and case studies on all relevant subject areas, including the 1984 Cable Act. Chapters in *All about Cable* deal extensively with cable television's regulatory history, federal and state regulation of the cable industry, cable television franchising and local cable regulation, pay cable regulations, and business aspects of cable television.

Ira C. Stein's *Cable Television* is no less comprehensive in its coverage of the many legal and regulatory matters related to cable. Stein does follow a more rigidly defined structure that includes commentary and case studies under such chapter headings as cable television history, video technology, federal regulation, copyright, franchise regulation, financing, cable system purchase and sale, cable system construction, utility pole attachments, easements, programming, subscribers, personnel, advertising, public access, and telecommunications. Each chapter contains appendices with legal documents and forms relevant to the chapter's subject matter.

Brenner and Price's *Cable Television and Other Nonbroadcast Video: Law and Policy* varies from the other two books only in degree. The only method of separation that becomes readily apparent is the attention that Brenner/ Price pay to electronic media delivery systems apart from cable. Individual chapters in *Cable Television and Other Nonbroadcast Video* are devoted to law and regulatory matters associated with such delivery systems, SMATV and DBS in particular. Other chapters in the Brenner/Price book are organized to provide the same comprehensive examination of cable law and regulations as the Hamburg and Stein books. Included here are chapters on cable technology, the 1984 Cable Act and its regulatory predecessors, program content regulation, subscriber rate regulation, franchise renewal, copyright, franchise fees and taxes, and privacy.

Hamburg concludes *All about Cable* with an extensive array of appendices that include federal cable rules and regulations; assorted state regulatory documents affecting cable television; examples of such documents as program license agreements, leased channel agreements, and cable network advertising agreements; and the 1984 Cable Act. Stein's *Cable Television* concludes with copies of the FCC cable regulations, miscellaneous contract provisions, and a glossary of cable terms. One very important feature of the Hamburg, Stein, and Brenner/Price books is their loose-leaf construction that makes it possible to add updated inserts whenever necessary.

A three-volume set of books by Charles D. Ferris, Frank W. Lloyd, and Thomas J. Casey entitled *Cable Television Law* may exceed the Hamburg, Stein, and Brenner/Price books as a comprehensive guide to cable law and regulations. *Cable Television Law* ranges far and wide to cover regulation of all video technologies to some extent, but as its title suggests, the book's volumes concentrate on cable television. Part 1 of volume 1 is devoted to broadcast television regulation, while part 2, which begins in volume 1 and concludes in volume 2, belongs to cable. Every facet of federal regulatory jurisdiction is explored here. Parts 3, 4, and 5 of *Cable Television Law* are all in volume 2. Part 3 is devoted entirely to regulatory matters concerning electronic media other than cable and broadcast television. The final two parts contain commentary on selected legal problems of cable television and other video technologies—antitrust, theft of service, defamation, securities laws, and tax issues—and on international developments in cable television. *Cable Television Law*'s third volume is an appendix that contains, among other items, copies of statutes (Communications Act, Cable Act, and Copyright Act), regulations, and federal and state forms related to cable television. It is, in a word, complete. Like Hamburg, Stein and Brenner/Price, the authors of *Cable Television Law* promise frequent updates to the basic text with summaries and comments on leading court cases and decisions, and regulatory and congressional developments affecting cable.

Certainly not to be overlooked is *Broadcasting/Cablecasting Yearbook*. This publication contains an annual review of federal cable television rules, regulations, and policy developments.

Cable Communication by Thomas F. Baldwin and D. Stevens McVoy provides a very solid chapter on cable law and regulations. The chapter opens with an overview of the cable policy structure—who regulates what and who contributes to creating cable policy—and then proceeds to describe federal, state, and local policies generally applicable to cable. Baldwin/McVoy also examine the 1976 Copyright Law and the purpose of the Copyright Royalty Tribunal and close with a discussion of cable-related First Amendment issues.

An outstanding case study text for cable television law and regulations is Charles M. Firestone and Nicholas Johnson's *Cases and Materials on Communications Law and Policy*. The second volume of this three-volume set is devoted exclusively to cable television and new video systems. Most major decisions that have affected cable television (for example, franchising, signal carriage, and program content) since the early 1970s are represented here, published either in their entirety or edited to include only the essentials.

A series of books that must be considered the most current and most thorough source of information about cable television law and regulations are those published periodically by the Practising Law Institute (PLI). The books (actually handbooks) are essentially a compilation of articles, reports, judicial and regulatory documents, and assorted commentary pertaining to specific subjects (cable television being only one of several subjects addressed) and meant as study material for PLI meetings in New York City. The books are available for purchase by nonmembers of PLI.

The PLI books serve as an annual review of important legal matters related to mass communication in general or to cable television in particular. Books in the first category still have considerable content related to cable. Even a cursory description of all the important cable-related items contained in these books would be a monumental task, so what follows is a list of the most important PLI books covering the years 1980 through 1986. The titles are listed chronologically. Publication dates are provided unless the date is a part of the title. Each title is preceded by the serial number assigned by the PLI. Specific content per title from the PLI books appearing in this list is cited by PLI serial number following this list.

No. 125, *Communications Law 1980*, vol. 2

No. 129, *Current Development in CATV 1981*

No. 137, *Antitrust, the Media, and the New Technology*, 1981

No. 139, *Ninth Annual Communications Law Institute*, 1981, vol. 1

No. 154, *Communications Law 1982*, vol. 2

No. 158, *Cable Television in a New Era*, 1983

No. 164, *New Program Opportunities in the Electronic Media*, 1983

No. 165, *Campaign '84: Advertising and Programming Obligations of the Electronic Media*, 1983

No. 169, *Communications Law 1983*, vol. 2

No. 188, *Communications Law 1984*, vol. 1

No. 194, *The New Era In CATV: The Cable Franchise Policy and Communications Act of 1984*

No. 200, *A Practical Guide to the Cable Communications Policy Act of 1984*

No. 214, *Cable Television: Retrospective and Prospective*, 1985

No. 232, *Communications Law 1986*, vol. 2

Antitrust (137, 154, 158, 214, 232)

Cable Act of 1984 (194, 200, 214)

Copyright (129, 158)

Economics/finance (158, 214)

First Amendment (154, 169, 214, 232)

Franchising (129, 154, 158, 194, 200, 214, 232)

Labor relations (214)

Overview of regulatory framework (125, 154, 169, 188, 214)

Ownership (158)

Pole attachment (129)

Political campaign announcement/programs (165)

Public access (129)

Videotex (125)

Vernone Sparkes's "Cable Television in the United States: A Story of Continuing Growth and Change" in *Cable Television and the Future of Broad-*

casting, edited by Ralph M. Negrine, is one of several chapters in the Negrine book that look at cable television development worldwide. The Sparkes chapter provides some general history of U.S. cable development, but it concentrates on policy and regulatory history. The last portion of the chapter is devoted to a discussion of cable television's social and economic impact.

Franchising

Three of the most important resource books for information regarding cable television franchising are Hamburg's *All about Cable*, Stein's *Cable Television: Handbook and Forms*, and Brenner/Price's *Cable Television and Other Nonbroadcast Video: Law and Policy*, all of which were mentioned under the previous heading. The three books cover practically every aspect of cable, but their chapters on franchising are thorough descriptions of the process.

All About Cable includes not only a chapter on cable franchising and local regulation, but also one on state regulation of cable. Morton Hamburg looks specifically at the structure and operation of two state regulatory commissions, those of New York and Massachusetts. The franchising chapter defines the process in every detail, moving the reader from the initial appointment of an advisory committee to selecting a franchisee, formulating the franchise agreement, and franchise renewal. Hamburg includes a model franchise proposal and makes suggestions on what components the proposal should contain. He concludes with comments on legal challenges such as antitrust suits that franchising authorities might confront. The appendices to *All about Cable* are an especially important feature. They contain federal cable regulations, the Cable Communications Policy Act of 1984, state regulatory commission documents, a cable franchising workbook, and copies of program-related agreements and contracts.

Ira Stein's *Cable Television: Handbook and Forms* covers much the same territory as Hamburg but concentrates more on the application of the 1984 Cable Act to the franchising process. He looks at recent developments in antitrust law and cable television, First Amendment issues and cable, and the franchise negotiating process. Stein includes a franchise agreement and ordinance as an appendix to his book.

Brenner and Price include two important cable franchise chapters in *Cable Television and Other Nonbroadcast Video*. The first provides a specific grounding in the fundamentals of franchising—its establishment, enforcement, and modification. The second chapter moves beyond the initial franchise to concentrate on franchise renewal. Especially notable here is the emphasis on how the 1984 Cable Act applies to the refranchising process.

While these three books are thorough in their discussions of franchising, they present information in a somewhat legalistic language. Much more readable—and almost as thorough—is the franchising chapter in Thomas F. Baldwin and D. Stevens McVoy's *Cable Communication*. This book has also been noted previously for its general textbook format. Baldwin/McVoy survey the franchising process by providing a detailed description of all components of the process, especially the provisions to be included in a franchise agreement and ordinance. They make reference to actual cable franchising that has occurred in several markets. The appendices to *Cable Communication* include samples of local public access channel rules, procedures for assessing community needs for cable television, and a copy of the National League of Cities Code of Good Cable Television Franchising Conduct.

Jean Rice has edited an excellent cable information sourcebook in *Cable TV Renewals and Refranchising*. The ten chapters of the book, all written by cable television professionals, include a comprehensive discussion of municipal considerations in cable franchise renewals; cable programming and technology; franchise renewals from the legal, franchising authority, and cable operator's perspectives; service to rural areas; access channels; consumer privacy; leased channel policy; and competing electronic media in the marketplace. Rice includes a very helpful appendix with information on "Requesting Proposals for Cable Television Systems: A Model for Municipal Governments." The model was prepared by the National Federation of Local Cable Programmers to serve as a sample structure for local cable franchising officials.

The Cable Television Information Center (CTIC) has prepared a two-volume *CTIC Cablebooks* set to assist members of the public in creating cable television policy. The first *CTIC Cablebook* volume, *The Community Medium*, edited by Nancy Jesuale and Ralph Lee Smith is noted elsewhere in this reference guide. Volume two, *A Guide for Local Policy*, edited by Nancy J. Jesuale, Richard M. Neustadt and Nicholas P. Miller, is described below. According to the CTIC staff, the *CTIC Cablebooks* "are a result of our involvement with local officials who have successfully addressed the touchy issues of regulatory policies, privacy, censorship, local ownership, free ('universal') service, citizen access to the system, educational uses, and much more" (p. xiii). Commentary in *A Guide for Local Policy* is brief but covers a lot of territory. The book's first three chapters describe the rationale for regulation—federal, state, and local—the franchising process, and the creation of a local cable television ordinance. Later chapters cover such matters as public ownership of cable television systems, cable rate regulation, franchise enforcement and franchise renegotiation, access matters, and antitrust issues and consumer issues in cable television. Two appendices in *A Guide for Local Policy* contain Joseph W. Way, Jr.'s "Actors in the Industry," a list of the agencies and regulatory bodies affecting cable television policy nationally and locally, and Sharon A. Briley's "Index of State Franchising Statutes."

Herbert S. Dordick's *Public Television and Cable: New Working Opportunities in the Franchising and Refranchising Process* has been written as a guide

or handbook for public television (PTV) station managers who must represent the needs of their stations and the cable television role that public
broadcasting should play in local cable franchise negotiations. The book is
touted as a "how-to" guide for PTV station managers with advice drawn
from the experiences of managers who already have been involved in the
franchise process.

Publications of the Practising Law Institute (PLI) also contain valuable
information on cable television franchising as well as antitrust matters affecting local franchising authorities. All the PLI publications pertaining to
cable were noted earlier in this chapter. Those with specific content having
to do with franchising are especially important because of the many actual
franchise-related documents and the diversity of issue-related commentary
they contain.

Chapters in three books examine cable television franchising in a more
narrative style than the above books. David K. Speaker and David Z.
Wirtschafter's "Cable Television Franchising" in the *1983 Entertainment,
Publishing, and the Arts Handbook,* edited by Michael Meyer and John David
Viera, looks at franchising case studies in several markets and focuses es-
pecially on the political nature of cable franchising.

A companion piece to the Speaker/Wirtschafter essay updates matters by
looking at the state of cable television franchising in 1984. Randall Paul
Sherman's "Blue Skies, Going Away? Directions in the Cable Television
Industry" in Michael Meyer and John David Viera's *1984 Entertainment,
Publishing, and the Arts Handbook* assesses the less-than-glowing progress
that cable television franchising made in one year by following the same
case study format as Speaker/Wirtschafter. Sherman contends that there is
much evidence to support the comments of critics who were saying that
"cable's importance has been overestimated, and it is no longer a 'good'
business" (p. 119).

Antitrust and Local Government: Perspectives on the Boulder Decision, edited
by James V. Siena, is a book whose twenty essays all relate to the *Boulder*
case. Some of the most noted jurists in the country comment on the implications of the decision and on antitrust matters in general. All of the
essays appearing here are extensions of papers first developed for a National
League of Cities–sponsored "Local Government and the Antitrust Laws"
conference held in 1982 in Dallas.

A close examination of the excesses of politics and the cable television
franchising process is the subject of Ronald Garay's "Politics and Cable
Television: The Case of Houston, Texas" in *Communication Yearbook 7,*
edited by Robert Bostrom. The essay describes the unusual cable franchising
practices that were used by the Houston, Texas, City Council. The major
portion of the article analyzes the antitrust case, *Affiliated Capital Corporation
v. City of Houston,* that was instituted by one potential cable system operator

whose franchise application was excluded illegally from Houston City Council consideration.

The influence of local policymakers on the future direction that cable television as well as other electronic media will take is examined in Mark A. Greenwald's "The Telecommunications Role of Local Government" in *Communications and the Future*, edited by Howard F. Didsbury, Jr. Greenwald says that just as municipal governments had to plan for housing and transportation in the past, so they must now plan for public access to communications or information. He investigates the local government's parameters for such a role under the major headings of policy concerns, economic concerns, and sociological concerns.

First Amendment

The entire content of Ithiel de Sola Pool's *Technologies of Freedom* focuses on the strain between regulating electronic media and the First Amendment protection for those media. Chapter 7 of the book looks specifically at cable television and at the development and application of cable regulation as it relates to First Amendment matters. The author says, "The time has come to bury the old cliche that spectrum is a scarce resource. It is an abundant resource, but a squandered and misused one. Like any resource, it is limited, but like such other communications resources as paper, trees, printing presses, wires, or television sets, it is plentiful" (p. 151). Pool goes on to comment that deregulatory measures and court decisions regarding cable television "have let stand assumptions about the legitimacy of content regulation that derive from problems of early broadcasting" (p. 166). He concludes, "There is nothing about spectrum technology that today mandates bureaucratic control of what is transmitted by cable. There need be no scarcity of capacity or access. The law that governs print can become the law that governs those who communicate on cable channels too" (p. 166).

George H. Shapiro, Philip B. Kurland, and James P. Mercurio note that the underlying thesis of their book *'CableSpeech': The Case for First Amendment Protection* "is that communication by cable television must be free from governmental interference if we are to preserve and pass on the great freedoms we enjoy in this nation" (p. viii). The authors advance the philosophical arguments for full First Amendment protection of cable television. They examine major First Amendment court decisions and their application to cable, narrate cable television regulatory history, and then survey decisions and regulatory positions in these areas: obscenity and indecency, fairness doctrine and political advertising, mandatory access requirements, must-carry rules, cable subscriber rates, limits on cable system ownership. Also briefly examined are regulatory positions on such matters as franchise fees, cable system capacity and cable system service areas.

Patrick Parsons states in his book *Cable Television and the First Amendment* that, although cable is becoming increasingly a major part of our media lives, we nevertheless "have no clear notion of the constitutional rights of those who own, program, and view the medium. In the past," Parsons continues, "the First Amendment rights of the system owner and operator were sacrificed for the benefit of the community. Now the pendulum is swinging back, and soon the community may have very little say in what the local cable system distributes or refuses to distribute" (p. 9). Parsons has produced a thorough and very readable explanation of the evolution of cable television's First Amendment position. He looks closely at the regulatory, constitutional, and philosophical bases of that position as he makes his way toward creating a First Amendment model that is most applicable to cable's current and future media role.

Returning to the broader scope of the Ithiel de Sola Pool book in its look at all the emerging electronic media but approaching the subject in a law school casebook format is T. Barton Carter, Marc A. Franklin, and Jay B. Wright's *The First Amendment and the Fourth Estate*. This book examines how the U.S. Supreme Court has applied First Amendment principles to the new and emerging media. While the authors do refer to some major Supreme Court First Amendment decisions pertaining to cable television in particular, their main purpose here seems directed more toward describing cable television, its history, its operation and its regulation.

Denise M. Trauth and John L. Huffman, in a monograph entitled "Obscenity and Cable Television: A Regulatory Approach," explore the complex matter of regulating cable program content that is considered by some standards as unsuitable for viewing. The two authors review the major cases that have thus far focused on efforts either to prohibit or curtail cable system operators from providing channel space for adult programming. The substance of this monograph is framed within three basic questions: "[I]s adult cable programming susceptible to regulation? Can material that would not be considered obscene were it shown in a movie theatre be prohibited from cable distribution? And, if this sort of material can be regulated, what form would that regulation take?" (pp. 2–3).

Interactive Cable and Privacy

"Challenges to the protection of personal privacy posed by two-way information technology" (p. vii) is what David H. Flaherty says *Protecting Privacy in Two-Way Electronic Services* is all about. Flaherty sets his discussion in the context of interactive cable television and says that among other things his book "attempts to demonstrate to the public, legislators and industry policymakers the need for a critical awareness of the inherent threats to privacy embodied in specific new technologies" (p. 3). Once having looked at the prospects for privacy invasion, *Protecting Privacy* then evaluates various policy remedies that either already exist or are in a proposal stage. "This book does not emphasize the many positive aspects of two-way systems," says Flaherty, "but instead focuses on the risks users face in losing control of information about themselves as they make use of these desirable and beneficial services" (pp. 3–4).

Copyright

A good overview of copyright legislative and regulatory history and current application of copyright law and regulation to cable is provided by Stein's *Cable Television: Handbook and Forms* and Brenner/Price's *Cable Television and Other Nonbroadcast Video* noted earlier. Stein's chapter 4 and Brenner/Price's chapter 9 look extensively at the 1976 Copyright Act and the compulsory license affecting cable television system operators.

Several PLI publications also contain a good collection of information about not only the compulsory license, but also the Copyright Royalty Tribunal's function, legal documents and forms having to do with copyright liability, and court decisions affecting cable and copyright. The reader should refer to the General Survey, Cable-Specific part of this chapter for the specific PLI titles that contain the copyright content.

A book chapter, "A Pavan for Print: Accommodating Copyright to the Tele-Technologies" by U.S. Register of Copyrights David Ladd, appears in *Cable Television: Media and Copyright Law Aspects*, edited by H. Cohen Jehoram. Ladd's essay on cable copyright is a straightforward overview of the subject, with comments on the status of U.S. cable, court decisions affecting cable copyright, and the current state of copyright protection as guaranteed by the compulsory license, and a description of computation procedures for calculating copyright fees. Brief comments are also included here on congressional efforts to alter the requirements of the compulsory license.

Program Market Competition

A "merger analysis" is the subject of Lawrence J. White's "Antitrust and Video Markets: The Merger of Showtime and The Movie Channel as a Case Study" essay in the *1985 Entertainment, Publishing, and the Arts Handbook*, edited by John David Viera and Michael Meyer. White investigates the complex merger plan announced in late 1982 whose objective was the combination of major pay cable components ranging from program production entities to distribution entities. The author analyzes the application of the Clayton Antitrust Act to the business arrangement that he describes in these terms:

It entailed the outright merger of two providers of pay programming services (horizontal competitors), Showtime and TMC; it involved the addition of two movie studios (horizontal competitors), Universal and Paramount, to the joint venture involving a third studio (Warner) that already controlled one programming service (TMC) and that would now control both; and the programming services were major purchasers of major theatrical films from the studios, so customer-supplier (vertical) relationships were also involved. (p. 372)

Government Documents

The content of *Freedom of Expression*, transcripts of hearings conducted by the Senate Committee on Commerce, Science, and Transportation, includes comments on governmental control and regulation of media content, particularly in regard to new or emerging electronic media. Especially good are comments on the subject coming from William Van Alstyne (pp. 103–12) and Harry E. Smith of CBS Inc. (pp. 35–50).

Hearings conducted by the Senate Subcommittee on Criminal Law of the Committee on the Judiciary in mid–1985 addressed the concerns of many citizens about the appearance of adult programming—labeled as pornographic by some—on cable television systems. The specific legislative intent of the hearings, whose transcript is entitled *Cable-Porn and Dial-a-Porn Control Act*, was for support of a bill (S. 1090) introduced by Senator Jesse Helms (R-N.C.) to broaden section 1464, title 18 of the U.S. Code that currently prohibits the broadcast of "obscene, indecent, or profane language by means of radio communication" to include the transmission of such language by means of cable television as well.

The testimony and inserts of hearings conducted by the Subcommittee on Telecommunications, Consumer Protection, and Finance of the House Committee on Energy and Commerce appear in *Unauthorized Reception of Subscription Television*. These hearings were conducted to examine the need and intent of H.R. 4727 that would establish penalties for violations of the Communications Act provision that prohibits unauthorized reception of pay television signals. While the substance of these hearings pertains mostly to noncable pay systems, the implications for cable television, especially pay cable, are obvious.

The remainder of the government documents noted in this section all pertain in one degree or another to cable television copyright matters. To begin, there is the general oversight hearings testimony and inserts that comprise the content of *Copyright Office, the U.S. Patent and Trademark Office, and the Copyright Royalty Tribunal*. The hearings, conducted by the Subcommittee on Courts, Civil Liberties, and the Administration of Justice of the House Committee on the Judiciary, contain excellent extended remarks and accompanying charts, diagrams, and the like from Wilbur D. Campbell on "The Operation of the Copyright Royalty Tribunal" (pp. 85–128).

Oversight of the Copyright Act of 1976 (Cable Television) is the title of the transcript of hearings conducted by the U.S. Senate Committee on the Judiciary whose main purpose was to examine provisions of the Copyright Act dealing with secondary transmission by cable television systems and the cable compulsory license. Included here are excellent statements with accompanying inserts from the National Telecommunications and Information Administration' (NTIA) Dale N. Hatfield (pp. 80–93), Register of Copyrights David Ladd (pp. 94–194), Motion Picture Association of America (MPAA) president Jack Valenti (pp. 211–51), and NAB president Vincent T. Wasilewski (pp. 259–95).

The content of *Copyright/Cable Television*, part 1, consists of testimony from hearings conducted by the Subcommittee on Courts, Civil Liberties, and the Administration of Justice of the U.S. House Committee on the Judiciary on a collection of House measures introduced to amend provisions of the 1976 Copyright Law. The cable television compulsory license is the item that generated the most comments from witnesses. Although testimony is spread throughout the hearings transcript, several remarks stand out for their substance and their accompanying illustrative data. Most notable is the testimony of MPAA president Jack Valenti (pp. 58–126), Baseball Commissioner Bowie Kuhn (pp. 132–85), NAB president Vincent Wasilewski (pp. 192–344), Recording Industry Association of America (RIAA) president Stanley M. Gortikov (pp. 394–457), NCTA president Thomas E. Wheeler (pp. 479–514), Turner Broadcasting System president R. E. Turner III (pp. 659–75), Association of Independent Television Stations president Herman W. Land (pp. 831–47), and Register of Copyrights David Ladd (pp. 900–1005). Part 2 of the above hearings continues in the same context with additional testimony and data presented by Wheeler (pp. 1272–87), Valenti (pp. 1289–1334), Wasilewski (pp. 1342–56), Ladd (pp. 1387–1409), Kuhn (pp. 1417–31), and Turner (pp. 1465–73).

The House Judiciary Committee reports favorably on H.R. 5949 in *Cable Television Copyright Act Amendments*. The purpose of the bill, as explained in the report, is to amend the 1976 Copyright Law "with respect to limitations on exclusive rights to secondary transmission of copyrighted broadcasted material by cable television systems, to provide statutory syndicated exclusivity protection, [and] to amend the Communications Act of 1934 to provide a statutory provision regarding the compulsory carriage of broadcast signals by cable television systems" (p. 1). *Cable Copyright Legislation*, containing the testimony from hearings conducted by the Subcommittee on Telecommunications, Consumer Protection, and Finance of the House Committee on Energy and Commerce, also examines H.R. 5949 and deals with its provisions on copyright liability of cable television system operators for programs imported to their systems and on syndicated program exclusivity protections. Provisions in H.R. 5949 regarding syndicated program rights and cable television's must-carry rule are the subject of hearings conducted jointly by the U.S. Senate Committee on Commerce, Science, and Transportation and the Committee on the Judiciary and published under the title *Cable Copyright and Signal Carriage Act of 1982*.

Testimony that contains general oversight reports on copyright issues affecting cable television and other media and the accomplishment of the U.S. Copyright Office and Copyright Royalty Tribunal (CRT) appears in transcripts entitled *Copyright Office/Copyright Royalty Tribunal* of hearings conducted by the U.S. House Subcommittee on Courts, Civil Liberties, and the Administration of Justice. More general oversight comments on copyright matters appear in *Oversight of the Copyright Office and the Copyright Royalty Tribunal*, transcripts of Subcommittee on Patents, Copyrights, and Trademarks of the U.S. Senate Committee on the Judiciary hearings.

The subject of hearings conducted by the Subcommittee on Patents, Copyrights, and Trademarks of the U.S. Senate Committee on the Judiciary and whose transcripts comprise *The Free Market Copyright Royalty Act of 1983* is consideration of S. 1270 to revise the compensation method adopted by the CRT in compensating copyright holders of material carried on distant signals imported by local cable television systems. The same Senate sub-committee published the proceedings of a Fort Lauderdale, Florida, sym-posium on public policy implications of copyright law and its application to new technology under the title *Proceedings of the Congressional Copyright and Technology Symposium*. The latter portion of the symposium report (pp. 123–82) is devoted to the mass media.

Hearings to consider H.R. 2902 and H.R. 3419 to revise the rate structure that the CRT requires to be applied to cable television systems that carry imported distant signals or superstations are the subject of transcripts en-titled *Copyright Royalty Fees for Cable Systems*. The hearings, conducted by the Subcommittee on Courts, Civil Liberties, and the Administration of Justice of the U.S. House Committee on the Judiciary, solicited excellent testimony in the prepared statements of MPAA president Jack Valenti (pp. 113–45), Register of Copyrights David Ladd (pp. 163–92), NAB Copyright Committee chairman David Polinger (pp. 204–24), and Baseball Commis-sioner Bowie Kuhn (pp. 257–88). Also included are memoranda on the two bills submitted by the Turner Broadcasting System (pp. 344–403), MPAA (pp. 404–25), and United Video (pp. 426–54); a reprint of the article "Co-pyright, Cable, the Compulsory License: A Second Chance" by David Ladd, Dorothy M. Schrader, David Leibowitz, and Harriet L. Oler (pp. 455–528) in *Communications and the Law*; statements on the matter appearing in the *Federal Register* (pp. 529–70); and reprints of a number of court de-cisions involving copyright and cable television system importation of dis-tant signals (pp. 596–686).

Most oversight hearings are routine, but the ones conducted by the Sub-committee on Courts, Civil Liberties, and the Administration of Justice of the U.S. House Committee on the Judiciary and whose published transcript is entitled *Copyright Royalty Tribunal and U.S. Copyright Office* were far from routine. These hearings focused on the controversial and problematical function of the CRT. Subcommittee chairman Robert W. Kastenmeier (D-Wis.) set the tone of the hearings by saying that he had "little doubt that the Tribunal is in dire need of reform." He continued, "The subcommittee has had a classic case of a broken agency on its hands. I do not know whether the agency is broken beyond repair." Congressman Kastenmeier then stated the purpose of the hearings as an inquiry into "whether the [CRT] generally is effective and whether the Commissioners' relative lack of expertise, . . . in copyright law has hurt the Tribunal in terms of its deliberations; whether judicial review has been meaningful; [and] whether the absence of clear guidance from Congress on how the Tribunal shall make rate decisions creates a statutory defect that ought to be rectified" (pp. 1–2). Needless to say, the operation and structure of the CRT are given a thorough review during the course of these hearings.

CRT Reform and Compulsory Licenses contains hearings conducted by the Subcommittee on Courts, Civil Liberties, and the Administration of Justice of the U.S. House Committee on the Judiciary that continue the critical review of the CRT. These particular hearings considered H.R. 2752 and H.R. 2784 and had as their chief function an examination of the usefulness of the CRT with an eye to abolishing the agency, given its inattention by the White House, the inexperience of its political appointees, and the agency's small staff and low funding.

Periodical Articles

Most articles noted here are found in law journals and reviews and have a relatively general subject focus, given the ever-changing nature of cable law and regulations. Jill Stern, Erwin Krasnow, and R. Michael Senkowski's "The New Video Marketplace and the Search for a Coherent Regulatory Philosophy" provides a thorough overview of competing electronic delivery systems and offers commentary on new theories of electronic media regulation. Different approaches to cable regulation amid the influence and competition of other media are found in Neil Hamilton's "Implications for Economic Regulation of Cable Television." Tracing the evolution of cable television regulation is "A Review of Federal, State, and Local Regulation of Cable Television in the United States" by Adrian E. Herbst, Gary R. Matz, and John F. Gibbs. The role served by the judiciary in establishing regulatory boundaries for the FCC's oversight of cable television appears in Jonathan Mallamud's "Courts, Statutes, and Administrative Agency Jurisdiction: A Consideration of Limits on Judicial Creativity."

William Owen Knox questions the constitutionality of cable franchising in "Cable Franchising and the First Amendment: Does the Franchising Process Contravene First Amendment Rights?" Also addressing the same matter are William E. Lee's "Cable Franchising and the First Amendment" and Donald Cook's "Cable Television: The Constitutional Limitations of Local Government Control." How cable franchising requirements conflict with cable system construction is viewed in Alida Camp's "Anti-Cream-

Skimming Regulations: Do They Infringe Cable Television's First-Amendment Rights?"

Antitrust litigation has accompanied cable system monopoly charges in recent years. Exploring the antitrust subject are Michael Botein's "Cable Television Franchising and the Antitrust Laws: A Preliminary Analysis of Substantive Standards" and Paul S. Ryerson's "Cable Television Franchising without Antitrust Immunity: The Aftermath of *Boulder*." Antitrust is viewed from a forum perspective as Robert Blau and Michael O. Wirth respond to Thomas W. Hazlett's position in "The Policy of Exclusive Franchising in Cable Television."

Christine Gasser comments on freedom of expression relative to cable in "Cable Television: A New Challenge for the 'Old' First Amendment." Douglas H. Ginsburg's "Rights of Excess: Cable and the First Amendment" and Glen O. Robinson's "Cable Television and the First Amendment" also concentrate on freedom of expression matters. The future of local regulation of cable program content is examined in John W. Witt's "Cable Television Content Regulation after *Crisp*: Is There Anything Left?" Roland S. Homet, Jr., comments on the First Amendment protection of commercial access to cable in " 'Getting the Message': Statutory Approaches to Electronic Information Delivery and the Duty of Carriage," and Mark Mininberg addresses the public access requirement for cable systems in "Circumstances within Our Control: Promoting Freedom of Expression through Cable Television."

The issue of regulatory control over indecent cable program content has been examined by several authors. Chief among the articles appearing on the subject are Jessica Sporn's "Content Regulation of Cable Television: 'Indecency' Statutes and the First Amendment," and Lynn D. Wardle's "Cable Comes of Age: A Constitutional Analysis of the Regulation of 'Indecent' Cable Television Programming."

Kenneth M. H. Hoff concentrates on cable privacy matters raised by interactive services and proposes a model privacy act in "Two-Way Cable Television and Informational Privacy." Additional comments on the cable privacy subject appear in John M. Wegner's "Home Interactive Media: An Analysis of Potential Abuses of Privacy."

Finally, issues surrounding cable copyright are addressed by Leslie Swackhamer in "Cable-Copyright: The Corruption of Consensus" and by Ralph Oman, whose "The Compulsory License Redux: Will It Survive in a Changing Marketplace?" looks at how the copyright compulsory license has fared in doing what it was meant to do.

THE 1984 CABLE ACT

Creation and Consideration

The Cable Communications Policy Act of 1984 is the progeny of several bills introduced in the U.S. House and Senate over the past few years. The bills have been either cable-specific, in that their content carried provisions applicable only to cable television, or divided between other forms of telecommunications media (primarily telephone) and cable, with provisions most often applicable to the division of services for which each medium would be responsible. Often, provisions of one bill among those related to this subject have closely resembled those of another, since the intent of both was essentially the same. Also, several of the bills not being acted upon during one Congress were reintroduced almost intact but with a different number assigned to them during a subsequent Congress.

Those bills that are most important in the legislative history of the Cable Act are S. 622 (introduced during the 96th Congress), S. 898 and S. 2172 (introduced during the 97th Congress), and S. 66 and its companion bill H.R. 4103 (introduced during the 98th Congress—S. 66 on 26 January 1983 and H.R. 4103 on 6 October 1983). The text of the Cable Act derives mainly from S. 66 as passed by the U.S. Senate on 14 June 1983 and approved by the U.S. House on 11 October 1984.

Government Documents: S. 622, S. 898, and S. 2172

Hearings on S. 622 were conducted by the Communications Subcommittee of the Senate Commerce, Science, and Transportation Committee during April, May, and June 1979. Four volumes of testimony and related information resulted from the hearings. All volumes are found under the general title *Amendments to the Communications Act of 1934*. Parts (or volumes) 2, 3, and 4 collectively focus most heavily on cable television. Part 2 covers hearings conducted in April and May 1979. Testimony during these hearings related almost exclusively to regulation of domestic and international common carriers and the telephone industry. The one exception is a small portion (pp. 841–942) devoted to telephone-cable television competition. A supplementary report by the Teleprompter Corporation on that subject, "Exclusion of Potential Competition from Community Antenna Television (CATV)" (pp. 850–87), is also included here.

Part 3 of *Amendments to the Communications Act of 1934* contains testimony and supplementary inserts from May and June 1979. Some of the more substantive matters covered during testimony included cable copyright royalty payments, economic impact of cable on other local media, and impact of cable television on professional sports. Insertions of special note included in part 3 are a report entitled "Effect of Cable Carriage of Distant Signals on the Audience and Revenue of Local Independent Television Stations," parts 1 and 2 (pp. 2208–95), prepared by Roger Cooper and Associates, and a report by the Young and Rubicam advertising agency on cable television's impact on advertising (pp. 2354–59). Only brief attention is given to cable television in part 4 of the Communications Subcommittee hearings. This volume covers hearings conducted in June 1979. Cable-related comments are directed primarily toward government-mandated access channels (pp. 2518–45).

The Senate Communications Subcommittee considered S. 898 during hearings on 22 June 1981. Portions of the published hearings, *Rural Telecommunications*, contain testimony on cable television availability in rural areas and telephone company cross-ownership of cable systems (pp. 28–65). The Senate Committee on Commerce, Science, and Transportation issued a report on S. 898 entitled *Telecommunications Competition and Deregulation Act of 1981* on 27 July 1981. Only a small portion of the document (pp. 54–59) explains those provisions of the bill affecting cable television. S. 898 was introduced for floor debate on 5 October 1981. Due to what Senator Barry Goldwater (R-Ariz.) considered insufficient attention to cable television during Senate hearings, he introduced an amendment to delete S. 898 provisions pertaining to cable. Senator Goldwater's amendment (No. 541) was approved by a 59–34 vote on October 6.[65]

Hearings by the Senate Communications Subcommittee conducted in April 1982 applied to consideration of S. 2172. *Cable Television Regulation— Part 2* contains testimony from those hearings related to cable television local regulation and ownership, investment requirements for cable, cable television competition in local markets, and restrictions on cable carriage of professional sports events. S. 2172 was reported from committee on 10 August 1982. The report, *Cable Telecommunications Act of 1982*, contains the most comprehensive examination of cable television regulatory needs and policy revisions prior to consideration and passage of the 1984 Cable Act.

Government Documents: Supplemental Hearings

Other congressional hearings were conducted during 1981 and 1982 that, although unrelated to specific legislation, nonetheless contributed important information toward later cable television legislation. The first such series of hearings was conducted by the Subcommittee on Telecommunications, Consumer Protection, and Finance of the House Energy and Commerce Committee in June and July 1981 and published under the title *Telecommunications Miscellaneous—Part 1*. Pertinent subject matter covered in hearings testimony pertains to cable television's economic impact on broadcast television, cable television ownership, municipal ownership of cable television systems, and general problems of local cable system franchising (pp. 486–684).

Both the Senate Commerce, Science, and Transportation Committee and the House Subcommittee on Telecommunications conducted hearings outside of Washington, on cable television system franchising. The Senate committee's hearings occurred in January 1982 in Seattle, Washington, and in February 1982 in Albuquerque, New Mexico. Testimony primarily from municipal and cable television officials in these two locations was published in *Cable Television Regulation—Part 1*. The House subcommittee hearings were conducted in Chicago in March 1982. Testimony from the hearings appears in *Cable Franchise Investigation: Local Participation*. The document's title reflects the hearings' general subject matter, but specific attention is paid to minority participation in the cable television industry.

Finally, hearings on H.R. 1155, a bill not intended to affect cable television regulation per se but rather to increase minority ownership and participation in the cable industry, were conducted in Chicago by the House Telecommunications Subcommittee in June 1983. Hearings testimony was published under the title *Parity for Minorities in the Media*. Comments focus primarily on minority problems in the media and enforcement of FCC equal employment opportunity rules. Supplementary inserts include "Cable System Employment 1980–1981, A Report on the Status of Minorities and Women" by Janice M. Engsberg, Allan T. Walters, and Gracie B. Nettingham (pp. 32–115); a National Association of Broadcasters report on minority ownership and employment status in the broadcasting and cable television industries (pp. 147–67); a report entitled "Minority Business Involvement in the Telecommunications Industry" prepared by Resources Inc. of Washington, D.C. (pp. 192–280); and a study prepared by Allen S. Hammond entitled "Now You See It, Now You Don't: Minority Ownership in an 'Unregulated' Video Marketplace" (pp. 281–346).

Government Documents: S. 66 and H.R. 4103

Hearings on S. 66, the bill that upon amendment would become the Cable Act, were conducted by the Senate Communications Subcommittee of the Committee on Commerce, Science, and Transportation in February 1983. Hearings testimony appears in *Cable Telecommunications Act of 1983*. Major comments center on cable television deregulation, division of local and federal regulatory jurisdiction, and cable television competition with other emerging media.

S. 66 was reported from committee on 27 April 1983 under the report title *Cable Telecommunications Act of 1983*. Senate deliberation on S. 66 followed on June 13 and 14, with the bill's passage occurring on the 14th.[66]

Hearings on H.R. 4103, the companion bill to S. 66, were held in May, June, and November 1983. Testimony and supplemental material were published under the title *Options for Cable Legislation*. Matters discussed cover a broad range of topics, including the pros and cons of the NLC-NCTA compromise agreement on cable system franchising; the effects of current and projected cable television regulations on the cable industry, municipalities, consumers, and the economic marketplace in general; the cost of cable service; the nature of cable television program content; cable television access channels and facilities; the impact of interactive cable television services on the telephone industry; and the role of cable television in competition with other emerging electronic media delivery systems.

Options for Cable Legislation also contains several important supplementary items. Among them are a research report, "Competitive Policy Considerations in Cable Television Franchising," by Bruce M. Owen and Peter

R. Greenhalgh (pp. 69–117); "Critique of 'The Cost of Cable Television Regulatory and Franchise Requirements: A Preliminary Analysis,' " prepared by Hyman Goldin and Yale Brauenstein for the Telecommunications Research and Action Center in response to an earlier NCTA-commissioned study (pp. 330–45); a report by Robert M. Entman entitled "Ain't Misbehavin'? Cable Television Franchising and the Case for Local Deregulation" (pp. 346–409); and a study, "Cable, Content Regulation, and the First Amendment," by Henry Geller and Donna Lampert (pp. 446–97).

The House Committee on Energy and Commerce reported H.R. 4103 under the title *Cable Franchise Policy and Communications Act of 1984* on 1 August 1984. The full House deliberated on H.R. 4103 but tabled the bill on October 1 in favor of the Senate's S. 66. However, reservations about some of the provisions of the Senate bill delayed final House approval until a conference committee could consider House amendments to the measure.[67] On 11 October 1984 the Senate agreed to the House amendments and added several more amendments to S. 66 before returning the bill to the House for final approval on the same day.[68]

Periodicals/Newspapers

Three periodicals that provide the most substantive and comprehensive information about the Cable Act are *Multichannel News*, *CableVision*, and *Broadcasting*. Articles from each overlap at times, especially when devoted to specific legislative events that occurred during committee deliberations on cable measures. Each periodical, however, devotes some space to analytical pieces or commentary dealing with three primary topics: the NLC-NCTA negotiations, reaction to matters occurring at various stages of congressional activity surrounding cable legislation, and postenactment assessments of the Cable Act's impact on the cable television industry in particular and the telecommunications industry in general.

Implementation and Reaction

Government Documents

The Cable Communications Policy Act of 1984 was published as Public Law 98–549.[69] The law became effective sixty days after its 30 October 1984 enactment. In order to bring FCC rules into specific compliance with the Cable Act, the commission established a rulemaking proceeding in December 1984. *Implementing the Provisions of the Cable Communications Policy Act of 1984* contains the FCC's proposed new rules and rule revisions. After an FCC review of comments on the matter, the rules appeared in their final form in *Implementation of the Provisions of the Cable Communications Policy Act of 1984*.

Books

The PLI books mentioned earlier contain an assortment of material that not only traces the history of the Cable Act but also provides excellent commentary on the important implementation phases of that history. Two of the PLI books, *Communications Law 1983*, vol. 2 (no. 169), and *Communications Law 1984*, vol. 1 (no. 188), carry pieces by former FCC chairman Richard Wiley under the same title, "The Media and the Communications Revolution: An Overview of the Regulatory Framework and Developing Trends." Both pieces are written in outline form and serve as an overview of the purpose for federal regulation of cable television and as a review (as of October 1983 for no. 169 and October 1984 for no. 188) of applicable cable television rules. Important FCC and judicial citations to cases affecting cable television regulation also accompany the Wiley pieces.

Three later PLI books are even more content-specific regarding the Cable Act. *The New Era in CATV: The Cable Franchise Policy and Communications Act of 1984* (no. 194) carries several pieces presented in survey-outline fashion examining application of the Cable Act and the changes that the law will require in municipal cable television regulation. A companion book in terms of subject matter is *A Practical Guide to the Cable Communications Policy Act of 1984* (no. 200). This book provides information of a similar nature to *The New Era in CATV* but includes pieces covering a greater range of commentary on the Cable Act. The more recent publication date of the latter book makes its content somewhat more timely. Both books carry copies of pertinent government documents related to the Cable Act. *The New Era in CATV*, for instance, includes a copy of the FCC document no. 84–1296, *Amendment of Parts 1, 63, and 76 of the Commission's Rules to Implement the Provisions of the Cable Communications Policy Act of 1984*, released on 11 December 1984, with a copy of the Cable Act appended. Also included is a copy of the House committee report on H.R. 4103 released on 1 August 1984 entitled *Cable Franchise Policy and Communications Act of 1984*. A third PLI book, *Cable Television: Retrospective and Prospective* (no. 214), carries articles, commentary, and documents on a number of cable television legal and regulatory matters in the light of the implementation of the Cable Act. The book's appendices carry copies of the Cable Act, excerpts from congressional debate on the act, and FCC rulemaking related to the Cable Act.

Another book that follows the format of PLI books is *The Cable Communications Policy Act of 1984*. Included in this book are brief reports and comments, generally in outline form, on a number of subjects that together form a comprehensive picture of how the Cable Act is to be applied to various cable television practices. Some examples of the content are G. Todd Hardy's "1984 Cable Act—Enforceability and Modification of Existing Franchises: An Operator's Perspective"; George H. Shapiro's "Renewal of Franchise Procedures under the New Act"; and Paul Rodgers' "Catchall Provisions of the New Act."

One of the outstanding sources for information on Cable Act implementation and for cable television law and regulations in general is Ferris,
Lloyd, and Casey's *Cable Television Law*, noted earlier in this chapter. The
authors were prompt in preparing a supplement booklet on the Cable Act
soon after the law's enactment.

Of equal significance are three other excellent books, also mentioned
earlier, whose content reflects changes in cable regulations as a result of the
Cable Act's passage. Brenner/Price's *Cable Television and Other Nonbroadcast
Video: Law and Policy* was written after the act became effective and has
what is perhaps the most comprehensive statement of the law's impact upon
various facets of the cable business. Both the Hamburg *All about Cable* and
the Stein *Cable Television: Handbook and Forms* have been updated since their
original publication to include regulatory changes resulting from the Cable
Act.

Cynthia Pols, Norman M. Sinel, and Paul S. Ryerson have edited *Cable
Franchising and Regulation: A Local Government Guide to the New Law* as a
guidebook for local municipal officers and attorneys who must cope with
interpreting the 1984 Cable Act provisions regarding cable franchise matters.
The book's aim is to provide a "starting point for a full understanding" of
the rights and responsibilities of municipal officials under the act so as "to
prevent cable operators from taking unfair advantage of the complexities
of the new law" (pp. ii–iii). *Cable Franchising and Regulation* is divided into
four sections. Section 1 summarizes the Cable Act's legislative history.
Section 2 summarizes the major provisions of the act, and section 3 addresses
key issues arising from the act. The final section contains a copy of the
Cable Act itself.

In what could be described as a miniversion of the preceding book, Robert
G. Finney's "Cable Communications Policy Act of 1984" summarizes the
major components of the Cable Act, its history, and what its impact likely
will be on key players in the cable arena. Finney's essay appears in the *1985
Entertainment, Publishing, and the Arts Handbook*, edited by John David Viera
and Michael Meyer.

Periodical Articles

There has been too little time since the Cable Act became law to assess
its full impact. However, several articles, most of them from law journals
and reviews, attempt to at least project some possibilities onto the future
cable television regulatory landscape. Joseph R. Fogarty and Marcia Spielholz's "FCC Cable Jurisdiction: From Zero to Plenary in Twenty-Five
Years" and Daniel L. Brenner and Monroe E. Price's "The 1984 Cable Act:
Prologue and Precedents" create the context of pre- and post-Cable Act
regulation to examine what regulatory trends might now be expected. While
Fogarty and Spielholz confine their attention primarily to the evolution of
the FCC's regulatory jurisdiction over cable television and how the Cable

Act has altered or is likely to alter that jurisdiction, Brenner and Price broaden their attention, focusing on the Cable Act's preemptive impact on state and local regulatory authority.

Michael A. McGregor's "Will the Real Cable Television Industry Please Stand Up: The Divergent Regulatory Treatment of the Cable Television Industry prior to the Cable Communications Policy Act of 1984" perhaps should be read before reading either the Fogarty/Spielholz or Brenner/Price articles. Taking into account the Cable Act's future regulatory impact and how the FCC may apply the act's provisions to the cable television industry, McGregor examines past FCC policy decisions regarding the industry and finds an inconsistent history in policy formulation and application, based primarily on the commission's characterizations of an industry that is described at one time as strong and vigorous and at others as weak and struggling. The purpose of McGregor's article is to sort out the FCC's paradoxical characterizations.

Several other articles take different directions from those just mentioned. Michael Meyerson's "The Cable Communications Policy Act of 1984: A Balancing Act on the Coaxial Wires" provides an overview of three major considerations in the Cable Act: (1) federal jurisdiction over cable television in general, (2) the relationship between the cable television system operator and local government agencies, and (3) cable television and individual rights of access and privacy protection. R. Clark Wadlow and Linda M. Wellstein review the Cable Act along with judicial pronouncements such as occurred in the *Preferred* and *Quincy* decisions and comment on how all of these will influence the future development of cable television in "The Changing Regulatory Terrain of Cable Television." Similar matters, particularly in regard to the effect that the Cable Act and recent court decisions will have on cable television's First Amendment protection, are explored in Rosemary B. Healy's "*Preferred Communications, Inc. v. City of Los Angeles*: Impact of the First Amendment on Access Rights of Cable Television Companies"; Alan F. Ciamporcero's "Is There Any Hope for Cities? Recent Developments in Cable Television Law"; Scott Sibary's "The Cable Communications Policy Act of 1984 v. the First Amendment"; and Mark J. Bernet's "*Quincy Cable* and Its Effect on the Access Provisions of the 1984 Cable Act."

Articles by Sheryl Snyder and Randy Welch look at the purely local angle of the Cable Act. Snyder's "The Cable Communications Policy Act of 1984: Major Changes for Local Governments and Cable Providers" highlights changes in cable television regulation that will affect cable system operators and local municipalities in Kentucky. Snyder's comments are, however, relevant to cable television systems and municipalities nationwide. Randy Welch's "Regulating Cable Television" points to problem areas that will remain in cable television regulation for some time to come, regardless of the success of the Cable Act. "Cable's growing technology and importance," says Welch, "make return bouts with state legislatures inevitable" (p. 27).

How local cable system operators and local municipal franchising authorities perceived their situations both before and after passage of the Cable Act was the subject of a survey conducted by Wenmouth Williams, Jr., and Kathleen Mahoney and reported in "Perceived Impact of the Cable Policy Act of 1984." The Cable Act's impact on the consumer in terms of privacy protection, satellite signal reception, program content control, subscription fees, and cable access services is briefly reviewed in Patrick B. McCauley and Laurie Orlando's "The Rights of the Consumer under the Cable Communications Policy Act of 1984."

Lawrence Blaskopf's "Defining the Relevant Product Market of the New Video Technologies" considers the complex requirement of the Cable Act that the FCC determine the nature of the competitive market in which local cable television systems operate in order to either allow or prohibit local franchising authorities' establishment of permissible subscriber rates. The FCC's part in establishing what Blaskopf calls a "relevant product market" has implications for future antitrust action. Subscriber rate oversight is also scrutinized in Ronald Berman's "The End of Government Regulation of the Rates Cable Television Services Charge Their Subscribers." Fees of a different nature are examined by David J. Saylor. In "Municipal Ripoff: The Unconstitutionality of Cable Television Franchise Fees and Access Support Payments" Saylor questions the legality of annual franchise fees and support fees to finance access facilities that cable system operators must pay municipalities.

Deborah A. George's "The Cable Communications Policy Act of 1984 and Content Regulation of Cable Television" addresses the problem of regulators attempting to define objectionable program content and prohibiting its airing by cable television systems in view of program content provisions of the Cable Act. While the scope of his article is more wide-ranging than that of the George article, Howard M. Kleiman explores some of the considerations of those individuals who constructed the Cable Act's program content provisions in his "Indecent Programming on Cable Television: Legal and Social Dimensions." William Hanks and Carolyn Hanks comment on what appears to be an incompatible relationship between state obscenity statutes pertaining to cable program content and federal jurisdiction over such matters as embodied in the Cable Act in "Federal Preemption of State Regulation of X-Rated Movies on Cable Television." Similar territory is covered in William E. Hanks and Stephen E. Coran's "Federal Preemption of Obscenity Law Applied to Cable Television."

The fundamental issues comprising the controversy that continues between owners of TVRO satellite dishes and cable, most often pay cable, program suppliers are nicely framed in Robert D. Haymer's "Who Owns the Air? Unscrambling the Satellite Viewing Rights Dilemma." Haymer places his comments within the context of the Cable Act provisions on the subject. Doing the same but with special attention to the freedom given by the Cable Act to the private household use of satellite-received programming is Richard L. Brown and Lauritz S. Helland's "Section 605 of the Communications Act: Teaching a Salty Old Sea Dog New Tricks." Terry S. Bienstock and Philip J. Kantor's "Unauthorized Interception of Satellite Programming: Does Section 705's 'Private Viewing' Exemption Apply to Condominium and Apartment Complexes?" takes yet another slant on Cable Act provisions regarding satellite-received programming.

NOTES

1. Joseph R. Fogarty and Marcia Spielholz, "FCC Cable Jurisdiction: From Zero to Plenary in Twenty-Five Years," *Federal Communications Law Journal* 37 (Winter 1985): 113.

2. *Cable Communications Policy Act of 1984*, Pub. L. no. 98–549, 98 Stat. 2779 (1984).

3. *Cable Television Report and Order*, 36 FCC 2d 143 (1972), reconsidered, 36 FCC 2d 326 (1972).

4. Senate Committee on Commerce, Science, and Transportation, *Cable Telecommunications Act of 1983*, 98th Cong., 1st sess., 1983, S. Rept. 98–67, p. 6.

5. Ibid.

6. Ibid., pp. 8–9.

7. Ibid., p. 9.

8. Erwin G. Krasnow, Lawrence D. Longley, and Herbert A. Terry, *The Politics of Broadcast Regulation*, 3d ed. (New York: St. Martin's Press, 1982), p. 26.

9. Senate Committee on Commerce, Science, and Transportation, *Cable Telecommunications Act of 1983*, p. 9.

10. House Committee on Energy and Commerce, *Cable Franchise Policy and Communications Act of 1984*, 98th Cong., 2d sess., 1984, H. Rept. 98–934, p. 21.

11. George Latimer, letter to U.S. Rep. John D. Dingell, 25 January 1984.

12. Craig Leddy, "Cable Deregulation Passes As Legislators Compromise," *Electronic Media*, 18 October 1984, p. 2.

13. "Cable's Cliffhanger," *Broadcasting*, 1 October 1984, p. 106.

14. "What the New Law Does," *Multichannel News*, 22 October 1984, pp. 1+.

15. "Cable Industry Is Ready to Roll," *Broadcasting*, 10 December 1984, p. 31.

16. Michael Botein, "Who Came Out Ahead in the Cable Act," *Channels*, March/April 1985, p. 14.

17. *Implementing the Provisions of the Cable Communications Policy Act of 1984*, 49 *Fed. Reg.* 48765, 14 December 1984.

18. "FCC Approves Rules That Will Deregulate 80 Percent of Systems," *Multichannel News*, 15 April 1985, p. 1.

19. *A Cable Primer* (Washington, D.C.: National Cable Television Association, 1981), p. 23.

20. Patrick D. Maines, "Cable Franchising Process Invites Political Folly," *Media Institute Forum*, May/June 1984, p. 1.

21. Clint Bolick, "Cable Television: An Unnatural Monopoly," Cato Institute Policy Analysis, no. 34, 13 March 1984, pp. 4–5.

22. House Committee on Energy and Commerce, *Cable Franchise Policy and Communications Act of 1984*, pp. 63–64.

23. Ibid., p. 26.

24. "Cable Op-City Relationships Seen Hinging on Court Cases," *Multichannel News*, 11 May 1987, p. 43.

25. Pub. L. no 95–234, 92 Stat. 33 (1978).

26. Fred Dawson, "Pole Attachment Politics," *CableVision Plus*, 30 July 1984, pp. 5–10.

27. *Federal Communications Commission et al. v. Florida Power Corporation et al.*, no. 85–1658, Slip Opinion, 25 February 1987.

28. Michael Botein, "Jurisdictional and Antitrust Considerations in the Regulation of the New Communications Technologies," *New York Law School Law Review* 25 (1980): 879.

29. *Community Communications Company, Inc. v. City of Boulder*, 455 U.S. 40 (1982).

30. *Preferred Communications, Inc. v. City of Los Angeles, California*, 754 F. 2d 1396 (1985).

31. *City of Los Angeles et al. v. Preferred Communications, Inc.*, No. 85–390, Slip Opinion, 2 June 1986.

32. Ronald Garay, "Politics and Cable Television: The Case of Houston, Texas," in *Communication Yearbook* 7, ed. Robert N. Bostrom (Beverly Hills, Calif.: Sage, 1983), pp. 443–61.

33. *Affiliated Capital Corporation v. City of Houston*, 735 F. 2d 1555, 1563 (1984).

34. Nicholas P. Miller and Larrine S. Holbrooke, "Cable and the Cities: A Clash of Rights," *Channels*, May/June 1985, p. 10.

35. Steve Weinstein, "Sex and Cable," *CableVision*, 11 February 1985, pp. 28–32; and Michael Meyerson, "Cable's 'New Obnoxiousness' Tests the First Amendment," *Channels*, March/April 1985, pp. 40–42.

36. "Decency Case," *Broadcasting*, 15 April 1985, p. 10.

37. 555 F. Supp. 1164 (1982).

38. "Appeals Court Agrees Utah Law Violates First Amendment," *Broadcasting*, 15 September 1986, p. 100.

39. John Wolfe, "Supreme Court Lifts Cloud over R Fare," *CableVision*, 13 April 1987, p. 18.

40. J. L. Freeman, "FCC, ACLU Testify against Cable-Porn Bill," *Multichannel News*, 5 August 1985, p. 8.

41. J. L. Freeman, "Meese Cites Cable TV in Naming Porno Panel," *Multichannel News*, 27 May 1985, pp. 1, 34.

42. 413 U.S. 15 (1973).

43. House Committee on Energy and Commerce, *Cable Franchise Policy and Communications Act of 1984*, pp. 69–70.

44. Richard M. Neustadt, Gregg P. Skall, and Michael Hammer, "The Regulation of Electronic Publication," *Federal Communications Law Journal* 33 (Summer 1981): 345.

45. Richard M. Neustadt, "Regulating Abundance," *Telecommunications*, September 1981, p. 53.

46. Deanna C. Nash and David A. Bollier, "Protecting Privacy in the Age of Hometech," *Technology Review*, August/September 1981, p. 67.

47. Gary Witt, "Who's Watching Whom?" *Cable Vision Plus*, 6 June 1983, pp. 5–8.

48. David R. Sidall, "Cable Television Compulsory Copyright License Fees for Retransmission of Programs on New (Post Malrite) Distant Broadcast Signals" (unpublished report, Congressional Research Service, 14 March 1983), pp. 3–11.

49. J. L. Freeman, "Cable Industry Targets Copyright Reform in '85," *Multichannel News*, 3 December 1984, pp. 11 +.

50. Les Brown, "The Coming Showdown between Cable and Broadcasting," *Channels*, July/August 1983, pp. 23–24.

51. *Quincy Cable TV, Inc. v. F.C.C.*, 768 F. 2d 1434 (1985).

52. "The Deal Is Done on Must Carry," *Broadcasting*, 3 March 1986, pp. 31–34.

53. "Cable Wins in Quincy," *Broadcasting*, 16 June 1986, p. 31.

54. William Mahoney, "Must-Carry Highlights," *Electronic Media*, 11 August 1986, p. 30.

55. "Cable Television; Amendment of the Commission's Rules Concerning Carriage of Television Broadcast Signals by Cable Television Systems," 51 *Fed. Reg.* 44606, 11 December 1986.

56. "Amendment of Part 76 of the Commission's Rules Concerning Carriage of Television Broadcast Signals by Cable Television Systems," 2 FCC Rcd. 603 (1987).

57. John Wolfe, "Key Congressmen Express Dismay at FCC Revision of Must-Carry," *Cable Vision*, 13 April 1987, p. 14.

58. Charles F. Luce, Jr., "Scuttling the Air Pirates: Theories of Pay Television Signal Theft Liability," *Communications and the Law* 4 (Fall 1982): 18.

59. John Wolfe, "The Cable Act and Cable Theft: Hopes Rest on Civil Case Impact," *Cable Vision*, 2 March 1987, p. 38.

60. Ibid.

61. Richard L. Brown and Lauritz S. Helland, "Section 605 of the Communications Act: Teaching a Salty Old Sea Dog New Tricks," *Catholic University Law Review* 34 (Spring 1985): 635.

62. "Earth Station Battle Goes to the Hill," *Broadcasting*, 10 March 1986, p. 35.

63. Albert Gore, Jr., "Protecting Fair Access to Cable Satellite Programming: The Satellite Television Viewing Rights Act of 1985," *Memphis State University Law Review* 15 (Spring 1985): 343–44.

64. J. L. Freeman, "Senate Kills Scrambling Bill on 54–44 Vote; HBO, Showtime Offer TVRO 'Electronic Lockbox,' " *Multichannel News*, 6 October 1986, p. 1.

65. *Congressional Record* 127 (daily ed., 5 October 1981): S11018; (daily ed., 6 October 1981): S11133–35.

66. *Congressional Record* 129 (daily ed., 13 June 1983): S8244–78; (daily ed., 14 June 1983): S8291–98, S8303–28.

67. *Congressional Record* 130 (daily ed., 1 October 1984): H10427–51.

68. *Congressional Record* 130 (daily ed., 11 October 1984): S14281–97; H12234–44.

69. 98 Stat. 2779.

BIBLIOGRAPHY

Books and Book Chapters

General Survey

Bittner, John R. *Broadcast Law and Regulation*. Englewood Cliffs, N.J.: Prentice-Hall, 1982.

Botein, Michael, and Michael B. Sprague. "Regulation of Telecommunications in the United States." In *Telecommunications for Management*, edited by Charles T. Meadow and Albert S. Tedesco. New York: McGraw-Hill, 1985.

Cass, Ronald A. *Revolution in the Wasteland: Value and Diversity in Television*. Charlottesville, Va.: University Press of Virginia, 1981.

Diamond, Edwin, Norman Sandler, and Milton Mueller. *Telecommunications in Crisis: The First Amendment, Technology, and Deregulation*. Washington, D.C.: Cato Institute, 1983.

Dolan, Edward V. *TV or CATV? A Struggle for Power*. Port Washington, N.Y.: Associated Faculty Press, 1984.

Franklin, Marc A. *Cases and Materials on Mass Media Law*. 3d ed. Mineola, N.Y.: Foundation Press, 1986.

Gillmor, Donald M., and Jerome A. Barron. *Mass Communication Law: Cases and Comment*. 4th ed. St. Paul, Minn.: West Publishing, 1984.

Heffron, Florence. "The Federal Communications Commission and Broadcast Deregulation." In *Communications Policy and the Political Process*, edited by John J. Havick. Westport, Conn.: Greenwood Press, 1983.

National Association of Broadcasters Legal Guide to FCC Broadcast Regulations. 2d ed. Washington, D.C.: National Association of Broadcasters, 1984.

Owen, Bruce M. "The Rise and Fall of Cable Television Regulation." In *Case Studies in Regulation: Revolution and Reform*, edited by Leonard W. Weiss and Michael W. Klass. Boston, Mass.: Little, Brown and Company, 1981.

Pember, Don R. *Mass Media Law*. 4th ed. Dubuque, Iowa: Wm. C. Brown, 1987.

Rice, David M., Michael Botein, and Edward B. Samuels. *Development and Regulation of New Communications Technologies*. New York: Communications Media Center of New York Law School, 1980.

Webbink, Douglas W. "The Recent Deregulatory Movement at the FCC." In *Telecommunications in the U.S.: Trends and Policies*, edited by Leonard Lewin. Dedham, Mass.: Artech House, 1981.

Zuckman, Harvey L., and Martin J. Gaynes. *Mass Communications Law in a Nutshell*. 2d ed. St. Paul, Minn.: West Publishing, 1983.

General Survey, Cable-Specific

Antitrust, the Media, and the New Technology. No. 137. New York: Practising Law Institute, 1981.

Baldwin, Thomas F., and D. Stevens McVoy. *Cable Communication*. Englewood Cliffs, N.J.: Prentice-Hall, 1983.

Brenner, Daniel L., and Monroe E. Price. *Cable Television and Other Nonbroadcast Video: Law and Policy*. New York: Clark Boardman Company, 1986.

Broadcasting/Cablecasting Yearbook. Washington, D.C.: Broadcasting Publications.

Cable Television in a New Era. No. 158. New York: Practising Law Institute, 1983.

Cable Television: Retrospective and Prospective. No. 214. New York: Practising Law Institute, 1985.

Campaign '84: Advertising and Programming Obligations of the Electronic Media. No. 165. New York: Practising Law Institute, 1983.

Communications Law 1980. Vol. 2. No. 125. New York: Practising Law Institute, 1980.

Communications Law 1982. Vol. 2. No. 154. New York: Practising Law Institute, 1982.

Communications Law 1983. Vol. 2. No. 169. New York: Practising Law Institute, 1983.

Communications Law 1984. Vol. 1. No. 188. New York: Practising Law Institute, 1984.

Communications Law 1986. Vol. 2. No. 232. New York: Practising Law Institute, 1986.

Current Development in CATV 1981. No. 129. New York: Practising Law Institute, 1981.

Ferris, Charles D., Frank W. Lloyd, and Thomas J. Casey. *Cable Television Law*. 3 vols. New York: Matthew Bender, 1985.

Firestone, Charles M., and Nicholas Johnson. *Cases and Materials on Communications Law and Policy*. 3 vols. Los Angeles, Calif.: UCLA School of Law, 1983.

Hamburg, Morton I. *All about Cable*. Rev. ed. New York: Law Journal Seminars-Press, 1985.

The New Era in CATV: The Cable Franchise Policy and Communications Act of 1984. No. 194. New York: Practising Law Institute, 1984.

New Program Opportunities in the Electronic Media. No. 164. New York: Practising Law Institute, 1983.

Ninth Annual Communications Law Institute. Vol. 1. No. 139. New York: Practising Law Institute, 1981.

A Practical Guide to the Cable Communications Policy Act of 1984. No. 200. New York: Practising Law Institute, 1984.

Sparkes, Vernone. "Cable Television in the United States: A Story of Continuing Growth and Change." In *Cable Television and the Future of Broadcasting*, edited by Ralph M. Negrine. New York: St. Martin's Press, 1985.

Stein, Ira C. *Cable Television: Handbook and Forms*. Colorado Springs, Colo.: Shepard's/McGraw-Hill, 1985.

Franchising

Baldwin. See entry under General Survey, Cable-Specific.

Brenner/Price. See entry under General Survey, Cable-Specific.

Dordick, Herbert S. *Public Television and Cable: New Working Opportunities in the Franchising and Refranchising Process*. Washington, D.C.: Corporation for Public Broadcasting, 1983.

Garay, Ronald. "Politics and Cable Television: The Case of Houston, Texas." In *Communication Yearbook 7*, edited by Robert Bostrom. Beverly Hills, Calif.: Sage, 1983.

Greenwald, Mark A. "The Telecommunications Role of Local Government." In

Communications and the Future, edited by Howard F. Didsbury, Jr. Bethesda, Md.: World Future Society, 1982.

Hamburg. See entry under General Survey, Cable-Specific.

Jesuale, Nancy J., and Ralph Lee Smith, eds. *A Guide for Local Policy*. Vol. II of *CTIC Cablebooks*. Arlington, Va.: Cable Television Information Center, 1982.

Rice, Jean, ed. *Cable TV Renewals and Refranchising*. Washington, D.C.: Communications Press, 1983.

Sherman, Randall Paul. "Blue Skies, Going Away? Directions in the Cable Television Industry." In *1984 Entertainment, Publishing, and the Arts Handbook*, edited by Michael Meyer and John David Viera. New York: Clark Boardman Company, 1984.

Siena, James V., ed. *Antitrust and Local Government: Perspectives on the Boulder Decision*. Cabin John, Md.: Seven Locks Press, 1982.

Speaker, David K., and David Z. Wirtschafter. "Cable Television Franchising." In *1983 Entertainment, Publishing, and the Arts Handbook*, edited by Michael Meyer and John David Viera. New York: Clark Boardman Company, 1983.

Stein. See entry under General Survey, Cable-Specific.

First Amendment

Carter, T. Barton, Marc A. Franklin, and Jay B. Wright. *The First Amendment and the Fourth Estate*. 3d ed. Mineola, N.Y.: Foundation Press, 1985.

Parsons, Patrick. *Cable Television and the First Amendment*. Lexington, Mass.: Lexington Books, 1987.

Pool, Ithiel de Sola. *Technologies of Freedom*. Cambridge, Mass.: Belknap Press, 1983.

Shapiro, George H., Philip B. Kurland, and James P. Mercurio. *'CableSpeech': The Case for First Amendment Protection*. New York: Harcourt Brace Jovanovich, 1983.

Interactive Cable and Privacy

Flaherty, David H. *Protecting Privacy in Two-Way Electronic Services*. White Plains, N.Y.: Knowledge Industry Publications, 1985.

Trauth, Denise M. and John F. Huffman. "Obscenity and Cable Television: A Regulatory Approach." *Journalism Monograph*, no. 95 (March 1986).

Copyright

Brenner/Price. See entry under General Survey, Cable-Specific.

Ladd, David. "A Pavan for Print: Accommodating Copyright to the Tele-Technologies." In *Cable Television: Media and Copyright Law Aspects*, edited by H. Cohen Jehoram. Boston, Mass.: Kluwer Law and Taxation Publishers, 1983.

Stein. See entry under General Survey, Cable-Specific.

Program Market Competition

White, Lawrence J. "Antitrust and Video Markets: The Merger of Showtime and The Movie Channel as a Case Study." In *1985 Entertainment, Publishing, and the Arts Handbook*, edited by Michael Meyer and John David Viera. New York: Clark Boardman Company, 1985.

Government Documents

U.S. House. Committee on the Judiciary. *Cable Television Copyright Act Amendments.* 97th Cong., 2d sess., 1982. H. Rept. 97–559, pt. 1.

_____. Subcommittee on Courts, Civil Liberties, and the Administration of Justice of the Committee on the Judiciary. *Copyright/Cable Television.* Pts. 1–2. 97th Cong., 1st–2d sess., 1981–1982. Hearing.

_____. *Copyright Office/Copyright Royalty Tribunal.* 98th Cong., 1st sess., 1983. Hearing.

_____. *Copyright Office, the U.S. Patent and Trademark Office, and the Copyright Royalty Tribunal.* 97th Cong., 1st sess., 1981. Hearing.

_____. *Copyright Royalty Fees for Cable Systems.* 98th Cong., 1st–2d sess., 1983–1984. Hearing.

_____. *Copyright Royalty Tribunal and U.S. Copyright Office.* 99th Cong., 1st sess., 1985. Hearing.

_____. *CRT Reform and Compulsory Licenses.* 99th Cong., 1st sess., 1985. Hearing.

_____. Subcommittee on Telecommunications, Consumer Protection, and Finance of the Committee on Energy and Commerce. *Cable Copyright Legislation.* 97th Cong., 2d. sess., 1982. Hearing.

_____. Subcommittee on Telecommunications, Consumer Protection, and Finance of the Committee on Energy and Commerce. *Unauthorized Reception of Subscription Television.* 97th Cong., 1st sess., 1981. Hearing.

U.S. Senate. Committee on Commerce, Science, and Transportation. *Freedom of Expression.* 97th Cong., 2d sess., 1982. Hearing.

_____. Committee on Commerce, Science, and Transportation and Committee on the Judiciary. *Cable Copyright and Signal Carriage Act of 1982.* 97th Cong., 2d sess., 1982. Joint Hearing.

_____. Committee on the Judiciary. *Oversight of the Copyright Act of 1976 (Cable Television).* 97th Cong., 1st sess., 1981. Hearing.

_____. Subcommittee on Criminal Law of the Committee on the Judiciary. *Cable-Porn and Dial-a-Porn Control Act.* 99th Cong., 1st sess., 1985. Hearing.

_____. Subcommittee on Patents, Copyrights, and Trademarks of the Committee on the Judiciary. *Oversight of the Copyright Office and the Copyright Royalty Tribunal.* 98th Cong., 1st sess., 1983. Hearing.

_____. *The Free Market Copyright Royalty Act of 1983.* 98th Cong., 2d sess., 1984. Hearing.

_____. *Proceedings of the Congressional Copyright and Technology Symposium.* 99th Cong., 1st sess., 1985. Committee Print.

Periodical Articles

Blau, Robert. "To Franchise or Not to Franchise: Is That Really the Question?" *Journal of Broadcasting and Electronic Media* 31 (Winter 1987): 95–97.

Botein, Michael. "Cable Television Franchising and the Antitrust Laws: A Preliminary Analysis of Substantive Standards." *Federal Communications Law Journal* 36 (December 1984): 253–82.

Camp, Alida. "Anti-Cream-Skimming Regulations: Do They Infringe Cable Television's First Amendment Rights?" *American Business Law Journal* 23 (Summer 1985): 203–55.

Cook, Donald. "Cable Television: The Constitutional Limitations of Local Government Control." *Southwestern University Law Review* 15 (1984): 181–215.

Gasser, Christine. "Cable Television: A New Challenge for the 'Old' First Amendment." *St. John's Law Review* 60 (Fall 1985): 114–43.

Ginsburg, Douglas H. "Rights of Excess: Cable and the First Amendment." *Communications and the Law* 6 (October 1984): 71–79.

Hamilton, Neil. "Implications for Economic Regulation of Cable Television." *William Mitchell Law Review* 10 (1984): 433–57.

Hazlett, Thomas W. "The Policy of Exclusive Franchising in Cable Television." *Journal of Broadcasting and Electronic Media* 31 (Winter 1987): 1–20.

Herbst, Adrian E., Gary R. Matz, and John F. Gibbs. "A Review of Federal, State, and Local Regulation of Cable Television in the United States." *William Mitchell Law Review* 10 (1984): 377–411.

Hoff, Kenneth M. H. "Two-Way Cable Television and Informational Privacy." *COMM/ENT Law Journal* 6 (Summer 1984): 797–836.

Homet, Roland S., Jr. " 'Getting the Message': Statutory Approaches to Electronic Information Delivery and the Duty of Carriage." *Federal Communications Law Journal*, 37 (April 1985): 217–92.

Knox, William Owen. "Cable Franchising and the First Amendment: Does the Franchising Process Contravene First Amendment Rights?" *Federal Communications Law Journal* 36 (December 1984): 317–35.

Lee, William E. "Cable Franchising and the First Amendment." *Vanderbilt Law Review* 36 (May 1983): 867–928.

Mallamud, Jonathan. "Courts, Statutes, and Administrative Agency Jurisdiction: A Consideration of Limits on Judicial Creativity." *South Carolina Law Review* 35 (Winter 1984): 191–293.

Mininberg, Mark. "Circumstances within Our Control: Promoting Freedom of Expression through Cable Television." *Hastings Constitutional Law Quarterly* 11 (Summer 1984): 551–98.

Oman, Ralph. "The Compulsory License Redux: Will It Survive in a Changing Marketplace?" *Cardozo Arts and Entertainment Law Journal* 5 (1986): 37–50.

Robinson, Glen O. "Cable Television and the First Amendment." *Communications and the Law* 6 (October 1984): 47–61.

Ryerson, Paul S. "Cable Television Franchising without Antitrust Immunity: The Aftermath of *Boulder*." *Urban Lawyer* 16 (Summer 1984): 387–422.

Sporn, Jessica. "Content Regulation of Cable Television: 'Indecency' Statutes and the First Amendment." *Rutgers Computer and Technology Law Journal* 11 (1985): 141–70.

Stern, Jill, Erwin Krasnow, and R. Michael Senkowski. "The New Video Marketplace and the Search for a Coherent Regulatory Philosophy." *Catholic University Law Review* 32 (Spring 1983): 529–602.

Swackhamer, Leslie. "Cable-Copyright: The Corruption of Consensus." *COMM/ENT Law Journal* 6 (Winter 1984): 283–324.

Wardle, Lynn D. "Cable Comes of Age: A Constitutional Analysis of the Regulation of 'Indecent' Cable Television Programming." *Denver University Law Review* 63 (Winter 1986): 621–95.

Wegner, John M. "Home Interactive Media: An Analysis of Potential Abuses of Privacy." *Journal of Broadcasting and Electronic Media* 29 (Winter 1985): 51–63.

Wirth, Michael O. "Comment on 'The Policy of Exclusive Franchising in Cable Television.' " *Journal of Broadcasting and Electronic Media*, 31 (Winter 1987): 98–101.

Witt, John W. "Cable Television Content Regulation after *Crisp*: Is There Anything Left?" *Urban Lawyer* 17 (Spring 1985): 277–97.

THE CABLE COMMUNICATIONS POLICY ACT OF 1984: BIBLIOGRAPHY

Creation and Consideration

Government Documents

U.S. House. Committee on Energy and Commerce. *Cable Franchise Policy and Communications Act of 1984.* 98th Cong., 2d sess., 1984. H. Rept. 98–934.

————. *Options for Cable Legislation.* 98th Cong., 1st sess., 1983. Hearing.

————. Subcommittee on Telecommunications, Consumer Protection, and Finance of the Committee on Energy and Commerce. *Cable Franchise Investigation: Local Participation.* 97th Cong., 2d sess., 1982. Hearing.

————. *Parity for Minorities in the Media.* 98th Cong., 1st sess., 1983. Hearing.

————. *Telecommunications Miscellaneous—Part 1.* 97th Cong., 1st sess., 1981. Hearing.

U.S. Senate. Committee on Commerce, Science, and Transportation. *Cable Telecommunications Act of 1982.* 97th Cong., 2d sess., 1982. S. Rept. 97–518.

————. *Cable Telecommunications Act of 1983.* 98th Cong., 1st sess., 1983. S. Rept. 98–67.

————. *Cable Television Regulation—Part 1.* 97th Cong., 2d sess., 1982. Hearing.

————. *Telecommunications Competition and Deregulation Act of 1981.* 97th Cong., 1st sess., 1981. S. Rept. 97–170.

————. Subcommittee on Communications of the Committee on Commerce, Science, and Transportation. *Amendments to the Communications Act of 1934.* Pts. 2–4. 96th Cong., 1st sess., 1979. Hearing.

————. *Cable Telecommunications Act of 1983.* 98th Cong., 1st sess., 1983. Hearing.

————. *Cable Television Regulation—Part 2.* 97th Cong., 2d sess., 1982. Hearing.

————. *Rural Telecommunications.* 97th Cong., 1st sess., 1981. Hearing.

Implementation and Reaction

Government Documents

Federal Communications Commission. *Implementing the Provisions of the Cable Communications Policy Act of 1984.* 49 *Federal Register* 48765, 14 December 1984.

_____. *Implementation of the Provisions of the Cable Communications Policy Act of 1984.* 50 *Federal Register* 18637, 2 May 1985.

Books

The Cable Communications Policy Act of 1984. New York: Harcourt Brace Jovanovich, 1985.

Cable Television: Retrospective and Prospective. No. 214. New York: Practising Law Institute, 1985.

Communications Law 1983. Vol. 2. No. 169. New York: Practising Law Institute, 1983

Communications Law 1984. Vol. 1. No. 188. New York: Practising Law Institute, 1984.

Ferris/Lloyd/Casey. See entry under General Survey, Cable-Specific.

Finney, Robert G. "Cable Communications Policy Act of 1984." In *1985 Entertainment, Publishing, and the Arts Handbook*, edited by John David Viera and Michael Meyer. New York: Clark Boardman Company, 1985.

Hamburg. See entry under General Survey, Cable-Specific.

The New Era in CATV: The Cable Franchise Policy and Communications Act of 1984. No. 194. New York: Practising Law Institute, 1985.

Pols, Cynthia, Norman M. Sinel, and Paul S. Ryerson, eds. *Cable Franchising and Regulation: A Local Government Guide to the New Law.* Washington, D.C.: National League of Cities, 1985.

A Practical Guide to the Cable Communications Policy Act of 1984. No. 200. New York: Practising Law Institute, 1984.

Stein. See entry under General Survey, Cable-Specific.

Periodical Articles

Berman, Ronald. "The End of Government Regulation of the Rates Cable Television Services Charge Their Subscribers." *Cardozo Arts and Entertainment Law Journal* 5 (1986): 157–93.

Bernet, Mark J. "*Quincy Cable* and Its Effect on the Access Provisions of the 1984 Cable Act." *Notre Dame Law Review* 61 (1986): 426–39.

Bienstock, Terry S., and Philip J. Kantor. "Unauthorized Interception of Satellite Programming: Does Section 705's 'Private Viewing' Exemption Apply to Condominium and Apartment Complexes?" *Entertainment and Sports Law Journal* 3 (Spring 1986): 107–113.

Blaskopf, Lawrence. "Defining the Relevant Product Market of the New Video Technologies." *Cardozo Arts and Entertainment Law Journal* 4 (1985): 75–103.

Brenner, Daniel L., and Monroe E. Price. "The 1984 Cable Act: Prologue and Precedents." *Cardozo Arts and Entertainment Law Journal* 4 (1985): 19–50.

Brown, Richard L., and Lauritz S. Helland. "Section 605 of the Communications Act: Teaching a Salty Old Sea Dog New Tricks." *Catholic University Law Review* 34 (Spring 1985): 635–70.

Ciamporcero, Alan F. "Is There Any Hope for Cities? Recent Developments in Cable Television Law." *Urban Lawyer* 18 (Spring 1986): 369–92.

Fogarty, Joseph R., and Marcia Spielholz. "FCC Cable Jurisdiction: From Zero to

Plenary in Twenty-Five Years." *Federal Communications Law Journal* 37 (Winter 1985): 113–29.

George, Deborah A. "The Cable Communications Policy Act of 1984 and Content Regulation of Cable Television." *New England Law Review* 20 (1984–1985): 779–804.

Hanks, William E., and Stephen E. Coran. "Federal Preemption of Obscenity Law Applied to Cable Television." *Journalism Quarterly* 63 (Spring 1986): 43–47.

Hanks, William, and Carolyn Hanks. "Federal Preemption of State Regulation of X-Rated Movies on Cable Television." *Mass Comm Review* 12 (1985): 18–22.

Haymer, Robert D. "Who Owns the Air? Unscrambling the Satellite Viewing Rights Dilemma." *Loyola of Los Angeles Law Review* 20 (November 1986): 145–79.

Healy, Rosemary B. "*Preferred Communications, Inc. v. City of Los Angeles*: Impact of the First Amendment on Access Rights of Cable Television Companies." *Catholic University Law Review* 35 (Spring 1986): 851–82.

Kleiman, Howard M. "Indecent Programming on Cable Television: Legal and Social Dimensions." *Journal of Broadcasting and Electronic Media* 30 (Summer 1986): 275–94.

Krug, Peter. "Cable Television Franchise Fees for General Revenue: The 1984 Cable Act, Wisconsin Law, and the First Amendment." *Wisconsin Law Review* (1985): 1273–1303.

McCauley, Patrick B., and Laurie Orlando. "The Rights of the Consumer under the Cable Communications Policy Act of 1984." *Michigan Bar Journal* 65 (November 1986): 1112–15.

McGregor, Michael A. "Will the Real Cable Television Industry Please Stand Up: The Divergent Regulatory Treatment of the Cable Television Industry prior to the Cable Communications Policy Act of 1984." *COMM/ENT Law Journal* 8 (Fall 1985): 33–54.

Meyerson, Michael. "The Cable Communications Policy Act of 1984: A Balancing Act on the Coaxial Wires." *Georgia Law Review* 19 (Spring 1985): 543–622.

Saylor, David J. "Municipal Ripoff: The Unconstitutionality of Cable Television Franchise Fees and Access Support Payments." *Catholic University Law Review* 35 (Spring 1986): 671–704.

Sibary, Scott. "The Cable Communications Policy Act of 1984 v. the First Amendment." *COMM/ENT Law Journal* 7 (Spring 1985): 381–415.

Snyder, Sheryl. "The Cable Communications Policy Act of 1984: Major Changes for Local Governments and Cable Providers." *Kentucky Bench and Bar* 49 (January 1985): 11 + .

Wadlow, R. Clark, and Linda M. Wellstein. "The Changing Regulatory Terrain of Cable Television." *Catholic University Law Review* 35 (Spring 1986): 705–36.

Welch, Randy. "Regulating Cable Television." *State Legislature* 11 (January 1985): 26–30.

Williams, Wenmouth, Jr., and Kathleen Mahoney. "Perceived Impact of the Cable Policy Act of 1984." *Journal of Broadcasting and Electronic Media* 31 (Spring 1987): 193–205.

Chapter Five

VIDEOTEX

ISSUE OVERVIEW

There is nothing simple about videotex. Its function, its economics, its regulation, and its impact (or presumed impact) on humankind is shrouded in a maze of complexity. Even the definition of "videotex" is anything but simple. For starters, videotex can be considered a generic term for a system that allows a home subscriber access via an interactive wired medium to numerous computer data bases for alphanumeric and graphic display of the accessed information on a television screen. Cable television's coaxial wire obviously could be that medium. As such, videotex stands to be one of the most significant and advanced services available to cable television subscribers.

There are some problems, however, that presently cloud the future of videotex as a cable service. Most of these are extrinsic to the technology of the delivery medium and will be identified later. The one intrinsic problem is that the interactive wire that enters the subscriber's home to provide the videotex service need not be supplied by a cable television company. It just as easily could be supplied by a telephone company. That fact alone has brought the cable television industry and the telephone industry head-to-head competitively and will fashion the development of videotex in this country for some years to come.

A discussion of specific issues related to videotex follows shortly, but first, more needs to be said about what videotex is, where it came from, and what it can do. According to one source, videotex is an umbrella term that consists of several basic types:

Viewdata is fully-interactive videotex. The user's requests for services or information are actually sent to, received by, and acted upon by the system computer. In North America, the terms 'videotex' and 'videotext' have become synonymous with view-data.

Teletext is pseudo-interactive or broadcast videotex. While the user can select the information or service to be received, only a one-way communication link is involved.[1]

In its chronological development videotex is characterized as a "third generation data transmission system." The first generation is "roll-a-text," which is used by many cable systems for transmitting continuous data or graphics and which may not be accessed by viewers. Teletext is a second-generation system with limited access as indicated above.[2]

There is yet a third typology for identifying videotex that, given the stages through which videotex has evolved, may be the most significant. This typology breaks videotex into four categories based on the kind of service rendered and the place where the service is rendered. The categories are "consumer videotex" (general-interest data available in the home), "business videotex" (specialized business data available in the office), "public-access videotex" (specialized general-interest data available in public places), and "organizational videotex" (specialized in-house organizational data available in the workplace).[3]

The terms "videotex" and "videotext" are interchangeable at present. The terms "videotex" and "teletext" also appear to be interchangeable in the literature, but as mentioned earlier and as noted below, the functions of the two systems are quite distinct technically:

Teletext information is usually transmitted over the vertical blanking interval (VBI) of a television signal (the black bar visible when vertical hold isn't working); the data in the VBI can then be translated into textual and graphics information by a teletext decoder. But teletext can also be sent on a subcarrier of an FM or television broadcast signal or even on a whole cable television channel.

Videotex may be carried over telephone lines, cable television, or optical fiber. It can also be transmitted via satellite. In addition, a hybrid system, consisting of a one-way broadcast signal to a teletext receiver with return communication through the telephone, has also been developed.[4]

Development

The first videotex system was developed by engineers of the British Post Office in the early 1970s. The British Broadcasting Corporation (BBC) began experimental broadcasts using the system, and by 1976 the BBC had launched the first commercial videotex service, called CEEFAX. Three years prior to the launch of CEEFAX the French had begun experiments with a similar videotex system, Antiope. By 1978 the Canadian Department of Communications had announced the creation of its Telidon videotex system. Not until 1980 did videotex experiments begin in the United States. They commenced when AT & T teamed with Knight-Ridder for testing of a telephone-based videotex system in Coral Gables, Florida.[5]

One of the major benefits of videotex was seen in its providing access to data bases throughout the world. Though the possibility existed, the technical hurdle of incompatible systems had to be overcome. European countries once more took the lead in this matter by developing the first integrated videotex network in 1983. The following year the United States and Canada created their own network, agreeing to adopt the common videotex standard called the North American Presentation Level Protocol Syntax (NAPLPS).[6]

Application Advantages and Disadvantages

Videotex applications have been classified under five headings: "retrieval (news, sports, weather, travel schedules, stock market reports), computing (computer-assisted instruction, management information services, income-tax aids), transactional (teleshopping, telebanking), messaging, and down-line loading (transmitting telesoftware programs to intelligent terminals)."[7] Specific services provided by some U.S. videotex systems have included burglar/fire alarms; games; wedding, birth, and engagement announcements; restaurant specials; school luncheon menus; and a method for users to design and send electronic valentines. A survey conducted among subscribers to the Times Mirror Videotex Service in Los Angeles to rank the system's most essential services yielded the following results: "games (79 percent), shopping/product information (72 percent), bill-paying at a bank (71 percent), late-breaking news (60 percent), education for children (57 percent) and electronic mail (56 percent)."[8]

Videotex carries with it a tremendous potential for data base suppliers. Moreover, videotex has great potential for advertisers. One advertising agency representative noted, for example, that videotex advertisements could be updated instantly at minimal cost for price change and inventory change information. The videotex advertisement will be there at the command of the system subscriber to access information when needed. Finally, advertising messages could be "layered" with several "pages" of information, each page providing greater detail than the previous page for those wishing more information about an advertised product or service.[9] Videotex is likely best suited for direct marketer advertising, although at least one videotex service plans to approach "national advertisers, financial services and retailers as potential advertisers." Advertising rates will be "based on the number of subscribers viewing a particular ad, or, for direct marketers, on the number of orders placed through the service."[10]

One of the chief attributes of videotex lies in its capabilities as an electronic publisher. As such, it offers advantages over print in "speed, selectivity, personalization of information and the maintaining of wide-ranging, comprehensive collections of data." The speed advantage is an obvious reference to the ability of videotex to circumvent all the steps in print publishing and physical delivery that require so much time and effort. Selectivity refers to the videotex subscriber's ability to seek out specific information that he wants or needs without having to wander through pages of text and advertising. Access to data collections heretofore unavailable need not be explained as another obvious advantage, but the personalization of information pertains to the subscriber's ability to compile information in a way that would otherwise require purchase of several newspapers or magazines.[11]

Videotex offers the possibility for far-ranging services to meet the needs of specific categories of users. Educators and students, for instance, would have videotex access to libraries. The handicapped would have access to information that might otherwise be unobtainable. Farmers and business executives alike could access needed information instantly via videotex. This public service potential of videotex may be its greatest asset.[12]

The major disadvantage in videotex is its technical limitations. After all, a television screen does not hold nearly the amount of copy found on the page of a newspaper or magazine. Also, the videotex subscriber may only view one page at a time, whereas a print media user may view more. Perhaps the biggest disadvantage with videotex is that it is not portable. One must view the screen from one location only. The other disadvantages of videotex of a nontechnical nature are the inability of editors to order or prioritize news items—something that readers often rely upon—and the cost of subscribing to a videotex service. That cost can exceed by five to fifty times the cost of a newspaper, magazine, or book, none of which require special hardware for content access.[13]

Economics

Money is a factor that is manifested in several ways with regards to videotex. First comes the millions of dollars being invested in developing videotex systems by such corporate giants as Dow Jones, IBM, and Sears and consortiums formed by AT & T, Chemical Bank, Time Inc., and Bank of America.[14] Such expenditures are ironic given the failure in March 1986 of videotex services operated by two of the nation's largest newspaper chains—Times Mirror and Knight-Ridder. "After a decade of research, market trials, and actual service," the two companies gave up on videotex after spending an estimated $80 million between them.[15] That failure has not deterred other companies from investing in some three dozen new videotex ventures that, by late 1986, served an estimated one million subscribers.[16]

For all the money and effort, though, there are fewer subscribers in the home market than in the business market. Ironically, both kinds of subscribers have ignored the videotex systems that provide color and fancy graphics in favor of the simpler text-only systems, despite the fact that much of the money spent to develop videotex went into creating the more sophisticated but less popular technology. Economic forecasts that have painted a gloomy picture for videotex as originally envisaged now see a growth trend in the use of text-only systems.[17]

One matter that could work either to the advantage or disadvantage of videotex is its competition from computer interests. As stated by one authority:

The explosive growth of home computers has been accompanied by the rise of computer information networks. Such networks as CompuServe, The Source, and the Dow Jones Information Network serve hundreds of thousands of computer owners. They provide in-home banking and shopping, and allow you to purchase stocks, read the news, and play games—in short, everything videotex is supposed to do. The costs of these systems are not prohibitive either. . . . In addition, a home computer may be used for other purposes.[18]

An executive with the Commodore International computer company went so far as to say that videotex will enter the mainstream consumer market only through its convergence with the home computer. He remarked that videotex "should be seen as an extension of computer services, rather than as a separate industry."[19]

The encroachment of home computers into the videotex market raises as many questions for cable television as the competition from the telephone industry. A computer keyboard, monitor, and modem facilitate the same kind of access/display capability, once linked to a data base by telephone's interactive wire, as a cable television–supplied videotex service.

The uncertainty surrounding videotex has caused some concern within the publishing industry, conceivably the industry that eventually will supply much of the content for videotex services. Publishers are most concerned over the kind of financial returns to expect from videotex. For newspaper and magazine publishers in particular, reliance on advertising income as a traditional base of support might not be as substantial with videotex, since advertisers are as yet reluctant to spend advertising dollars to reach a very limited audience. The need for advertisers to support a service that has yet to attract enough subscribers to interest them has been described as the "classic chicken-and-egg dilemma."[20]

Whether and when videotex accelerates its entry into the consumer marketplace depends to a great extent on the natural rate of acceptance of new technology, the identification of the videotex subscriber, and the marketing skills of those providing the videotex services. Regarding the rate of acceptance, technological forecasters suggest that twenty years is the typical length of time needed for new technology to mature. If that is so, then videotex should become accepted and profitable in the 1990s. One analyst has also said that in order for videotex to succeed, the technology must become more user-friendly.[21]

Identification of the proper market is also necessary if videotex is to succeed. Market analyst Gary Arlen predicts that "the growing number of single-person households, shrinking family size and the greater devotion to useful leisure time will 'accelerate acceptance of teleservices.' " Moreover, says Arlen, "children now growing up in homes with computers will be the main teleservice buyers in the 1990s."[22] Here is another assessment of who the videotex subscriber most likely will be:

The people who will be spending money to use videotex services subscribe to a new set of values. Many will already own videogames, VCRs, and home computers. Their young children will be taught basic programming in the earliest grades. Since many of these people already work in the information sector of the economy, they will have an interest in, and some familiarity with, new technology. Many will come from two-paycheck families. They will be accustomed to other forms of retailing, such as shopping by mail and direct response advertising. They will have money, but very little time, because both husband and wife are working full-time at jobs outside the home. This itself has important implications for the places they shop, their purchasing decisions, shopping hours, and use of media. Because videotex is dynamic and interactive, it fits well into this new lifestyle.[23]

How does the videotex industry reach the potential subscriber and convince him of the technology's worth? A marketing expert suggests several key ingredients in selling videotex. First, the market must be well researched to determine who is most likely to subscribe. Second, the marketer must define in precise terms what services videotex can provide and why they are important. Third, subscriber contact must be maintained for service needs, for assistance with problems, and to maintain good customer relations in order to prevent subscription cancellation. Fourth, pricing must be simple and logical. Finally, videotex should be promoted as an extension of the home computer.[24]

Whether the preceding will be successful as a marketing strategy is yet to be seen. The videotex industry has already learned at least two costly lessons in judging the receptiveness of the American public to videotex. First, "It is virtually impossible to create popular demand for an expensive new product that is available in only a few localities." Second, "While Americans will pay a small sum each month for an entertainment service such as cable TV, and a large sum for innovative entertainment equipment such as videocassette recorders, they are more cautious about plunging money into revolutionary information technologies."[25]

Regulation

There are several regulatory matters pertaining to videotex, most of which fall into First Amendment categories. Because videotex is analogous to publishing, many feel that the same First Amendment content protection that applies to the print media should apply to videotex. However, given the transmission of videotex via regulated media, there is some confusion over whether electronic media–oriented regulation should apply to cable entirely or in part or not at all. Especially worrisome to legal authorities is how equal opportunity rules for political candidates and the fairness doctrine, provisions of which are spelled out in the Communications Act of 1934 (as amended), will apply to videotex. Applications of defamation laws and copyright laws raise a similar concern.

Perhaps of most concern to videotex supplier as well as consumer are questions surrounding privacy protection.

Videotex providers could invade subscribers' privacy simply by divulging information as to what items individual subscribers had requested. There might be an invasion of privacy merely by compiling such records. In other words, the system operator could keep track of what information you were looking at. Where a system provides for in-home shopping or electronic funds transfers, the information it could compile is frightening. Financial data, personal net worth, shopping habits, etc.— all could be subject to public view.[26]

Some states have already enacted legislation to ensure videotex subscriber privacy protection. Local cable franchising authorities have also written privacy protection clauses into franchise agreements.[27] The Videotex Industry Association (VIA) has prepared voluntary guidelines pertaining to privacy matters. The guidelines list five instances when videotex operator-collected data on subscribers may be used: "(1) to provide service in response to a subscriber's request; (2) to maintain technical operations; (3) to prevent illegal or unauthorized use of the videotex system; (4) to manage and operate billing and accounting systems; and (5) to conduct market research in order to compile bulk information." The VIA requires that disclosures of any other nature be allowed only with subscriber consent. A court order for release of otherwise protected information would be allowed only after notice to the affected videotex subscriber, according to the VIA.[28]

Newspaper publishers who lease channel space from cable television system operators are presented with some special legal problems. One of these is the control that could be exercised over a newspaper's videotex service content by a cable franchising authority. Might a city council attempt to place special requirements on the content that would infringe upon First Amendment rights of a publisher? Another problem pertains to assumption of liability for advertising contracts when an advertisement fails to air due to a system malfunction. Would the newspaper or the cable company be responsible? Yet a third problem arises from the total freedom that a cable company might be willing to grant a newspaper for its leased videotex channel. Would that then identify the cable television system as a common carrier, and if so, would it then open the system to regulations applicable to common carriers?[29]

Effects

An important question has been posed about videotex and its role in the social milieu: "Society has reached an important decision point. Should we allow a technology like videotex to transform society seemingly at will, or should we direct the change process triggered in part by videotex toward goals consistent with our present values?"[30]

The complexion of any social transformation that might occur as a result of videotex is speculative, although there are some changes that we might anticipate. In home and family life, for instance, such services as tele-shopping and telebanking could result in more time at home and less time on the highway. Videotex services could also provide information that would allow individuals to work at home and to learn at home. In such cases parents could spend more time at home with their young children, and older children could spend more time with the family. There are un-desirable effects of this videotex-induced togetherness, though. Persons who are at home constantly tend to get onto other family members' nerves. Competition for use of a single videotex unit in the same household might also result in family squabbles.

The greater learning opportunity that would result from using videotex is certainly a benefit, as is the interaction that might occur between parent and child when using videotex for instructional purposes. Videotex would also benefit the learning-impaired and the physically handicapped by pro-viding specialized and easily accessible information sources. The one major disadvantage of videotex as an instructional tool is the elimination of peer interaction—an important component in socialization.[31]

While we weigh the advantages and disadvantages of videotex for indi-viduals, some consideration should be given to the economic ramifications of changing lifestyles. What will be the impact of teleshopping and tele-banking on employees of financial institutions and businesses who no longer will have clientele to serve? What will happen to libraries when books are no longer circulated or read? What will happen to cash flow in a society where exchange of money will become entirely an electronic transaction?[32] How will the publishing industry adapt in an age of electronic publication? The task will not be simple, as noted in this article excerpt from *Business Week*: "Embracing the new electronic technology will certainly be no easy feat for publishers. They will have to rethink completely their product and marketing strategies and learn new editorial and management skills—in short, overhaul their entire corporate culture."[33]

Much in the context of the social impact of videotex is based upon universal acceptance and utilization of the videotex technology. Acceptance on this scale might not be the case, at least not in the near future, for several reasons. As already noted, the high cost of videotex services and the availability of videotex in only a few locations have already limited its use. These limitations likely will not change for some time to come. There are two other reasons that videotex may not become a household fixture for awhile. Both deal with human nature.

For one thing, the ways persons use printed publication sources are habitual; and habits are hard to break. Individuals read newspapers, for example, while drinking their morning coffee or while riding the bus or subway to work. Moreover, we do not so much seek out information as we come upon it as we leaf through pages of a newspaper or magazine.[34] Through casual browsing we are informed of things that we otherwise would have missed had we gone straight to the item or items of most interest. Videotex will not allow as much convenience in manner of access nor will it allow a user to browse. To use videotex will require forming new habits.

Human nature will form another impediment to videotex acceptance through a common fear that many experience in using new technology. A research project in Michigan proved the point. Subjects were asked to familiarize themselves with and to use an experimental videotex system there.[35] Those who expressed discomfort with computers generally expressed apprehension with using the computerlike videotex system, even though the particular system required limited skills in accessing data.[36]

Several clinical terms for computer fear, among them "cyberphobia," "technophobia,"[37] and "computer anxiety," may be collectively defined as a helpless feeling experienced by a person when confronting a computer because he thinks he will "never be able to figure it out."[38] The malady is prevalent in a sizable portion of society and has even spawned at least one "how-to" book with suggestions on overcoming computer anxiety.[39] The key to ridding society of this phobia appears to be simply waiting for the next generation of individuals to enter adulthood. According to at least one authority, children seem to have few fears of technology and indeed are fascinated by such things as computers.[40] The comfort that these future adults find with computers will likely transfer to an interest in and a utilization of videotex.

SOURCE OVERVIEW

Books and Book Chapters
General Survey

The most comprehensive book available on videotex is *The World Videotex Report*. This massive volume (866 pages) is a compilation of papers presented at two 1983 videotex conferences, one in New York City and the other in Amsterdam, and covers subjects ranging from *A* to *Z* about the development and status of videotex in the United States and abroad. Some of the eighty-six papers will be cited under later headings, but for a general overview of videotex in the United States the following are suggested: Haines B. Gaffner's "What Is This Thing Called Videotex?" Walter S. Ciciora's "Pixels and Bits—How Videotex Works," Michael Mensh's "The Case for Videotex," and Gary H. Arlen's "The End of the Beginning: What Will We Do with What We Learned on the Trial Trail?"

Antone F. Alber's *Videotex/Teletext: Principles and Practices* is the complete book on videotex. The first five of the twelve chapters in *Videotex/Teletext* define the technologies and how they function and describe their applications. The next four chapters describe the commercial and economic aspects of videotex/teletext, management of videotex/teletext systems, and system pricing and marketing. Chapter 10 looks at such special issues as videotex/teletext regulation and policies, security and privacy, and social implications both affected by and affecting the introduction of the technologies into society. Chapter 11 of *Videotex/Teletext* examines behavioral factors affecting users of the technologies. The book's final chapter projects the use of videotex/teletext into the future. Alber concludes his book with a glossary of videotex/teletext terms.

Paul Hurly, Matthias Laucht, and Denis Hlynka write in the preface to *The Videotex and Teletext Handbook* that the handbook "will introduce readers to the facts and the myths, the potential promises and the perils that videotex information technology offers" (p. vi). *The Videotex and Teletext Handbook* begins by discussing factors that led to the development of videotex and then moves to an examination of specific videotex applications, the technical operation of videotex systems, and issues associated with videotex application. The handbook concludes with several appendices that contain a videotex bibliography, videotex privacy guidelines, information on videotex trial operations, and a videotex glossary.

Efrem Sigel's *The Future of Videotext* is divided into two parts, with the first part consisting of the author's general introduction to videotex—descriptions and definitions of videotex system terms, history of videotex development, a discussion of the advantages and disadvantages of videotex, and a table with information regarding videotex systems around the world. One chapter of the Sigel book describes and illustrates how videotex works, while a later chapter focuses on the nature of videotex information services, their costs, and their comparisons with similar services provided by other media. Jeffrey Silverstein provides an important chapter in *The Future of Videotext* devoted exclusively to videotex in the United States. Included here is information on the medium's integration into the established communications industry of this country, regulatory problems faced by U.S.

videotex, and profiles of selected companies involved in videotex. The second part of Sigel's book looks at videotex use in other countries.

Efrem Sigel edited an earlier book entitled *Videotext: The Coming Revolution in Home/Office Information Retrieval*. This is a very basic overview of videotex/teletext development internationally, with several authors contributing chapters on individual countries. Sigel's "Videotext in the U.S." chapter provides a very straightforward, nontechnical glimpse of videotex experimentation in this country.

Interactive Videotex: The Domesticated Computer is Dimitris N. Chorafas' excellent textbook overview of videotex system operation. He describes the technical operation of videotex and illustrates the utility of videotex by describing the application successes of foreign videotex systems.

James Martin offers some solid information on all phases of videotex (or viewdata, as he prefers to call it) in *Viewdata and the Information Society*. Martin describes videotex technology, the videotex services available, and the effects of videotex on various commercial, economic, and social institutions. Martin concentrates on European videotex systems since they were the ones most commercially successful at the time his book was written. One of the outstanding features of *Viewdata and the Information Society* is the abundance of color pictures throughout the book that illustrate how information actually appears on the videotex screen.

Rudy Bretz's *Media for Interactive Communication* is a technical book on various interactive media systems describing how they function and how they are used. One of the book's chapters concentrates on the Warner Amex QUBE system, and another concentrates on videotex.

Chapter 3 of Diane Gayeski and David Williams' *Interactive Media* gives the reader a thorough grounding in videotex technology. The authors define videotex terminology, describe its technology, and comment on how videotex services both in the United States and abroad are utilized.

For short takes there is Vincent Mosco's "What Is Videotex?" in *Transmission*, edited by Peter D'Agostino, which examines videotex and what other countries are doing with it. Albert S. Tedesco's "Videotex" in his and Charles T. Meadow's *Telecommunications for Management* describes the history of videotex, the technology of videotex system components, videotex user characteristics, barriers to videotex adoption, and business and public policy issues related to videotex. Tedesco's treatment is brief, very technical, and very theoretical in nature. Finally, Michael Nyhan, Robert Johansen, and Robert Plummer's "The USA" in *Viewdata in Action*, edited by Rex Winsbury, discusses what is happening with videotex in this country and why its development has been so sluggish in comparison with videotex and teletext activity in Great Britain.

Chapters on videotex in several other books are short but generally descriptive of the technology's operation. Efrem Sigel and Joseph Roizen's

"Videotext" in *The Video Age: Television Technology and Applications in the 1980s* introduces the subject by describing the components of a videotex system, the use of videotex, and its future prospects. Frederick Williams devotes a portion of *The Communications Revolution* to an explanation of what videotex is and what it does. He discusses videotex services, compares the technology's capabilities to those of print, and looks at the impact of videotex on the print media. A short section in the NAB's *New Technologies Affecting Radio and Television Broadcasting* examines what impact videotex will likely have upon the broadcast media and the costs and benefits of videotex service to the consumer.

Several textbooks offer general information about videotex, but the two listed below offer the most. Lynne Schafer Gross refers to videotex throughout *The New Television Technologies* but devotes one chapter to an extended look at the technology by examining videotex system components, costs, available services, and the history of videotex development in Europe and the United States. She then briefly addresses such videotex-related subjects as economic viability, competition, copyright, privacy, and social effects. An account devoted primarily to the technical operation of videotex and teletext appears in George E. Whitehouse's *Understanding the New Technologies of the Mass Media*.

Applications and Utilization

One of the most comprehensive books on videotex application is *The World Videotex Report*, noted earlier. Several essays included in the book cover most of the application territory under three category headings: "Electronic Publishing"; "Transactional Videotex: Telebanking"; and "Transactional Videotex: Teleshopping." Examples of essays appearing under the first heading are Neil Kuehnl's "Videotex and Magazines: This Month's Edition" and Darby Miller's "The Role of Videotex in the Multimedia Company." The second heading on telebanking is represented by Frank J. Schultz's "The Place for Videotex in the Bank of the Future." The final heading is represented by essays having an advertising or marketing theme, such as Walter S. James's "The Use of Videotex as an Advertising Medium" and David M. Simons' "Is Videotex a Medium for Your Message?"

John Tydeman, Herbert Lipinski, Richard P. Adler, Michael Nyhan, and Laurence Zwimpfer's *Teletext and Videotex in the United States* presents the findings of a study conducted to assess the predicted impact of videotex and teletext in this country in the coming two decades. The book's chapters address three specific topics: the state of videotex and teletext internationally and the market potential for the technology in the United States, probable technological developments for videotex and user application, and the public policy issues and social issues surrounding the use of videotex and teletext.

Dimitris N. Chorafas' *Interactive Message Services: Planning, Designing, and Implementing Videotex* examines videotex utilization primarily in business and industry. The book is thorough, with many excellent charts and diagrams to illustrate videotex uses, but has a decidedly technical orientation.

The role of videotex as a technology for electronic publication and its image as that of either a complementary or competitive medium relative to the print media are matters addressed in the following collection of books. To begin with, David A. Patten's *Newspapers and New Media* places videotex in the context of other new and emerging electronic media to examine how these combined technologies are changing or will change established media such as newspapers. Patten says, "Established media willing to confront and take up the challenge of the new media must learn new ways of thinking about media and journalism"; his book provides "a context within which such thinking can be translated into action as well as guidelines for determining the direction such action should take" (p. 13).

Electronic Publishing Plus, edited by Martin Greenberger, contains a number of essays first developed for a research forum organized by the Annenberg School of Communications' Washington Program in Communications Policy Studies. The essays, all written by prominent authorities in their respective areas, fall into six major sections: "The Consumer," "The Industry," "The Supplier," "Intellectual Property," "Public Regulation," and "The Public Interest." A sampling of the essays comprising *Electronic Publishing Plus* includes Everett M. Rogers' "Acceptance of the New Technologies," Ronald E. Rice's "Implications of the Media Habit for Electronic Publishing," and Harry E. Smith's "Taking Videotex to Market."

While David H. Weaver's *Videotex Journalism* reports on a study of the use, adoption, and effects of videotex and teletext in other countries, the information here has direct application to the same matters in this country. What Weaver suggests is that videotex has some distance to go before it can prove itself a worthy competitor to existing news media.

The Print Publisher in an Electronic World, edited by Claire Green, includes the published proceedings of a 1980 conference on electronic publishing. Short essays in the book present the views of various representatives from the publishing business on how videotex along with other electronic means of publication will impact upon the newspaper, magazine, and book publishing industry. One of the book's chapters, by Efrem Sigel, concentrates on videotex, but videotex is generally incorporated into discussions of all the new or emerging electronic media.

Benjamin M. Compaine says in "Videotex and the Newspaper Industry: Threat or Opportunity" in *Understanding New Media: Trends and Issues in Electronic Distribution of Information*, edited by himself, that persons in the newspaper business should be cautious about their assessments of what direction videotex will take and what impact the technology will have on publishing. Compaine examines the status of videotex and then elaborates on several forces—regulation and methods of transmission, standardization and compatibility, physical delivery, degree of advertiser support, development of cultural pulls and resistance, and others—that will affect future directions in videotex and newspaper competition.

Moving from the publishing to the utilization of the published product category is Kathleen Criner's "Videotext: Implications and Applications for Libraries" in Donald W. King et al.'s *Telecommunications and Libraries.* Criner discusses uses of videotex data bases and future possibilities for such use.

Two chapters on videotex application are included in *Information and Behavior,* edited by Brent D. Ruben. The first, "The Impact of New Technology on the Acquisition, Processing, and Distribution of News," is Jerome Aumente's commentary on the integration of journalism and videotex. The second chapter is David Bloomquist's "Videotex and American Politics: The More Things Change...." Bloomquist examines the role videotex will play in this country's political process and institutions.

Stephen K. Badzik's "Videotex: Blessing or Bane for the 'Boob Tube'?" in Howard F. Didsbury, Jr.'s *Communications and the Future* looks at the role of videotex in the home and in family life, education, and leisure activities. Badzik says that his essay "seeks to identify some of the sociocultural issues that should be considered not only by commercial and governmental policymakers but by individual consumers, whose future may be radically affected by videotex" (p. 123).

T. Andrew Finn and Concetta M. Stewart create a videotex application typology and then discuss service applications under each heading in "From Consumer to Organizational Videotex Applications: Will Videotex Find a Home at the Office?" in *Communication Yearbook 9,* edited by Margaret L. McLaughlin. The two authors contend that videotex may be used most effectively for information management and retrieval in the business place.

Business and Economics

Lawrence Strauss says that his *Electronic Marketing: Emerging TV and Computer Channels for Interactive Home Shopping* "examines a number of key elements that are crucial to the development of electronic marketing over the next decade" (p. ix). Although Strauss looks at cable television in general and videotex in particular, there appears to be a concentration on the latter, as in a portion of chapter 5, "Time Sharing, Videotext, and Other Two-Way Electronic Marketing Systems," where the author describes the development and testing of videotex systems and comments on the future market for videotex, the technology's economic status, and advantages and disadvantages of videotex.

M. Christopher Lockhart's *The Advertiser's Place in the Evolution of Videotex* serves two purposes. First, it introduces potential videotex advertisers and marketers to the technology by defining terms and explaining how videotex systems operate. Second, Lockhart's book explores methods of best utilizing videotex for advertising.

Cable/Videotex: A Compendium for Direct Marketers, edited by R. C. Morse and Karen L. Burns, was mentioned in a previous chapter of this reference guide and is noted here for its many brief essays devoted to examinations of videotex marketing potential. Examples of commentary on application techniques for videotex marketing are Larry T. Pfister's "Videotex—The Bridge between Consumers and the Objects of Their Interests," John S. Warwick's "Videotex—Psychographic Marketing for the Motivated Consumer," and Sarah Ordover's "Direct Marketing and the Economics of Videotex."

Two articles on videotex marketing, Mark Kriss's "The Race for Market Share in Consumer Videotex" and David M. Simons' "Selling Videotex," appear in the aforementioned *World Videotex Report.*

Law and Regulations

Richard M. Neustadt's *The Birth of Electronic Publishing* contains an overview of regulatory policy issues pertinent to electronic publishing. The book's content is basic, opening with a description of what videotex and teletext are, moving to a history of the technology's development, and then giving a description of U.S. electronic publishing systems and experiments. Neustadt continues with a review of U.S. communication regulatory policies in general and then specifically as they relate to electronic publishing. Some of the book's chapters are devoted to electronic publishing and privacy, defamation and obscenity, copyright, piracy, and retransmission.

"Videotex and Teletext: The Problem of Regulation" by Tony Rimmer appears in Jerry Salvaggio's *Telecommunications: Issues and Choices for Society.* The essay carries an excellent description of the regulatory implications that loom in the future for electronic publishing. Rimmer explains that the objective of his essay is "to review communication law as it applies to the electronic publisher and consider whether this form of publishing might bring the newspaper within the regulatory scope of the Federal Communications Commission" (p. 106).

A portion of a chapter appearing in John Wicklein's *Electronic Nightmare: The New Communications and Freedom* (noted in greater detail under the next heading) explores electronic newspaper experimentation and asks' who will control the content of such newspapers, who will set content standards, and what will be the role of the government in regulating those standards?

Another contribution from the previously mentioned *World Videotex Report* is Richard M. Neustadt's "Videotex Industry Association Model Privacy Guidelines for Videotex Systems."

Uses and Content Effects

A very critical examination in ominous tones of the role of videotex in society appears in Vincent Mosco's *Pushbutton Fantasies.* Mosco claims that while the technology's impact is positive for some, it could be negative for others. *Pushbutton Fantasies* provides critical commentary on the entire political and economic structure that fosters a technology like videotex and on what the technology does to the social structure.

John Wicklein contends in his *Electronic Nightmare: The New Communications and Freedom* that the emergence and spread of new technology use, with the technology's interactive capabilities, might result in the loss of our individual liberties if the technology comes under the control of a single all-powerful overseer. Two of the book's chapters concentrate on videotex. In chapter 3 Wicklein looks at the development of and problems associated with videotex in Europe and the United States but spends a major amount of space on the potential control over the consumer's access to information that may result from using a videotex data base. The gist of Wicklein's chapter 4 is described under the preceding heading.

David M. Dozier and Ronald E. Rice's "Rival Theories of Electronic Newsreading" in Rice's *The New Media* examines the process of consumer adoption and use of videotex in the context of applicable mass communication theory. The piece has a very theoretical orientation but offers a unique view of how videotex in comparison with the print media will be utilized as an information-delivery system.

Periodical Articles

An excellent but somewhat technically oriented general article on videotex is Darby Miller's "Videotex: Science Fiction or Reality?" Roy D. Bright's "Videotex: An Interactive Information System" and Del Myers' "Corporate Videotex Is Growing Quietly But Steadily" examine corporate videotex, especially the variety whose service is supplied more by telephone companies than by cable television systems. Philippe Durand reports on application experiments for videotex use in educational, library, handicapped, agricultural, community, and governmental services in "The Public Service Potential of Videotex and Teletext."

Who videotex subscribers are likely to be and what they are likely to expect from videotex are explored in John A. Ledingham's "Are Consumers Ready for the Information Age?" Which of two kinds of videotex services, one providing news or one providing business and market data, would be most attractive to persons involved in agribusiness is the subject of research reported by James S. Ettema in "Videotex for News and Business Data." Susan T. Eastman and Donald E. Agostino report in "Commanding the Computer: Functions and Concepts of Videotex Technology for Eighth-Grade Students" their results from a study to ascertain how videotex may be incorporated into the classroom environment.

A sampling of videotex uses and effects research results appears in the following articles. Mickie Edwardson, Kurt Kent, and Maeve McConnell's "Television News Information Gain: Videotex versus a Talking Head" compares subject recall of news content between videotex as the news source and a newspaper as the news source. Consumer attitudes toward videotex are the subject of Lucy L. Henke and Thomas R. Donohue's "Teletext Viewing Habits and Preferences," and Jacalyn Klein Butler and Kurt M. Kent present results from a Florida survey to determine whether individuals would be willing to replace the newspaper with videotex as a news medium in "Potential Impact of Videotext on Newspapers." The matter of consumer attitude toward videotex adoption is examined once more in Kalle J. Heikkinen and Stephen D. Reese's "Newspaper Readers and a New Information Medium: Information Need and Channel Orientation as Predictors of Videotex Adoption."

Andrew J. Siegel provides an overview of regulatory policy issues related to videotex in "Videotex: We Have Seen the Future and It Is Murky." Covering similar territory but on a much greater scale is Anne W. Branscomb's "Electronic Publishing: A Global View of Videotex." A series of articles by noted legal authorities comprise the *Federal Communications Law Journal*'s "Symposium on Legal Issues in Electronic Publishing." These articles provide a comprehensive survey of all major videotex policy issues.

A description of how videotex is likely to affect consumers is outlined in Paul Hurly's "The Promises and Perils of Videotex." Hurly addresses such videotex-related issues as privacy and security, participatory democracy, and information handling. Mindy Elisa Wachtel's "Videotex: A Welcome New Technology or an Orwellian Threat to Privacy?" views the issues attendant upon the use of videotex technology to invade personal privacy. This issue and more are explored in "The Videotex Industry: Social Control and the Cybernetic Commodity of Home Networking" by Kevin Wilson. Wilson expands his investigation of videotex and the role it will play as a component of information networking to videotex development worldwide. His article, however, concentrates quite heavily on the United States.

NOTES

1. Paul Hurly, "The Promises and Perils of Videotex," *Futurist*, April 1985, pp. 7–8.

2. Andrew J. Siegel, "Videotex: We Have Seen the Future and It Is Murky," *Communications and the Law* 8 (April 1986): 3–4.

3. T. Andrew Finn and Concetta M. Stewart, "From Consumer to Organizational Videotex Applications: Will Videotex Find a Home at the Office?" in *Communication Yearbook 9*, ed. Margaret L. McLaughlin (Beverly Hills, Calif.: Sage, 1986), pp. 806–8.

4. Darby Miller, "Videotex: Science Fiction or Reality?" *BYTE*, July 1983, pp. 43–44.

5. Efrem Sigel, *The Future of Videotext* (White Plains, N.Y.: Knowledge Industry Publications, 1983), p. 2.

6. Hurly, "Promises and Perils," p. 10.

7. Ibid., p. 7.

8. Siegel, "Videotex," p. 4.

9. Watson S. James, "The Use of Videotex as an Advertising Medium," in *The World Videotex Report* (Middlesex, England: Online Publications, 1984), p. 767.

10. Cleveland Horton, "New Life for Videotex," *Advertising Age*, 6 April 1987, p. 84.

11. Sigel, *Future of Videotext*, pp. 3–4.

12. Philippe Durand, "The Public Service Potential of Videotex and Teletext," *Telecommunications Policy* 7 (June 1983): 149–62.

13. Sigel, *Future of Videotext*, pp. 4–6.

14. Gary Arlen, "High Rollers with High Hopes," *Channels Field Guide '87*, pp. 86–87.

15. Catherine L. Harris et al., "Two Videotex Heavyweights Quit—$80 Million Lighter," *Business Week*, 31 March 1986, p. 31.

16. Arlen, "High Rollers," p. 86.

17. Catherine L. Harris, "For Videotex, the Big Time Is Still a Long Way Off," *Business Week*, 14 January 1985, p. 128.

18. Siegel, "Videotex," pp. 4–5.

19. "The Changing Priorities of Videotex," *Broadcasting*, 1 July 1985, p. 64.

20. "Publishers Go Electronic," *Business Week*, 11 June 1984, pp. 84–90.

21. David Stoller, "Setting the Videotex Stage," *CableVision Plus*, 6 December 1982, pp. 6–8.

22. Ibid., p. 14.

23. Martin Nisenholtz, "The Product Development Process," in *The World Videotex Report* (Middlesex, England: Online Publications, 1984), p. 771.

24. David M. Simons, "Selling Videotex," in *The World Videotex Report* (Middlesex, England: Online Publications, 1984), pp. 847–52.

25. Ralph L. Lowenstein and Helen E. Aller, "The Inevitable March of Videotex," *Technology Review*, October 1985, pp. 26–27.

26. Siegel, "Videotex," pp. 8–10.

27. C. David Rambo, "Electronic Publishers Face Legal Questions on Variety of Issues," *Presstime*, October 1982, p. 7.

28. Richard M. Neustadt, "Videotex Industry Association Model Privacy Guidelines for Videotex Systems," in *The World Videotex Report* (Middlesex, England: Online Publications, 1984), pp. 319–22.

29. Rambo, "Electronic Publishers," pp. 5–6.

30. Hurly, "Promises and Perils," p. 7.

31. Stephen K. Badzik, "Videotex: Blessing or Bane for the 'Boob Tube'?" in Howard F. Didsbury, Jr., ed., *Communications and the Future* (Bethesda, Md.: World Future Society, 1982), pp. 123–32.

32. John Tydeman, Hubert Lipinski, Richard P. Adler, Michael Nyhan, and Laurence Zwimpfer, *Teletext and Videotex in the United States* (New York: McGraw-Hill, 1982), pp. 258–62.

33. "Publishers Go Electronic," p. 85

34. John Carey, "Videotex: The Past as Prologue," *Journal of Communication* 32 (Spring 1982): 80–83.

35. Tony Atwater, Carrie Heeter, and Natalie Brown, "Foreshadowing the Electronic Publishing Age: First Exposures to Viewtron" (unpublished paper presented

at the International Communication Association Annual Conference, Honolulu,
Hawaii, May 1985), pp. 3–4.

36. Ibid., p. 14.

37. Mark Schwed, "Technophobes More Afraid as Time Passes—Rapidly,"
Houston Chronicle, 27 October 1985, sec. 9, p. 17.

38. Lisa Jennings, "One New Social Ill Is 'Computer Anxiety,' " *Houston Chron-icle*, 15 July 1984, sec. 1, p. 6.

39. Jeff Berner, *Overcoming Computer Fear* (Berkeley, Calif.: SYBEX, 1984).

40. Schwed, "Technophobes More Afraid," sec. 9, p. 17.

BIBLIOGRAPHY

Books and Book Chapters

General Survey

Alber, Antone F. *Videotex/Teletext: Principles and Practices.* New York: McGraw-
Hill, 1985.

Bretz, Rudy. *Media for Interactive Communication.* Beverly Hills, Calif.: Sage, 1983.

Chorafas, Dimitris N. *Interactive Videotex: The Domesticated Computer.* New York:
Petrocelli Books, 1981.

Gayeski, Diane, and David Williams. *Interactive Media.* Englewood Cliffs, N.J.:
Prentice-Hall, 1985.

Gross, Lynne Schafer. *The New Television Technologies.* 2d ed. Dubuque, Iowa:
Wm. C. Brown, 1986.

Hurly, Paul, Matthias Laucht, and Denis Hlynka. *The Videotex and Teletext Hand-book.* New York: Harper & Row, 1985.

Martin, James. *Viewdata and the Information Society.* Englewood Cliffs, N.J.: Prentice-
Hall, 1982.

Mosco, Vincent. "What Is Videotex?" In *Transmission*, edited by Peter D'Agostino.
New York: Tanam Press, 1985.

National Association of Broadcasters. *New Technologies Affecting Radio and Television
Broadcasting.* Washington, D.C.: National Association of Broadcasters, 1981.

Nyhan, Michael, Robert Johansen, and Robert Plummer. "The USA." In *Viewdata
in Action*, edited by Rex Winsbury. London: McGraw-Hill, 1981.

Sigel, Efrem. *The Future of Videotext.* White Plains, N.Y.: Knowledge Industry
Publications, 1983.

Sigel, Efrem, ed. *Videotext: The Coming Revolution in Home/Office Information Re-trieval.* White Plains, N.Y.: Knowledge Industry Publications, 1980.

Sigel, Efrem, and Joseph Roizen. "Videotext." In *The Video Age: Television Tech-nology and Applications in the 1980s.* White Plains, N.Y.: Knowledge Industry
Publications, 1982.

Tedesco, Albert S. "Videotex." In *Telecommunications for Management*, by Charles
T. Meadow and Albert S. Tedesco. New York: McGraw-Hill, 1985.

Whitehouse, George E. *Understanding the New Technologies of the Mass Media.* En-glewood Cliffs, N.J.: Prentice-Hall, 1986.

Williams, Frederick. *The Communications Revolution.* Rev. ed. New York: Mentor, 1983.
The World Videotex Report. Middlesex, England: Online Publications, 1984.

Applications and Utilization

Aumente, Jerome. "The Impact of New Technology on the Acquisition, Processing, and Distribution of News." In *Information and Behavior*, vol. 1, edited by Brent D. Ruben. New Brunswick, N.J.: Transaction Books, 1985.

Badzik, Stephen K. "Videotex: Blessing or Bane for the 'Boob Tube'?" In *Communications and the Future*, edited by Howard F. Didsbury, Jr. Bethesda, Md.: World Future Society, 1982.

Bloomquist, David. "Videotex and American Politics: The More Things Change . . . ." In *Information and Behavior*, vol. 1, edited by Brent D. Ruben. New Brunswick, N.J.: Transaction Books, 1985.

Chorafas, Dimitris N. *Interactive Message Services: Planning, Designing, and Implementing Videotex.* New York: McGraw-Hill, 1984.

Compaine, Benjamin M. "Videotex and the Newspaper Industry: Threat or Opportunity." In *Understanding New Media: Trends and Issues in Electronic Distribution of Information*, edited by Benjamin M. Compaine. Cambridge, Mass.: Ballinger, 1984.

Criner, Kathleen. "Videotext: Implications and Applications for Libraries." In *Telecommunications and Libraries*, edited by Donald W. King et al. White Plains, N.Y.: Knowledge Industry Publications, 1981.

Finn, T. Andrew, and Concetta M. Stewart. "From Consumer to Organizational Videotex Applications: Will Videotex Find a Home at the Office?" In *Communication Yearbook 9*, edited by Margaret L. McLaughlin. Beverly Hills, Calif.: Sage, 1986.

Green, Claire, ed. *The Print Publisher in an Electronic World.* White Plains, N.Y.: Knowledge Industry Publications, 1981.

Greenberger, Martin, ed. *Electronic Publishing Plus.* White Plains, N.Y.: Knowledge Industry Publications, 1985.

Patten, David A. *Newspapers and New Media.* White Plains, N.Y.: Knowledge Industry Publications, 1986.

Tydeman, John, Hubert Lipinski, Richard P. Adler, Michael Nyhan, and Laurence Zwimpfer. *Teletext and Videotex in the United States.* New York: McGraw-Hill, 1982.

Weaver, David H. *Videotex Journalism.* Hillsdale, N.J.: Lawrence Erlbaum Associates, 1983.

Business and Economics

Lockhart, M. Christopher. *The Advertiser's Place in the Evolution of Videotex.* Hoffman Estates, Ill.: BL Associates, 1983.

Morse, R. C., and Karen L. Burns. *Cable/Videotex: A Compendium for Direct Marketers.* Monograph series, vol. 6. N.Y.: Direct Mail/Marketing Association, 1982.

Strauss, Lawrence. *Electronic Marketing: Emerging TV and Computer Channels for*

Interactive Home Shopping. White Plains, N.Y.: Knowledge Industry Publications, 1983.

The World Videotex Report. See entry under General Survey.

Law and Regulations

Neustadt, Richard M. *The Birth of Electronic Publishing.* White Plains, N.Y.: Knowledge Industry Publications, 1982.

Rimmer, Tony. "Videotex and Teletext: The Problem of Regulation." In *Telecommunications: Issues and Choices for Society*, by Jerry Salvaggio. New York: Longman, 1983.

Wicklein, John. *Electronic Nightmare: The New Communications and Freedom.* New York: Viking Press, 1981.

The World Videotex Report. See entry under General Survey.

Uses and Content Effects

Dozier, David M., and Ronald E. Rice. "Rival Theories of Electronic Newsreading." In *The New Media*, by Ronald E. Rice. Beverly Hills, Calif.: Sage, 1984.

Mosco, Vincent. *Pushbutton Fantasies.* Norwood, N.J.: Ablex Publishing, 1982.

Wicklein. See entry under Law and Regulations.

Periodical Articles

Branscomb, Anne W. "Electronic Publishing: A Global View of Videotex." *Federal Communications Law Journal* 36 (September 1984): 119–47.

Bright, Roy D. "Videotex: An Interactive Information System." *Telephony*, 2 January 1984, 90–96.

Butler, Jacalyn Klein, and Kurt M. Kent. "Potential Impact of Videotext on Newspapers." *Newspaper Research Journal* 5 (Fall 1983): 3–12.

Durand, Philippe. "The Public Service Potential of Videotex and Teletext." *Telecommunications Policy* 7 (June 1983): 149–62.

Eastman, Susan T., and Donald E. Agostino. "Commanding the Computer: Functions and Concepts of Videotex Technology for Eighth-Grade Students." *Journal of Research and Development in Education* 19 (1986): 49–57.

Edwardson, Mickie, Kurt Kent, and Maeve McConnell. "Television News Information Gain: Videotex versus a Talking Head." *Journal of Broadcasting and Electronic Media* 29 (Fall 1985): 367–78.

Ettema, James S. "Videotex for News and Business Data." *Telecommunications Policy* 9 (March 1985): 41–48.

Heikkinen, Kalle J., and Stephen D. Reese. "Newspaper Readers and a New Information Medium: Information Need and Channel Orientation as Predictors of Videotex Adoption." *Communication Research* 13 (January 1986): 19–36.

Henke, Lucy L., and Thomas R. Donohue. "Teletext Viewing Habits and Preferences." *Journalism Quarterly* 63 (Autumn 1986): 542–45, 553.

Hurly, Paul. "The Promises and Perils of Videotex." *Futurist*, April 1985, 7–13.

Ledingham, John A. "Are Consumers Ready for the Information Age?" *Journal of Advertising Research* 24 (August/September 1984): 31–37.

Miller, Darby. "Videotex: Science Fiction or Reality?" *BYTE*, July 1983, 42–56.

Myers, Del. "Corporate Videotex Is Growing Quietly But Steadily." *Telephony*, 2 January 1984, 70–76.

Siegel, Andrew J. "Videotex: We Have Seen the Future and It Is Murky." *Communications and the Law* 8 (April 1986): 3–11.

"Symposium on Legal Issues in Electronic Publishing." *Federal Communications Law Journal* 36 (September 1984): 148–224.

Wachtel, Mindy Elisa. "Videotex: A Welcome New Technology or an Orwellian Threat to Privacy?" *Cardozo Arts and Entertainment Law Journal* 2 (1983): 287–312.

Wilson, Kevin. "The Videotex Industry: Social Control and the Cybernetic Commodity of Home Networking." *Media Culture and Society* 8 (January 1986): 7–39.

APPENDIX: Association and Agency Addresses

Listed below are addresses and phone numbers for associations and agencies where cable and videotex information might be located.

Cable Television Information Center
  1500 N. Beauregard St., Suite 205
  Alexandria, Va. 22311
  (703) 845–1705

Cabletelevision Advertising Bureau
  757 Third Ave.
  New York, N.Y. 10017
  (212) 751–7770

Community Antenna Television Association
  P.0. Box 1005
  Fairfax, Va. 22030
  (703) 691–8875

Federal Communications Commission
  1919 M St., N.W.
  Washington, D.C. 20554
  (202) 632–7260

Foundation for Community Service Cable Television
  5010 Geary Blvd., Suite 3
  San Francisco, Calif. 94118
  (415) 387–0200

House Energy and Commerce Committee [Telecommunications, Consumer Protection, and Finance Subcommittee]
  Room 2125, Rayburn House Office Bldg.
  Washington, D.C. 20515
  (202) 225–2927

National Association of Broadcasters
  1771 N St., N.W.
  Washington, D.C. 20036
  (202) 429–5300

National Association of Regulatory Utility Commissioners
  1102 Interstate Commerce Commission Bldg., Box 684
  Washington, D.C. 20044
  (202) 898–2200

National Association of Telecommunications Officers and Advisors (an affiliate of
the National League of Cities)
  1301 Pennsylvania Ave., N.W.
  Washington, D.C. 20004
  (202) 626–3115

National Cable Television Association
  1724 Massachusetts Ave., N.W.
  Washington, D.C. 20036
  (202) 775–3550

National Federation of Local Cable Programmers
  906 Pennsylvania Ave., S.E.
  Washington, D.C. 20003
  (202) 544–7272

National League of Cities
  1301 Pennsylvania Ave., N.W.
  Washington, D.C. 20004
  (202) 626–3000

Senate Commerce Committee [Communications Subcommittee]
  Suite 508, Dirksen Bldg.
  Washington, D.C. 20510
  (202) 224–5115

Videotex Industry Association
  1901 N. Fort Meyer Dr., Suite 200
  Rosslyn, Va. 22209
  (703) 522–0883

INDEX

About the Author

RONALD GARAY, Associate Professor of Journalism at Louisiana State University, Baton Rouge, is the author of *Congressional Television: A Legislative History* (Greenwood Press, 1984), as well as articles on legal, political, and economic aspects of broadcasting.